Leadership on the Job

Leadership
on the Job

GUIDES TO GOOD SUPERVISION

Third Edition

edited by

William K. Fallon

A Division of American Management Associations

Library of Congress Cataloging in Publication Data
Main entry under title:

Leadership on the job.

Includes index.
1. Supervision of employees—Addresses, essays,
lectures.   2. Leadership—Addresses, essays, lectures.
3. Personnel management—Addresses, essays, lectures.
I. Fallon, William K.
HF5549.L36   1981   658.3'02   81-66224
ISBN 0-8144-5727-4   AACR2

Second Printing

Preface

We hear much about leadership today. When a political figure fails to do his job effectively, people say he lacks the ability to lead. Sometimes this ability is even offered as a panacea for our national and international problems: "What America needs now more than ever before is leadership!"

In the business world we hear similar comments: "I don't know how Jones got the job. He's certainly not a leader," or "She just isn't a good leader. That's all there is to it." Statements such as these raise some questions. What makes a good leader? Are leaders born or can they be made? Can one develop the qualities of leadership and, if so, how?

In this new version of a classic business book, more than 40 authors answer these questions and tell you much more about the qualities of leadership and the techniques of successful supervision. They present proven techniques of communication and personal development and offer practical discussions of the supervisor's expanding role along with workable suggestions for achieving better human relations. The selections are organized in six separate parts. The first part consists of seven chapters on the characteristics and styles of leadership and management. Here the reader learns what experts have to say about the qualities that make a leader and the different styles of management that may be acquired or developed. The next part consists of five chapters that stress the importance of communication as it pertains to leadership.

The third part consists of eight chapters on human resources management. These chapters deal with the methods that managers can use to motivate their subordinates and emphasize the fact that genuine leadership is *not* authoritarian dominance of people. The nine chapters that comprise the fourth part tell you how to manage your job so that it runs smoothly and efficiently. This part begins with advice from Peter F. Drucker on how to manage your boss and ends with a chapter on handling stress. Part Five covers all the special considerations involved in the management function, from nourishing the creative employee to dealing with sexual harassment. The final part deals with labor-management relations, a vital topic for many supervisors.

The book follows the general structure of the preceding edition, which was well received in both the management and academic communities. However, only two of the chapters from that edition have been retained. These pieces are every bit as cogent and timely today as when they were first published.

Thanks to all those at AMACOM, particularly Florence Stone, Bob Finley, Eileen Altman, and Elena Bose, who helped in developing this collection. We hope that it will serve you well as a ready source of information to help you do your job more quickly and easily with improved results.

William K. Fallon

Contents

Part One

CHARACTERISTICS AND STYLES

1

What It Takes
to Be a Leader

Louis Imundo

Is there such thing as a natural leader? People are not born leaders. They may have inherited or developed traits and characteristics that motivate others to identify with and be influenced by them. This phenomenon is a function of prevailing values and norms, which often change. Considerable research over the years has led to conclusions that people who exhibit certain traits and characteristics are more likely to succeed as leaders over the long run. The traits and characteristics of effective leaders are interrelated with the skill requirements for effective supervision. However, a number of distinct traits and characteristics can be correlated with leaders. These correlations can be made whether the leaders are formal, such as presidents and supervisors, or informal, that is, without organization title or sanctioning.

   People who become leaders tend to have a stronger level of drive

From *The Effective Supervisor's Handbook*. © 1980 AMACOM, a division of American Management Associations.

or perseverance than others. In the face of adversity or challenges, they persevere in order to reach a goal. Anyone who takes risks faces the possiblity of failure. When failures occur, leaders are able to analyze and learn from the failure and renew their efforts to reach a goal.

Effective leaders are skillful in communicating. They are able to identify with and relate to those with whom they interact. They are skillful in applying verbal and nonverbal techniques to influence others. They understand human behavior and how to influence. They are able to create conditions or situations where people's needs are met by following the leader.

Another characteristic of leaders is that they tend to display high achievement drives. High achievers not only compete against the standards of others, they develop their own standards. In a sense, their need to achieve can only be satisfied for short periods of time. High achievers are continually looking for new opportunities and challenges. These types of leaders may be very creative and bring success to themselves, others with whom they interact, and organizations; they can be an organization's worst liability. High achievers may exploit organizations and employees for the sake of personal gain. High achievers may also fail to recognize that they are different from other people and that other people may not be able to move at the speed and intensity that they move. This could lead to employees either withdrawing or rebelling.

Leaders display a high level of social and psychological maturity. This means that leaders not only know what to say and do, but how to say and do it. They have also developed an acute sense of timing; that is, when to say and do something. Many people have developed the skill to analyze problems and develop and implement solutions; but unless they know the right time to implement the solutions, they will not solve the problem. Supervisors who have had to negotiate, especially with union leaders in labor-management talks or grievance negotiations, learn to develop a sense of timing or they become ineffective.

Leaders display an ability to absorb and retain knowledge that is greater than that of followers, and they are usually more intelligent than those whom they lead. Intelligence and intellectual capacity, to a degree, are measurable. Standard IQ tests alone are insufficient. Intelligence is, in part, inherited. Intellectual development, however, is largely dependent upon stimulation, conditioning, practice, and reinforcement. Due to inheritance factors, one person may have a higher level of intelligence and even the capacity to learn more than others. However, if that intellect is not developed through stimulation and conditioning, its potential will not be realized. On the other hand, with proper stimulation, conditioning, practice, and reinforcement a person born with a lower level of intelligence could conceivably develop a much higher level than the person who started out with more.

Historically, societies have had a love-hate relationship with people who are more intelligent than the masses. Leaders at any level often find themselves simultaneously admired and respected, feared and hated. Leaders must be sensitive to the degree to which their intelligence arouses jealousy and fear among followers. It is well understood that the more inferior and threatened a person feels in the presence of someone else, the more he will try to avoid that person. If avoidance is difficult or impossible, nonviolent, or even violent, means may be used to remove the threat. Leaders should not hide their intelligence, but should be aware of how they display it.

Effective leaders have the self-confidence that allows them to take risks and accept responsibilities. Faceless bureaucrats, both in industry and government, tend to be risk avoiders and therefore avoid responsibility. As the late Harry S. Truman is reported to have said, "The buck stops here." Leaders, if they are to move forward, must be willing to assume risk and accept responsibility for success or failure.

Self-confidence is an important factor in a leader's willingness to make decisions. Decision making and responsibility go hand in hand. Leaders are the people who have to make key decisions. They must be able to absorb information, assess courses of action, weigh the risks, make the decisions, and assume the responsibility.

Leaders generally know how to conduct themselves when interacting with others. This does not mean a high level of social etiquette, although it does not hurt to have it. It does mean being able to control one's emotions without being unemotional. Joy, affection, tenderness, anger, resentment, and jealousy are all human emotions, and if they are not displayed, serious psychological problems may arise for supervisors and people with whom they have contact. The critical factor is knowing when, and to what degree, to display these normal emotions and feelings.

Another facet of effective leadership that is not often mentioned in management literature is a high level of moral integrity. Leaders set examples of behavior and are responsible for instilling a similar level of moral integrity in employees. The tragedy of Watergate and similar scandals are examples of the failure of leaders to have, and demonstrate through their actions, a high degree of moral integrity.

Leaders, particularly business and political leaders, must be able to function at a high level of moral integrity within the complex interrelationships of personal, religious, organizational, and societal values and prevailing law. They must also be able to predict and adapt to changes occurring in society.

DEVELOPING AN EFFECTIVE LEADERSHIP STYLE

As leaders, supervisors develop and employ various approaches to directing the activities of others. They may learn how to lead by following the examples of predecessors or other leaders, or they may develop their approaches by trial and error. Observation, training, evaluation, trial and error interact to shape a supervisor's approaches to leading and serve as feedback in developing the approaches or styles that work over the long run. There is no best approach because the effectiveness of any style is a function of three general interrelated variables. They are: (1) the traits, characteristics, and needs of leaders; (2) the traits, characteristics, and needs of followers; and (3) a broad range of environmental and situational variables.

Some people enjoy controlling the activities of others, but the degree to which they have a need to control varies widely. People are attracted to leadership roles in structured organizations such as the military, paramilitary organizations like police and fire-fighting units, or the clergy because the structure, symbolism, rituals, and uniforms satisfy their needs to lead in a directive or authoritarian manner.

People with different personalities and temperaments are at-tracted to leadership roles in organizations such as some universities, think tanks, and research laboratories because the comparatively loose structure, informality, and less rigidly defined roles satisfy their needs to lead in a less directive, more collegial, or participative manner. Because leaders have different traits, characteristics, personalities, and temperaments, their needs to lead in various ways vary widely. To be effective, leaders must be matched to environments where the approaches or styles they are most comfortable exhibiting will work to bring about positive results.

Leadership studies conducted over the past 50 years have shown that some people respond better to highly structured work environments with directive leadership while others respond better to unstructured work environments and nondirective leadership. Again, experience, personality, training, and other factors interplay to affect a person's needs to work under either structured or unstructured leadership. It is important that people be placed in work environments and under supervisors who will satisfy their needs.

Leadership styles in organizations are also affected by a broad range of environmental and situational factors, of which the following are some examples.

The leadership style exhibited by supervisors, up to the chief executive officer. (In some organizations leadership styles depend on the length of the shadow cast by the person in the top position.)

The degree of structuring and control of decision making by organizational procedures, regulations, and rules.

The presence of a union and negotiated labor-management agreement.

The level of danger present in the workplace.

The financial condition of the organization.

The organization's position in its industry.

The process of determining budget.

The supervisors' degree of responsibility and accountability.

The way in which work is scheduled.

Prevailing values, norms, attitudes, traditions, and past practices.

Legal constraints.

Technological constraints.

The degree of quality required in producing the product or service.

Size of the group.

The kind of behavior rewarded by the organization.

Leadership is too complex a process to be considered as just a function of a few variables. For this reason it is impossible to say conclusively that a particular style of leadership should be practiced by supervisors. What works for supervisors in one organization could bring disastrous results if applied in another organization. Leadership styles must be designed and tailored to fit.

Leadership effectiveness is broadly measured by the degree of cooperation supervisors get from employees in achieving organizational objectives within cost and time parameters. Supervisors can measure their own performance by comparing it to personal standards or expectations, or by using typical industry standards. Some of the specific performance criteria that should be measured, regardless of the setting are:

Quantity of production.

Quality of production.

Attendance of employees.

Degree of cooperativeness among employees.

Types and quantities of grievances filed.

Turnover of employees.

Cost of production.

Attitudes of informal group leaders.

Type and amount of upward communication.

Frequency of scheduled overtime.

Frequency of applying disciplinary action.

Degree of trust and confidence that exists between employees and management.

If the measurements of any one or combination of these factors do not meet, or exceed, the standards or expectations, supervisors must analyze the situation and determine the underlying causes of problems. Only then can a plan for corrective action be successfully formulated.

CHANGING LEADERSHIP STYLES

Supervisors, like most people, are creatures of habit. As such, they attempt to repeat behaviors that benefit them. However, changes in conditions, environment, or situation can necessitate changes in behavior. Supervisors do not always willingly change their behavior even when they recognize the need. Change can be forced upon people, but that can be a time-consuming and costly process. Long-run change can be best brought about if change is voluntary.

Suppose it is concluded that approaches to or styles of leading need to be changed. How can change be accomplished? The following conditions are necessary to successfully bring about a change.

The most important factor in the change process is the desire to change behavior itself. The stronger a person's motivation to change, the higher the probability of success. Changing basic leadership style is not easily accomplished and can be frustrating. Maintaining focus on the objective is important. Directly interrelated with a person's motivation to change is the support he or she receives from others, especially superiors. Having a superior who will support, guide, train, and counsel you is highly desirable. A supportive superior can help you in the difficult periods and give feedback as to progress or the lack of it. Honest and accurate feedback is essential in achieving goals.

In developing a plan for change, you must recognize and accept the type of leader you are. Looking in the mirror is not very helpful, because we don't see ourselves as others see us. We are judged not by what we say, but rather by what we do. Once the self-deception is removed, strategies and tactics for change can be developed. Implicit in planning for change is knowledge of leadership and the defining of a goal.

As the plan for change is implemented, the rate of progress must be measured. Short-range goals must be set and standards of measurement developed. For example, reduction in complaints per month, increased cooperation, or increasing the number of meetings with employees can be criteria for assessing progress.

The rewards, both intrinsic and extrinsic, must be available and distributed as change in behavior occurs. Intrinsic rewards are the rewards people give themselves. Extrinsic rewards are the rewards given by others. Praise, recognition, compensation increases, and prestige are the types of rewards that should be available.

Last, when expected change does not occur, disciplinary action with the objective of rehabilitation must be put into effect. Without the ability to reward or discipline, changing people's behavior will be difficult to achieve.

2

The Practice of Leadership

Ray A. Killian

The practice of leadership involves taking certain identifiable steps which, if performed skillfully, will result in maximum leadership influence and goal achievement. If these guidelines are disregarded, the results will not reach desired levels. The late Chester I. Barnard, former president of the New Jersey Bell Telephone Company and an outstanding thinker on management, suggested the following four factors in leadership behavior:

1. The determination of objectives.
2. The manipulation of means.
3. The instrumentality of action.
4. The stimulation of coordinated action.

The ten-step guide to leadership achievement which follows embodies these factors. This guide can be applied to most activities where the leader must utilize human resources to get the job done:

From *Managers Must Lead!*, by Ray A. Killian. © 1979 AMACOM, a division of American Management Associations.

1. *Establish goals*. Activity has no value until the reason for it has been identified. Leadership implies movement in some direction—but toward what destination? The first step is to determine the desired result. This could mean getting $100,000 in orders for the sales team, meeting a production quota for the assembly line, or winning the pennant for a major league ball club. In each case, planning, appropriate use of resources, and follow-through cannot be completed until the goal has been clearly identified. Once this has been done, everything else should focus on what is necessary to accomplish the required end.

2. *Communicate understanding of goals*. Once the leader has a clear understanding of the goal, *hir*** must use adequate means to communicate this understanding to the people who will help *hir* achieve the desired result. This could entail a simple explanation or an elaborately planned meeting and a lengthy presentation. In any case, the leader must take account of the fact that others' interests and responses are directly related to their understanding of the goal.

3. *Justify the effort and response requested*. After the goal is understood, its achievement requires response and effort from the group. This response may not be forthcoming without special effort by the leader. *Hir* must carefully gauge the amount of effort which will be needed, establish a clear picture of the job performance necessary, and set an appropriately devised program into motion, making certain to keep employees informed of the reasons for the goal and the potential benefits to those involved in the project. Success by its very nature hinges on the reaction of both the individual and the team. It is therefore a leadership responsibility to justify this response and bring it to bear effectively on the situation.

4. *Provide a roadmap to the goals*. Identifying and understanding the goals provide only the foundation for their achievement. Leadership must furnish the roadmap which indicates the proper paths to follow, the correct turns to take, and practical steps each person can

*Editor's Notes: AMACOM, with the full cooperation of Ray Killian, introduced a set of gender-free pronouns in *Managers Must Lead!* These pronouns are:
hir (pronounced "here" and replacing the forms *he/she* and *him/her*)
hirs (replacing *his/her* and *his/hers*)
hirself (replacing *himself/herself*)
The origin of these terms is explained fully in the Publisher's Note in *Managers Must Lead!*

take to accomplish the company objectives. This roadmap must offer all the information necessary for progress, and to a degree that minimizes uncertainties, delays, and distractions.

5. *Set resources into motion*. Battles have been lost, production schedules missed, and golden opportunities wasted because of inertia. Successful leadership recognizes that resources must be set into motion in the correct direction—things must be made to happen, effective teams must be organized, and initiative must be provided.

6. *Keep oriented toward the goal*. Undirected energy will fail to reach the target. When resources have been set into motion, the leader is responsible for keeping them oriented toward achievement of the desired result.

7. *Provide answers and set the example*. The best way to show people where to go is to lead them. The best way to get an enthusiastic response is to be enthusiastic. The best way to provide answers is to exert the effort necessary to find the answers. People are willing to follow the leader only when *hir* shows the desire to lead them toward their goal.

8. *Evaluate and improve all activities*. When a ship crosses the ocean, it has a destination. But its speed, position, course, and progress must be evaluated and adjusted often during the crossing to make certain it will reach the desired port. Human activity, too, seldom arrives at its goal without periodic appraisal of progress and adjustment of direction. The leader's responsibility is to provide this appraisal and determine what adjustments must be made.

9. *Recognize and commend progress*. People need to know how they are getting along and what progress they are making. The leader's responsibility is not so much to find fault as to guide *hirs* human and material resources toward the desired goal. Often, the most effective way to speed up what is being done is to give recognition and commendation to those who deserve it, and thus spur them to greater effort.

10. *Reward goal achievement appropriately*. Only the short-sighted leader fails to reward those who have contributed to the achievement of the goal. Proper rewards are the best assurance of future response and achievement. These rewards may be monetary or material, but of equal importance are ego satisfaction and recognition of individual contribution. The individual who gives this type of

recognition acquires a reputation as a good leader, increases his chances of success for *hirs* current project, and builds a sound foundation for future achievement.

KEYS TO IMPROVED LEADERSHIP

An essential characteristic of leadership is a striving for constant improvement. It follows that leaders themselves must constantly try to increase their own contribution. This does not occur by accident, but must be the result of a deliberate and carefully planned approach. Experience has shown that when leaders improve their knowledge and skills by following the rules, they increase their total contribution potential.

Be willing to accept additional leadership. A department head in a large general office was asked to assume responsibility for an additional segment of the work. Her reaction was that she didn't want it: She felt that she already had too much to look after, and that she couldn't take on additional work because she didn't have enough people or equipment to do it. What she failed to recognize was that if she agreed to do more work, the company expected to provide the necessary people and equipment. Yet this same woman was dissatisfied with her progress and salary.

Leaders who rise rapidly to higher positions of responsibility have one trait in common—a willingness to accept additional responsibility. Too many people make excuses for themselves by saying that they have too much to do already, that it will be too much trouble, or that is someone else's job. The successful leader recognizes that the only way to make a greater contribution is to accept greater leadership and work responsibility and, of course, to discharge that responsibility efficiently.

Surround yourself with capable people. All successful leaders realize somewhere along the way that they cannot handle all the details of their work themselves. The wise ones choose capable people to help get the job done. The abilities of these people do not detract from the leader's role; they contribute to it. And as their contributions increase, the leader reaches higher levels of accomplishment.

Be dissatisfied. The fatal blow to progress is self-satisfaction.

When leaders become smug about what they have accomplished, it is almost certain that they will make no further progress. Most executives look for leaders who are dissatisfied in their present positions in the hope that this dissatisfaction will bring about continuing improvement and growth.

After discussion, it was decided not to promote a line executive to the position of branch manager because he was too satisfied to bring sufficient drive to the job. The man was a college graduate, had a brilliant mind, possessed excellent ability, and was capable of accomplishing almost any goal. He was in his early forties, his children had finished college, and his wife had an excellent job. He was able to meet his financial responsibilities at his present salary level and could cope with the demands of his job with a minimum of exertion. He missed the promotion because he lacked sufficient ambition to be entrusted with more important responsibilities. Had he been dissatisfied with his present salary, with the results in his department, and with his present level of responsibility, he would have been a more aggressive leader and a prime candidate for promotion.

Put first things first. An effective leader has to have a sense of values that may be different from that of the employee. *Hir* must be able to give top priority to the most essential matters and not get sidetracked by details that will prevent *hir* from achieving the really important goals.

Most individuals find the time and the resources for the things they consider most important—whether it be fishing, golf, or professional improvements on the job. They do not necessarily have to choose between professional responsibilities and personal and professional lives.

Develop people. It is a basic human desire to want to improve, to make more money, and to become more professional in every activity. Some people have a capacity for self-motivation and can move forward to some degree by themselves. However, leaders need to recognize that one of their responsibilities is to accelerate the development of other people through training, example, and whatever other methods can do the job. The employee will be grateful for the assistance and will respond with respect and appreciation.

Design a blueprint for growth and stick to it. A contractor does not build a house without a blueprint. However, after the blueprint has been approved, *hir* must follow it unless there is sufficient reason for change, in which case new plans must be drawn. Leadership does not suddenly emerge from nowhere; it grows step by step. The blueprint should provide for this orderly development of leadership qualities.

LEADERSHIP AND EXECUTIVE GROWTH

John A. Patton said: "Ninety-nine percent of the people in this world want to be told what to do. Be in the other one percent." For those who have what it takes to be in the 1 percent group, the rewards are great in human satisfaction and material compensation. But this exclusive club is composed only of the ambitious, the dedicated, and those who are willing to follow the roadmap that leads to effective human leadership.

The opportunity to lead, to shape the lives of others, to provide an authentic service to people and enterprises, can be an experience equal in excitement and satisfaction to that offered by any sport or hobby. Take a new look at your leadership opportunity, plot a fresh and creative approach to it, elicit the mental and physical resources of your people, and your future can be one of unlimited possibilities.

3

Profile of a
Tough-Minded Manager

Joe D. Batten

A tough-minded and motivational climate is impossible without tough-minded and productive individuals. And, while we must recognize that there are many variations, shadings, and types of people who can measure up to the tough-minded business requirements of tomorrow, we need a comprehensive set of common denominators. The specifications which follow may seem unrealistically ideal, but a sizable number of people have made the grade and have repeatedly demonstrated that stretching toward ideals which may initially seem impossible is really very desirable. It is necessary, in fact, to create "stretch" for the person who in turn intends to stretch his subordinates. People with flabby mental and physical equipment simply cannot meet the national and international requirements of business in the world of tomorrow.

From *Tough-Minded Management*, by Joe D. Batten. © 1978 AMACOM, a division of American Management Associations.

AS INDIVIDUALS

Tough-minded managers must know themselves and be happy with what they are while at the same time building a healthy, calculated dissatisfaction with the status quo. They must realize, whether currently happy with their growth and caliber or not, that they must continue to grow, change, and stretch.

It is futile to point out that lots of nonmanagement people are more morose, disturbed, or neurotic than lots of management people. This has been tacitly implied throughout this book. But our concern in this particular context is management personnel, and we know it is naïve and silly to pretend that top executive status automatically implies optimum self-understanding, fitness, and effectiveness. People must take periodic, detailed inventories of themselves in terms of what they stand for, what they believe, what they can accomplish, what their strengths and weaknesses are, and what they put into life. The last-named point is perhaps most important. They must consider what they can give to life and derive from it rather than what *it* can give to *them*.

Here are some qualities of the ideal tough-minded executive as an individual, whether a man or a woman.

1. He practices self-discipline in terms of legal and ethical rules of conduct. He recognizes that a vigorous, outgoing, and sometimes ebullient way of life can only be possible and lasting as a product of such discipline.
2. He recognizes that developing and maintaining maximum physical fitness is an important requisite of mental health and acuity; that such fitness is not self-indulgence but part of an executive's obligation to his business, his employees, and his family. He becomes a bit of an authority on it and encourages his subordinates to do likewise. The development of the whole person is just lip service, he believes, without follow-through in terms of physical well-being.
3. He enjoys life—and people know it! The dour, scowling, formidable executive accomplishes little by his behavior except ulcers for his staff and himself.
4. His interests and activities may range widely or may center in

certain worthwhile areas. At his best, the truly broad-gauge executive reads widely and has his own private development program.

5. He has either developed or is moving toward a personal faith. He feels that religion is a personal thing, a way of living, and is tolerant of the views of others. (Usually such beliefs and a zest for life are closely related.)

6. He never apologizes for a thing before doing it; he apologizes only when he knows he has not done his best. He is impatient with apologists because their contribution is always negative.

7. He takes the stand that negativism is *never* justified. He knows that there are pluses and minuses in many situations but that the minuses can become pluses. Minuses are really only the absence of pluses.

8. He always wants to know the *why* of a happening and supplies the *why* conscientiously to others.

9. He predicates his actions on facts but, knowing that the variables often exceed the constants, he is not limited by them.

10. He is very much his own person and believes in God and himself.

11. He retains a healthy dissatisfaction with his abilities as a communicator. He knows eloquence is no substitute for understanding, erudition no guarantee of lucidity, volubleness no substitute for action. He does not confuse mere dialog with full communication.

12. He is impatient with old wives' sayings like, "You can't teach old dogs new tricks." He resolves to learn new things until the day he dies, and he knows he can. He retains his sense of wonder.

13. He slices right to the heart of problems and does something about them.

14. He knows that life without work is a short cut to deterioration.

15. He feels that a broad and eclectic fund of knowledge makes not only for a better generalist but also for a better specialist.

16. He is proud of his way of life and seeks to enrich the lives of others.

17. He does not confuse wit or intelligence with wisdom and strives steadily for greater wisdom.

18. He aims for a balanced existence in the full knowledge that wholesome recreation and rest habits enable him to do a better job.
19. He is impatient with the type of people who feel a harried expression and an ulcer are signs of success. He knows these people must grow up. He thinks laughter is great.
20. He is satisfied with nothing less than full success as a whole person.
21. He takes his work seriously but never himself.

AS MEMBERS OF SOCIETY

A lot of bunkum has been written about the business executive's role in society. Points of view have been thrust forward which vary from pole to pole. Some say business should abdicate its rights to big government; others feel that business should virtually replace government in many areas (and this may be so); while still others talk vaguely about a kind of partnershp heavily dominated by government.

It is the view of this book that government's role must change in expression and operation but not depart from basic principles. Our concepts of government must be fair and responsible as we move toward an increasingly cohesive world community, but this gradual transition must be accomplished in a statesmanlike way. Personalities and petty axes to grin will have no place tomorrow in either government or business. This calls for an enlightened and tough-minded citizenry of which business is a fully qualified representative.

Here are some specific things the tough-minded executive should do and is doing:

1. He lives integrity instead of relying on preachments.
2. He carries his emphasis on results over his community and industrywide activities.
3. He practices candor widely and reflects a true warmth of feeling toward his associates.
4. He has the guts to say what ought to be said. He realizes the time for permissiveness and apologetic behavior by business-men is long past (if it was ever appropriate).
5. He knows that the actions of a responsible executive are

contagious and that there is virtually no limit to potential accomplishment if a sufficient number of people live the precepts of tough-mindedness.

6. He is a humanitarian, but no one ever labeled a tough-minded executive a "do-gooder."

7. He believes that management by integrity can be a rallying point for true social, political, and economic progress.

8. He believes in trying to strengthen the caliber of political and municipal officials rather than just commenting on it caustically.

9. He knows it takes more courage and ability to strengthen our society than it takes to highlight its weaknesses.

10. When broad problems loom, he is not content simply to appoint a committee. He wants target dates set, objectives defined—then action.

AS A MANAGER

In his role within his own company, finally, the tough-minded person exemplifies all the principles of management by integrity as they have been set forth in these pages:

1. He takes steps to insure that the company's philosophy and objectives are researched, developed, and clearly communicated.

2. He insures that all employees know the *what, where, when, who, how,* and—above all—*why* of their jobs and the company.

3. He knows that people are more efficient and happy when they understand clearly what results are expected of them.

4. He insures that tailored procedures and techniques are installed to measure the contributions of all people and units to achieving the company's objectives, that compensation is related to performance.

5. He believes and lives the concept that the development of people, as a whole and in depth, pays real dividends to both the business and the individual.

6. He believes that everybody on the payroll should be held

accountable for accomplishment, that he must do the job or get out of it.

7. He makes certain that the statement, "Management is the development of people, not the direction of things," moves briskly beyond the lip-service stage and becomes completely understood and operational.

8. He knows that all personnel will contribute and receive more if they are helped to develop a clear feeling of purpose, direction, dignity, and expectations.

9. He knows that optimum results cannot be expected unless each employee receives all information appropriate to the results required of him.

10. He strives to develop in all personnel an awareness of the value of work *to them*.

11. He believes in utilizing all the modern management tools fully when appropriate, but he insists that they pay their way.

12. He knows that management by integrity is realistic and workable; that, in reality, there is no fit substitute for it.

13. He knows that changes in business and the world in general are inevitable, but he doesn't resist them. He anticipates the unfolding of the future, plans for it, and sets trends.

14. He requires and encourages a climate conducive to innovation in all facets of the business.

15. He cultivates a curiosity for new dimensions of knowledge and resists efforts to predicate plans on past and present knowledge only.

16. He believes our country is on the verge of increasingly dramatic breakthroughs in both technology and human understanding and wants to play a positive role in them.

17. He does not look to others to charge his battery but takes the necessary action to build in perpetuating values, inspiration, and intellectual enrichment.

18. He realizes that pressures in the work environment and within the person are caused almost completely by negativism, pessimism, and ungrounded fears. Accordingly, he makes sure that his own beliefs, energy, and positiveness flow out steadily to the extremities of the business. This calls for tough-mindedness of the highest order and is a never-ending challenge.

19. He increasingly relegates tools and techniques to their proper secondary role as he moves toward mature conceptual management. For concepts are part of the stuff of wisdom, and wisdom is the stuff of management.

20. He is not deterred by small people. He knows what he wants and what the organization needs, secures maximum participation from his key people, and moves ahead relentlessly toward the actual practice of management by integrity.

The *summum bonum* of this tough-minded profile is:

> *I will make the lives of others richer*
> *by the richness of my own.*

4

Leadership and Transactional Analysis

Heinz Weihrich

Few topics have received as much attention as leadership. Although managers perform various roles, perhaps none is as important as the role of organizational leader. It is generally recognized that in the study of leadership several sets of factors are important, such as forces in the manager, forces in the subordinates, and forces in the situation. There is no doubt that the leader's behavior and his use of authority in directing employees are critical in determining the effectiveness of the leadership pattern. Robert Tannenbaum and Warren Schmidt, in their classic article "How to Choose a Leadership Pattern" (*Harvard Business Review*, May–June 1973), present a variety of possible behaviors ranging from maximum use of authority with low degree of freedom for subordinates to minimum use of authority with high degree of freedom for subordinates. The different styles of managerial behaviors are charted in Figure 4-1.

Originally published as "How to Change a Leadership Pattern." From *Management Review*, April 1979.

Figure 4-1. Continuum of leadership behavior.

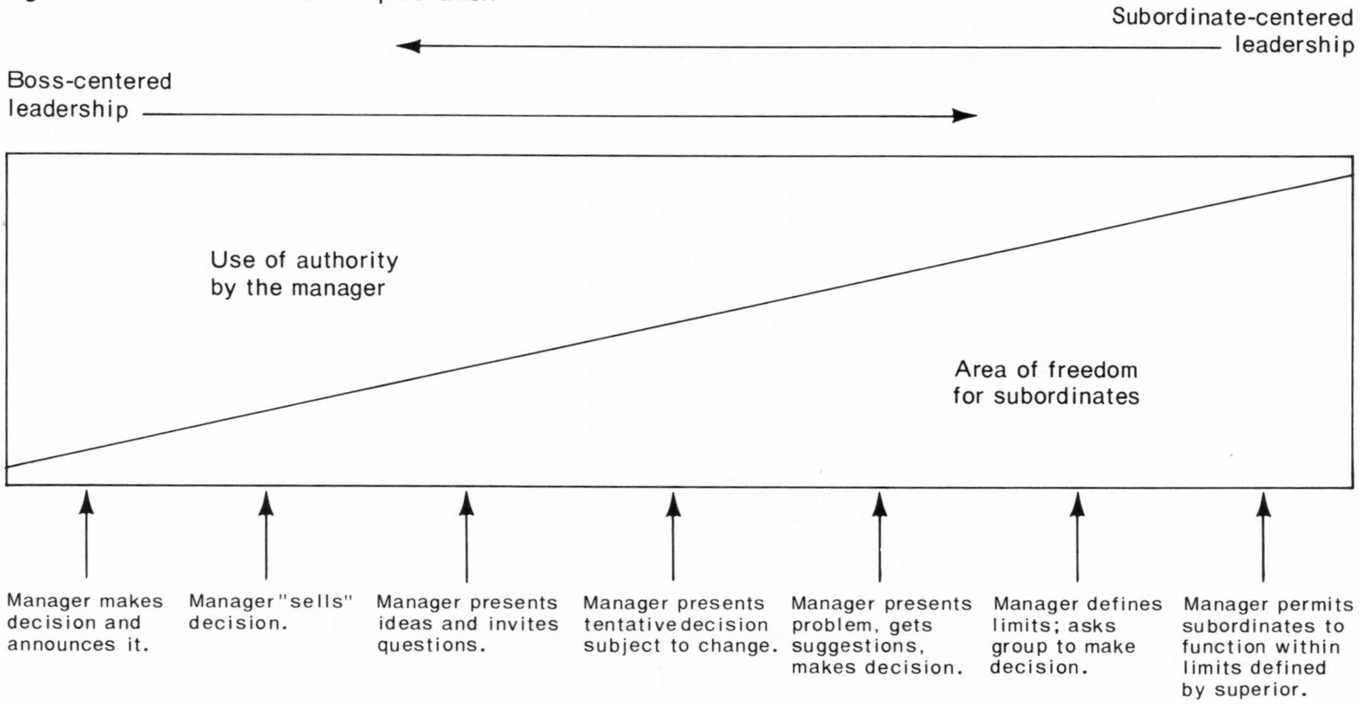

Boss-centered
leadership ———→

←——— Subordinate-centered
leadership

Use of authority
by the manager

Area of freedom
for subordinates

| Manager makes decision and announces it. | Manager "sells" decision. | Manager presents ideas and invites questions. | Manager presents tentative decision subject to change. | Manager presents problem, gets suggestions, makes decision. | Manager defines limits; asks group to make decision. | Manager permits subordinates to function within limits defined by superior. |

Although the model clearly shows that leadership behavior should be viewed on a continuum with different degrees of authority, it does not suggest how to *change* a leadership pattern. Fortunately, we have a tool that can assist a manager to alter behavior. By applying transactional analysis (TA), the manager can gain insights into his own behavior and that of subordinates, an advantage that may be the first step in changing behavior from an ineffective mode to one that fits the personality of the leader, the subordinates, and the situation.

The purpose of this article is to provide the missing link between TA and leadership by (1) explaining some basic TA concepts, (2) discussing the leadership patterns that may originate in one of the three ego states (the Parent, the Adult, or the Child), and (3) recommending ways to use TA for changing the leadership pattern.

THE EGO STATES IN TA

Transactional analysis was developed by the late Eric Berne and popularized in his book *Games People Play*. The general value of TA in improving communication soon became evident. More recently it has been shown that TA may also be used to improve appraisal. It also can be used to change leadership behavior.

TA consists of several parts: Structural analysis, which focuses on the ego states of individuals; the analysis of transactions, which emphasizes the interactions between individuals; the way time is structured, which includes the analysis of psychological games people tend to play; and finally the life positions one may adopt about oneself and others. This discussion, though, will emphasize the ego states, explained through structural analysis.

An ego state, according to Berne, is a consistent pattern of feelings and experiences directly related to a corresponding pattern of behavior. Each personality, then, consists of three ego states: the Parent, the Adult, and the Child. (These terms have nothing to do with age; they refer only to ego states.)

The *Parent* ego state may be seen, for example, in authoritative and even prejudiced behavior that is learned, to a large extent, from parents and other influential persons, especially during early life. A manager, then, operating in this ego state would make extensive use of authority, giving little freedom to subordinates. This would correspond to the left side of the model in Figure 4-1.

The *Adult* ego state, on the other hand is the rational part of the personality. The behavior includes, for example, information gathering and decision making based on a careful analysis of the facts. This ego state can be seen in a leadership behavior that may approximate the middle part and slightly to the right of the model in Figure 4-1.

The *Child* ego state—the third part of the personality—pertains largely to emotional aspects. It consists of the mental recordings of internal events. This ego state could probably be seen in the leadership behavior described at the extreme right side in the model.

The point is that the ego states of leaders may help to explain their behavior. TA facilitates the recognition of the ego states and provides us with the tools for changing one's leadership style to fit a variety of leadership situations.

LEADERSHIP BEHAVIOR: PARENT, ADULT, CHILD

Each ego state is a source of managerial behavior. The most likely relationships between the ego state and leadership style are summarized in Figure 4-2 in which popular—and shorter—labels are used to

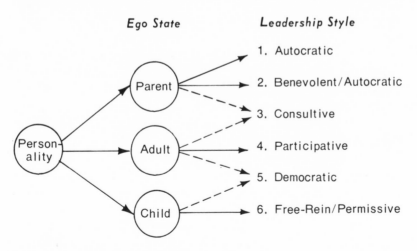

Figure 4–2. Personality and managerial leadership.

describe the managerial behaviors using different degrees of authority and the respective areas of freedom of subordinates.

1. *Autocratic leadership and the Parent ego state*. An autocratic leader operates primarily from the Parent ego state. In fact, this manager is often critical and even prejudiced in the relationship with subordinates. Authority, unfortunately, is often seen as the principal— if not the only—way to guide subordinates in their jobs.

Such a manager, for example, identifies the problems, objectives, and plans for the subordinates. He selects the course of action to be taken, and subordinates have few opportunities to participate in the decision-making process. Consequently, there is little commitment by subordinates to the aims of the organization. This leader may even use threats to get things done. Moreover, controls are rigid, and the manager acts as a judge in evaluating the performance of subordinates. In short, under this kind of leadership, subordinates have little freedom to influence their own work environment.

2. *Benevolent-autocratic leadership and the Parent ego state*. The benevolent-autocratic leader also operates primarily from his Parent ego state. More specifically, it is especially the Nurturing Parent ego state that establishes the relationship between the superior and subordinates. Such a manager will identify problems, objectives, and plans for the subordinates. He may ask for some inputs from his people, which, however, may or may not be seriously considered. Although there is some upward communication, information flow is primarily downward, and it is evident that this kind of leadership provides for rather limited freedom for subordinates.

3. *Consultive leadership: The Adult and Parent ego states*. A consultive manager presents ideas, invites questions from subordinates, and considers their inputs. This leader, for example, may use his Adult ego state to gather information necessary for decisions, although the decision might still be implemented through the Parent ego state.

A manager using the consultive leadership style provides a moderate number of opportunities to subordinates for participating in goal setting and the development of plans. Also, there is a considerable degree of integration of objectives and plans of various organizational units. Communication, in general, tends to flow fairly well, both vertically and horizontally. Further, subordinates do have some say in the evaluation of their own performance. In all, the consultive manager provides an environment that encourages problem solving and decisions based on objective facts, although the implementation of plans may still be done from the Parent ego state.

4. *Participative leadership and the Adult ego state*. This manager feels OK about himself and others. The leader, utilizing his Adult ego state, collects data relevant to the decision. Subordinates, on the other hand, have a great deal of freedom to participate in the identification of problems and in suggesting solutions. The leader and the followers jointly set objectives, jointly develop plans, and jointly evaluate alternative courses of action. The emphasis may be on the smooth functioning of the group with free flow of information. The organizational climate, then, is conducive to self-control and self-development, with a high degree of integration of individual needs and the demands on the organization. The leader's style, based on the Adult ego state, provides ample freedom for subordinates to utilize their potentials.

5. *Democratic leadership: Adult and Child ego states*. This manager uses less authority and gives even more freedom to subordinates than the participative leader. As a manager he may not even reserve the final decision-making authority. His aim is to get consensus among the group members. Although this leader may derive his behavior from the Adult ego state by using the group to collect relevant information, decisions will not always be based on the facts as seen by the manager; instead, group members may override the leader's decision because of the leader's emotional concern for consensus as an end in itself. It is quite possible, therefore, that such a leader may operate both from the Child ego state and from the Adult.

6. *Free-rein/permissive leadership and the Child ego state*. The leaders using this managerial style may make few decisions, leaving this to a great extent to subordinates. This manager uses a minimum amount of authority, giving maximum freedom to subordinates. He may avoid using power because of Not-OK feelings derived from his Child ego state. Or, it may simply be the result of a carefree attitude. There is little or no systematic effort by the leader to set objectives, identify problems, or develop plans. Subordinates may do as they wish. When creative ideas are developed by subordinates, they are seldom implemented. Further, this manager exercises little control

and does not hold subordinates accountable for results. A close look at such a manager reveals that his behavior originates primarily from the Child ego state, with decisions made on impulse rather than on a rational basis.

HOW TO CHANGE THE LEADERSHIP PATTERN

Leadership is a complex process. There is, however, general agreement that the leader is one who considers:

◊ The forces in himself or herself.
◊ The forces in those led—subordinates.
◊ The forces in the environment.

Clearly, to change the forces in the environment is often difficult, if not impossible, for the individual to initiate. On the other hand, to modify responses in the subordinates is not an insurmountable task. In fact, a manager can improve the interaction with his people by providing the proper stimulus to get a more effective response. Specifically, he can direct his message more frequently to the Adult ego states of subordinates, and the tools provided through TA can facilitate the interactions with employees.

Perhaps the easiest way to increase effectiveness is to begin with the leader. The individual who recognizes the ego state that gives rise to his leadership style will be able to better assess the forces not only in himself but also in subordinates and in the situation. More specifically, effective leader behavior requires (1) the recognition of one's own ego state, (2) the strengthening of the Adult ego state, (3) the identification of the ego state in others, and (4) the selection of the ego state demanded by the situation.

1. *Ego states in the leader*. There is no one best way to lead. Leadership style may range from one extreme, with the manager using a great amount of authority and leaving almost no freedom for subordinates, to the opposite end of the continuum, at which little authority is used by the manager, giving a great deal of freedom to subordinates.

The predominant ego state in the leader certainly influences his behavior. For example, the *autocratic* and even the *benevolent-*

autocratic leader probably sees the use of authority as the main tool to managing. This leadership pattern, however, can become especially dysfunctional if the base for behavior is the Prejudicial Parent ego state. Such a leader, for example, may have preconceived notions of the proper way of behaving. He does not recognize alternative ways of managing. The result is behavioral inflexibility.

Although the Parent ego state may be appropriate for some situations, problems usually occur if it is the only basis for directing subordinates. Such a leader may not recognize problems because his perceptions are dominated by his early experiences stored in the Parent ego state. Such perceptions may also inhibit the search for alternative solutions to a problem. In fact, his leadership style may result in a rigid, unimaginative organization. Also, since subordinates are not invited to participate in the decision-making process, they may not be committed to the aims of the organization. The problem is that such a manager may not even recognize the potentials of the subordinates and consequently will not utilize their full capacity.

It would be wrong to assume, however, that the leader operating from the Parent ego state is completely ineffective. Indeed, at times demanding authoriative direction, as in an emergency situation, this kind of leader can provide direction to a leaderless group. Similarly, the Nurturing Parent ego state may be appropriate for encouraging employees with Not-OK feelings to contribute to the organization. However, if this behavior becomes the predominant style, it may result in docile, dependent, yes-men employees.

Some managers take the other extreme and lead through the *free-rein/permissive* style, based on their Child ego state. It is true that, at times, this may result in creative ideas. However, in organizations it is also necessary that these innovative ideas become a reality and get implemented. Such a leader, unfortunately, may not give the required direction to subordinates. Objectives and plans may not be integrated with those of other departments. With poor standards, control is difficult and little accountability may be demanded from subordinates.

The *participative* manager, on the other hand, operates primarily from his Adult ego state. He feels OK about himself and others. Consequently, he is not threatened by the participation of subordinates in the decision-making process. In fact, he encourages subordinates to identify problems and to suggest solutions to overcome them. Goal setting and planning are done jointly by the manager and subordinates. Activities are coordinated with those of other organizational units. Specifically, the organization is seen as an interlocking, interdependent system in which all employees—managers and non-managers—contribute toward commom aims. Control information, for example, is collected on an objective basis. Similarly, subordinates are evaluated primarily on results rather than on personality traits.

One might incorrectly infer that the leadership style based on the Adult is the only way to manage. However, in a well-rounded personality all three ego states—the Parent, the Adult, and the Child—are important. Similarly, leadership styles ranging from auto-cratic to free-rein/permissive may be appropriate at times, depending on the subordinates and the situation, as will be discussed below. It is true, nevertheless, that too often the Adult is underutilized.

2. *The strengthening of the Adult.* The Adult ego state, like character, must be developed. This requires patience, confidence, supreme concern, and persistence. The Adult can be cultivated and utilized in several ways. By searching for the facts, preconceived notions may be uncovered. Thus, one may become aware, through the use of the Adult, when the Parent or Child responses are appropriate or when they are dysfunctional.

It is the Adult, then, that restrains the automatic Parent or Child responses. It is the Adult that asks probing questions, listens to new ideas, and tests them against reality. It is the Adult that initiates the setting of challenging, yet realistic objectives. It is the Adult that systematically searches for alternative courses of action and estimates their probability of success. It is the Adult that argues sincerely and courageously for an ethical, but perhaps unpopular, issue. It is the Adult that assumes responsibility for his own actions. Of course, such a manager may make mistakes; but he learns from them and then focuses on the future. In short, the OK manager operating from the Adult ego state feels confident, OK about himself, which allows him to select any of the three ego states appropriate to fit the occasion. And the selection is a conscious one, made through the Adult ego state.

3. *Ego states in subordinates.* The effective leader not only develops an awareness of his own ego states as sources of his behavior but also recognizes the ego states of followers. For example, the Not-

OK Child in the subordinate may need encouragement. Consequently, the leader, using his Nurturing Parent, can instill an OK-feeling in the subordinate by giving positive reinforcement. As the subordinate progresses toward a healthy self-image, the manager can direct his communication to the Adult ego state in the subordinate, promoting emphasis on objective data gathering and analytical decision making. This, of course, is the first step in the professionalization of employees and managers.

In general, a manager is more likely to address the interpersonal transaction to the Adult ego state of the employee if the subordinate:

◊ Has the knowledge and experience required to make the decision.

◊ Understands his goals and that of the organization so that he can use his Adult state to search for alternative ways to achieve the aims.

◊ Has had opportunities to prove that he is capable of making effective decisions.

◊ Has special (perhaps highly technical) knowledge the manager may not have.

◊ Can cope with uncertain situations by having a high tolerance for ambiguities.

In summarizing this section, it can be stated that managers too often direct the message—in TA terms, the transactional stimulus—to the Child ego state of their subordinates. This may be very ineffective because the new labor force is usually well educated, has high skills, and also demands responsibility. People can be professionalized by creating an environment in which the Adult ego state of subordinates is better utilized. This benefits both the organization and individuals, who can grow within the organizational environment.

4. *Ego states demanded by the situation*. Finally, the effective manager considers the situation when selecting the ego state for guiding subordinates. Thus, he might consider the type of organization, the nature of the tasks, and the problem itself.

Over time, organizations, like individuals, are guided by values and traditional ways of doing things. If, for example, the organizational climate discourages taking the initiative and finding new ways, then a sudden shift to a more participative leadership pattern will probably be met with skepticism. A subordinate, who has constantly heard the phrase, "We have always done it this way," will perhaps be difficult to convince that there are benefits in searching for different alternatives and experimenting with the new processes. Similarly, if a benevolent/ autocratic organization suddenly withdraws the traditional support, people will feel frustrated and helpless. The point, of course, is that people must be prepared for the change in organizational climate and values.

Another force in the situation is the nature of the task that demands different ego states as sources of leadership behavior. For example, people who have used a proven production process for many years may not see the value of questioning well-established methods even though new technology may be available. In contrast, a research group with a tradition of exploring new ideas and new ways of doing things may be prepared for a leadership style based on the Adult ego state of their boss.

Different problems may also demand different leadership styles. For example, in a situation with many possible alternatives, the Child and Adult ego state may be utilized effectively to find creative solutions. On the other hand, a fire in the building may require a strong direction from the boss's Parent ego state to guide employees to safety. At other times, the Adult may be appropriate for selecting from among many alternative courses of action. It is the Adult that guides the definition of the problem, the evaluation of the alternatives, and the selection of a course of action based on this analysis.

We can conclude, then, that the effective leader uses his Adult state to recognize the relevant factors such as the type of organization, the nature of the task, and the problem itself; and then selects the ego state appropriate to the situation.

5

Responsive Leadership: The Woman Manager's Asset or Liability?

Beverly Hyman

Ask yourself, Would you rather report to a man or to a woman? Most men and women still answer—a man. This comes as no great surprise. Men and women alike are resistant to change, and women's move into supervisory management represents a significant change for all of us in roles, rules, and norms.

Common perceptions of how the woman boss manages fall into two extreme stereotypes. Some of us see her as a Wagnerian Brunhild: tough, aggressive, unyielding, more autocratic than the autocratic male who was her model. More of us see the woman manager as a good worker but a weak, nonassertive leader. We fear that her early conditioning as a female, her needs to be liked, and her nurturance and concern for others will leave us in the frustrating vacuum created by inadequate leadership.

From *Supervisory Management*, August 1980.

As we move up the managerial ladder, leadership increasingly can be observed in a manager's pattern of communication. Fully 66 to 75 percent of a manager's time is spent in some form of interpersonal communication. The effectiveness of that communication, and therefore of the manager, depends on his or her communication style.

As women move into more and more managerial roles formerly occupied by men, some important questions about their communication style should be addressed:

1. Is there a difference between the way men and women managers communicate?
2. Do women managers pattern their communication style after male models or do they imitate traditional female models?
3. Do women managers have their own communication style?
4. How effective is the woman manager as a communicator?

MEN VERSUS WOMEN

In our culture, general differences between the way men and women communicate have been recorded. Men are more aggressive-assertive than women. You are more likely to hear your brother, your father, or your male boss say, "Do it, and do it now," than your sister, your mother, or your female boss. In spite of women's great reputation as talkers, men dominate conversations more than women. Men emerge more often as group leaders than women.

On the other hand, your own experience probably tells you that women generally reveal more information about their feelings, beliefs, and concerns than men. When you converse with most women you feel their need to insure that your conversation is interactive and positive in tone.

Male managers are said to be "strong silent types" whose communications emphasize task orientation and performance output. Female managers are said to be more people-oriented. They exceed males in communicating warmth, helpfulness, concern, and satisfaction. The woman manager, probably much like the women you know, is better at expressing and interpreting emotions of others than her male colleague.

This is probably not surprising to you since it reflects traditional cultural conditioning and even stereotypes. But it leaves many of us with serious questions about the effectiveness of women managers in getting the job done. Our fears and concerns for productivity levels, implementation of company rules and policies, and pursuit of organizational goals are raised when we hear that female managers are "more considerate" and "represent subordinates' interests more" than male managers.

Democracy was brought into the workplace decades before women began to make their recent entry into all levels of management. If concern and consideration for subordinates are all that women bring to their communications as managers, then they bring nothing new. It is true that male managers are less concerned and considerate, but male managers still rank above the normal population in communicating concern and satisfaction to others.

Fortunately, warmth and concern are only one aspect of the female manager's communication repertoire. In a study of the military, female army officers were found to be more considerate than males. (As you fondly reminisce about your male sergeant bellowing, "A ten shun!", your children and grandchildren are more likely hearing, "A ten shun, pleeze!") More important perhaps is that female army officers were rated more production-oriented than male officers. In two studies carried out in industrial settings, female managers were rated higher than males in conflict resolution and in concern for moving toward organizational goals and following rules and policies.

IMPACT ON SUBORDINATES

How do differences in male and female communication styles influence the subordinate on the job? How do these differences influence the way in which employee suggestions are received or whether they are received at all? How do the differences impact on performance-appraisal interviews? How do they affect the communication and carrying out of instructions on a production line?

John Baird and Patricia Bradley, in their book *Styles of Management and Communication: A Comprehensive Study of Men and Women*, attempted to answer some of these questions. The settings for their study included a medium-size midwestern hospital, the clerical departments of a large manufacturing firm, and the production lines of a small manufacturing firm. Their findings reveal that both male and female managers are above the normal population statistically in communicating "comfortableness, friendliness, and expressions of approval" to their subordinates.

If your mother, your wife, or your daughter is given to Sarah Bernhardt displays of emotion, do not be fooled. Women managers communicated no more emotional openness or drama than men. Managers of both sexes seem to feel that emotion and high drama are totally inappropriate to the managerial role.

Still, men and women managers communicated differently from one another in the study. The women did not imitate male models; they had their own communication style. Males were more dominant in their conversations and interviews with subordinates, they were quicker to challenge, and they directed the course of the conversation more.

Female managers in the study statistically supplied more information to subordinates than males. They stressed interpersonal relations, and they were more receptive to ideas and encouraged effort more.

Male subordinates' job satisfaction and morale were lower when they were supervised by male managers.

The same was true of female subordinates supervised by male managers. Female subordinates responded negatively to their male managers' patterns of directing the course of conversation and being quick to challenge. While female subordinates did not mind being dominated, they did mind being treated as so many cogs in the wheel. They needed and wanted to be heard.

Female managers were seen by both male and female subordinates as better communicators than male managers. The evidence clearly does not support our stereotypes of the female manager as either Brunhild, or Sarah Bernhardt, or Casper Milquetoast for that matter!

Martha Burrow's study *Developing the Woman Manager* supports this conclusion as well. While 60 percent of the managers who responded to the survey indicated that "working with women is the same as working with men," 23 percent who said they saw differences reported that women were "more dependable, more concerned, paid better attention to detail."

Put in the context of management theory, as one manager who responded to Burrow's survey wrote, women are "textbook 'people' managers."

SUMMING UP

In advocating a Theory Y approach to management, Douglas McGregor encourages all managers to provide workers with information about the different operations of the company. He argues in favor of our workers having greater input into the decision-making process. He encourages all managers to promote happy interpersonal relations.

In the same vein, Robert Blake and Jane Mouton, in *The Managerial Grid*, emphasize a "team style" approach to management that combines task and group orientations. Their management approach also includes workers in the decision-making process and establishing a climate of mutual trust, respect, and concern. In drawing the outline for "participative management" Rensis Likert, in *The Human Organization*, also describes the importance of worker participation with managers in decision making. Likert highlights the need for a climate of openness, candor, concern, and receptiveness.

Technological advances notwithstanding, management is still getting things done through people. Women managers seem to have their own uniquely feminine communication style that aids them in their efforts to accomplish this.

6

The Nonleaders: Incompetents and Other Bunglers

Donald T. Dalena
Richard I. Henderson

Over the past decade, declining levels of productivity and disappointing product quality have jolted senior management into taking a new look at the workplace. In the late 1960s, this investigation focused on the dissatisfied worker, who was thought to be suffering from various maladies that gave rise to such symptoms as blue-collar blues and white-collar woes. The underlying causes of these symptoms were attributed principally to unsatisfactory conditions existing around the nature of the work. Repetitive and routine work assignments were "identified" as two of the major culprits responsible for polluting the work climate. The true culprit, however, has often not been a boredom arising from work, but rather the treatment workers have received

From *Supervisory Management*, May 1976.

from their managers. Following are five kinds of managers who typify some of the worst kinds of treatment.

Abrasive Abe. This gentleman is an expert (often inadvertently) at rubbing folks the wrong way. He is armed with quick-lipped resistance to anything and everything. Contentious and quarrelsome, he is adept at opening wounds. He constantly wears the work group down; those under his sandpaper command often find themselves clashing with each other. Disagreement is common and there is a steady grinding on the nerves. Aspirin and tranquilizers find a good market among his subordinates.

Arrogant Al. Haughty, often with a visible swagger, this overbearing manager knows it all, has the right allies up the managerial ladder, and makes sure you know it. He is "the boss" and he is as quick with the discipline slip as the old sheriff in Tombstone Territory was with his six guns. He generates fear among his subordinates, and those working under his whip quickly become very cautious. They are experts at "beating the system"; they brag among themselves about how they sabotaged him.

The insecurity bred by Al's attitude breeds secret sabotage difficult to trace. To get even with this supervisor, workers become ingenious in figuring out ways to get back at the company without being caught.

Explosive Ella. Always annoyed and easily upset, she is at the ready for a flare-up. The worker with Ella for a boss doesn't make waves and never crosses her—in fact, he usually adopts a posture designed to pacify her before the fact. When things go wrong or a problem arises, the worker doesn't tell Ella. He knows that if he did, he'd be in for an angry outburst, fiery indignation, nit-picking, second-guessing, and a lot of static. The worker's motto with this kind of supervisor is, "Don't ask her for anything; figure it out yourself. Do the best you can, cover it up, and don't do anything that might annoy her."

Noncommitted Nora. The "I don't give a damn" syndrome is supposed to afflict only workers—but managers too suffer from it. This noncommitted manager has no respect for the worker and no allegiance to the organization. Her lack of concern for what happens is well known. Unwilling to accept responsibility for anything, she is all to happy for a subordinate to pick up the ball and run with it. Just don't expect her to give any directions or provide any blocking.

The mystery here is how this supervisor maintains her position. Her subordinates just cannot believe that higher management is too blind to see such incompetence. In fact, most workers think that this supervisor's seniors must be of the same ilk—which would explain why they don't recognize her.

Shaky Sam. Sam quivers and quakes like a dried-up oak leaf in January. He may once have been a vibrant manager, but either time has taken its toll or he should never have been in this position in the first place. Or he may have developed his gelatinous consistency as a result of threats, personal dislike, or misunderstanding from on high. He does not fully understand his duties or his assignments; his responsibilities often appear overwhelming. Since he doesn't know what to do, he is easily discouraged. Always fearful of doing something wrong, he becomes an expert at procrastination. Each new directive increases his worries. His lack of courage forces him to vacillate and question each action. His commands are weak; he lacks authority. He leans on his superior's orders for constant support and is all too happy to redelegate to his seniors any authority sent his way.

The marvel is that incompetents with such glaring faults get their jobs in the first place and then manage to hold on to them. A common reason is that these supervisors were once good workers, good technicians, good craftsmen, or good mechanics; because of their good work, they were promoted to supervisory positions. One day they were good workers; the next day, they became poor supervisors.

Competent supervisors are not made in heaven; they develop through continued organizational development and support. Organizations must provide individually designed help to transform people from good workers into good supervisors.

THE YARDSTICK

How do you or the supervisors who report to you measure up? Does your behavior ever mark you as an Abrasive Abe or one of his pals? You can use the supervisory responsibility checklist (Figure 6-1) to see how you or a subordinate supervisor is coming across to workers.

Senior managers are constantly being touted on the latest magic elixir to cure sick supervisors. The unhappy truth is that there are no such elixirs. Each illness has its individual roots; to be effective, any

Figure 6-1. Supervisory responsibility checklist.

Managerial Attributes	Abrasive	Arrogant	Explosive	Noncommitted	Shaky
Facilitates downward communication	Yes	No	Yes	No	Yes
Encourages upward communication	No	No	No	No	No
Values people	Yes	No	Yes	No	No
Builds motivating environment	No	No	No	No	No
Arouses respect of superiors	Yes	Yes	No	No	No
Arouses respect of peers	No	No	Yes	No	No
Arouses respect of subordinates	No	No	No	No	No
Inspires subordinates' confidence	No	No	Yes	No	No
Encourages worker self-involvement	No	Yes	Yes	Yes	No
Promotes positive creativity	No	No	Yes	Yes	Yes
Develops workers' sense of security	No	No	Yes	No	Yes
Builds teams	No	No	Yes	Yes	Yes
Minimizes negative creativity	No	No	Yes	Yes	Yes
Stimulates productivity	Yes	Yes	Yes	No	No
Understands job technology	Yes	Yes	Yes	No	Yes
Meets contingencies	No	No	Yes	Yes	No
Promotes quality work	No	No	Yes	No	Yes
Generates short-range efficiency	Yes	Yes	Yes	No	No
Generates short-range effectiveness	No	No	Yes	No	No
Plans long-range efficiency	No	No	No	No	No
Plans long-range effectiveness	No	No	No	No	No

cure must draw on the combined interest and effort of the supervisor himself and his organization.

The first step is for the individual supervisor to recognize his problem areas, accept the need for change, and express the desire to make improvements. The organization must help him identify his problem and decide which remedies in the organizational medicine cabinet are most likely to effect a cure. A review of the five incompetent managers and the diseases they carry into an organization may be helpful.

BICKERING AND STRIFE

A major disease touched off by the abrasive supervisor is dissension. The germs of strife and internal bickering can spread quickly throughout a work group. Individual discontent certainly results in decreased effectiveness (lowering the opportunity for individual goal achievement), although the abrasive supervisor who is technologically proficient can get the job done. This often results in the attainment of short-range efficiency (wise use of organizational resources), but may be detrimental to the long-range efficiency of his operation.

ANGER AND FEAR

Problems caused by the arrogant supervisor are deep and hidden. Although he may accomplish his duties and get the work done, he still inflicts grievous wounds. His subordinates are always angry. They live in fear and lack trust both in their superior and in the organization.

The arrogant supervisor presents the greatest challenge to workers. It is, however, definitely not a challenge that he would want them to live up to. Psychological warfare is used as a defense mechanism against him. His behavior sets off damage stemming from omission, wrong commission, and outright sabotage. If workers cannot directly harm him, they harm the company by damaging tools, machines, and products. On the surface, they go out of their way to please him by simulating the behavior he expects. Meanwhile, they avoid taking any initiative, demand numerous decisions of him, and follow with alacrity the decisions they know to be wrong.

The arrogant supervisor's superiors must let him know directly that they do not approve of such behavior. It does absolutely no good to beat around the bush with him. He must realize that there are no sacred cows in the organization and that although he makes an important contribution, he is still but one spoke in a big wheel—not the big wheel itself. If this supervisor cannot be retrained, he should be discharged. The tension created by the *explosive* supervisor leads to more problems. Keeping problems hidden may temporarily pacify him, but sooner or later the results of such action will cause more serious problems to surface and throw him into a frenzy. Though unintentional, his harassment of workers is nonetheless real. Workers are always on edge, forever off-balance; tending to overcorrect and overreact, they create even more potential for error.

Senior management will have to work closely with this supervisor. They must find ways to lower the pressure. A major pressure-reduction device is simply better communication from the upper levels—a better quality of information on what senior management expects of him and feedback on how well he is doing. When he succeeds, he should be praised; when he goofs, he should know it immediately. The best kind of feedback process for this kind of supervisor is one that lets him figure it out for himself—backed up with opportunities to resolve his unanswered questions through an "open door" to senior management. Interpretation or explanation by senior management goes a long way toward easing tension for this supervisor. A bit of confidence in him and less interference doesn't hurt either. Also, calling his attention to his character flaw could help him overcome it.

MULTIPLIED INDIFFERENCE

The unusual thing about the *noncommitted* supervisor is that he sometimes generates positive creativity among his work group by forcing them to solve workplace problems—they have to because he provides nothing. "You do your job, pal. Don't bother me and I won't bother you" is what he tells his workers. At other times, however, his "I don't give a damn" attitude either spreads indifference throughout the work group or, worse, generates negative creativity—the results of which are apparent in poor or unacceptable quality, high scrap losses, machine downtime, and customer complaints.

Organizations cannot permit an unenthusiastic manager to destroy employee initiative and creativity. They must institute drastic action. The first message to give him is, "Get your heart in or your body out." If this doesn't stimulate him, the organization must determine whether the next step is training, job relocation, or an exit interview.

If ever job and skill training have a purpose, it is with the *shaky* supervisor. He is a typical example of the "Peter Principle" (according to which, organizations tend to promote people to their level of incompetency). His problems and his intentions need to be understood before he's held accountable for something beyond his control. He needs understanding and encouragement as well as job-skills support. The training and development program must include sessions on interpersonal competency and interpersonal relations as well as the "nuts and bolts" of the job. Subordinates who have this kind of supervisor feel that he offers nothing. His recommendations go unheeded and, since he doesn't know how to fight for his rights or maneuver properly with the organization, the dirty jobs always get dumped on his subordinates. Feeling a lack of recognition and sensing unfair workload assignments, he may easily develop an adverse state of mental health, which leads directly to unacceptable performance and reduced levels of productivity.

If training and development programs are to be valuable, organizations must first identify and understand the basic factors underlying individual incompetencies and act to eliminate them. Once such individual corrective action is taken, more success can be expected from broadly based training programs that have general application.

The competent supervisor has the knowledge and ability to perform his assignment—and he knows it. He may occasionally be abrasive or blow his stack, or he may even display a shaky moment or two—but he is never noncommitted or arrogant. He understands his workers' strengths and recognizes their weaknesses. He knows the rules and has the ability to interpret them with sufficient flexibility to meet both worker and organizational needs. He relates to his workers in such a way that he is like them, yet his difference gains their respect to the point that they feel they want to imitate him.

7

Management Styles and the Human Component

Rensis Likert

Production data, the profit-and-loss statement, and similar measures are often used as performance criteria to assess the relative effectiveness of different management systems and leadership styles. But studies using these criteria have yielded conflicting results.

A major reason for the conflict is a serious inadequacy in the choice of criteria. Measurements of current earnings, production, and similar variables all ignore any changes that may have occurred in the human component of a department or firm and the subsequent impact these changes will have on the firm's performance and profitability.

When human component changes are taken into consideration, relatively consistent patterns of relationships generally emerge. Until investigators pay attention to these changes, their studies will continue

From *Management Review*, October 1977.

to lead to erroneous conclusions on the best style of leadership or management.

"QUICK AND DIRTY" APPROACH

Let's look at some data from a continuous process plant with about 600 employees. Top management was not satisfied with the productivity of the plant and brought in one of the best known management consulting firms to improve performance. This firm used what management consultants call the "quick and dirty" method. It analyzed the staffing of each department in the plant against standards the consultants themselves established and found about a third of the departments appreciably overstaffed.

Teams made up of persons from other departments, corporate or division staff, and the consulting firm were assigned to study each of these departments and recommend ways to reorganize the work to make excessive labor unnecessary. No one from the department being studied was a member of the team that developed the plan for that department.

After the plan for reorganizing the work of the department was prepared and approved, the department manager was ordered to introduce it and to eliminate the excess labor. This was done for each of the departments involved. The resulting savings in direct labor costs totaled approximately $250,000.

This highly authoritarian behavior by management was perceived as such by the employees. This is seen in Figure 7-1, which shows the profile of the key dimensions of the human component obtained *before* the cost-reduction program started, compared with the profile one year later, *after* the program was completed.

The employees in the departments affected saw all four measurements of supervisory leadership as even more authoritarian (lower scores on the profile) than they had been before the cost-reduction effort was started. In terms of Systems 1, 2, 3, and 4, the management system and leadership style of the affected departments shifted closer to System 1. (System 1 is punitive authoritarian; System 2, benevolent authoritarian; System 3, consultative management; and System 4, a participative group model.)

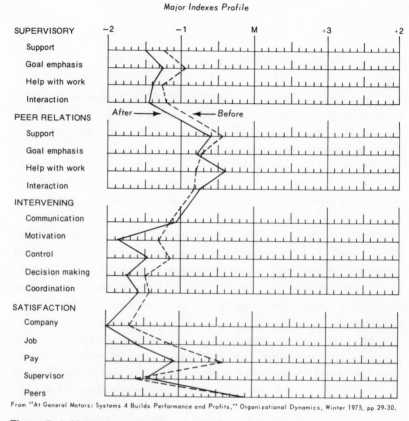

Figure 7–1. Human organization variables in departments where high cost-reduction effort was applied.

Looking only at costs and earnings, the results show that the shift toward System 1 brought improved productivity. The employees in the affected departments also perceived that peer help with work (the extent to which employees help each other in getting the work done) and peer interaction (team building and teamwork) improved.

However, a careful look at Figure 7-1 shows that this increase in teamwork and cooperation among the employees was accompanied by a substantial drop in their motivation to produce. These employees also felt that after the cost-control steps were imposed, the company had less capacity to exercise influence (control) on what occurred in the departments (relating to such matters as productivity and scrap loss) than previously. They also were less satisfied with company, job, and pay.

These changes in perceptions and reactions caused by the authoritarian cost-reduction program were not limited to the employees in the affected departments. They spread to all employees, as shown by the profiles in Figure 7-2. The differences in scores between *before* the cost-reduction program started and *after* it was over are significant at the 0.01 level or less for the following variables: peer help with work, peer interaction, motivation, control, and satisfaction with company, job, and pay.

Note the pattern: As the total group of employees became less satisfied with the company, their job, and their pay, they became less motivated to produce and their teamwork and group loyalty increased. This pattern of alienation among the employees restricts output. The workers evidently felt that the company would be unable to stop the restriction of output because management had lost some of its control. The human component of the plant had become less productive than before the cost-reduction effort was undertaken and management had less power to manage.

TIME LAG IN MANIFESTATION OF ADVERSE DATA

Managers and researchers misinterpret cause-and-effect relationships because of the lag in time between changes in the human component variables and changes in the productivity and financial variables. Research shows that any deterioration in the human component, such as occurred in this plant, is not likely to manifest itself in performance data until several months, or even years, have elapsed. Consequently, the management of this plant had no immediate evidence of the adverse changes that had occurred in the production capability of the plant's human component.

As soon as an analysis of the measurements of the human component of the plant revealed these changes, the results were reported to the plant manager and his staff and to the corporate

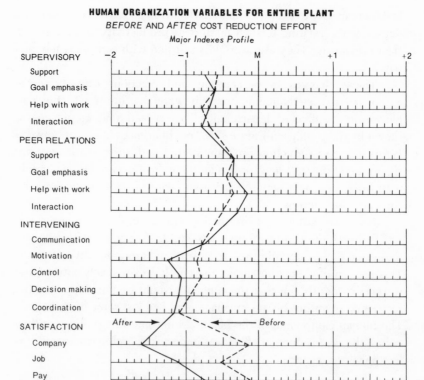

HUMAN ORGANIZATION VARIABLES FOR ENTIRE PLANT
BEFORE AND *AFTER* COST REDUCTION EFFORT
Major Indexes Profile

From "At General Motors: Systems 4 Builds Performance and Profits," *Organizational Dynamics*, Winter 1975, pp 29-30.

Figure 7–2. Human organization variables for entire plant.

executive vice president and divisional staff in charge of the division of which the plant was a part. They were interested in the results, but apart from the director of industrial relations, they treated the human organization measurements as of little consequence. From their point of view, the important fact was the $250,000 in labor savings that had been achieved.

A general feeling prevailed that the measurements of the human component had to be incorrect since they were getting higher productivity and lower costs from the plant's personnel. Even if the measurements were correct, management felt that the deterioration in the human component of the plant did not affect—and was not likely to affect—productivity and costs. As a consequence, in these circumstances it took no action.

The management of the division overseeing this plant was under considerable pressure from top corporate executives to improve earnings. To achieve that goal rapidly, it applied the same pressure-oriented cost-reduction program used in the first plant to two other plants. Again, there were immediate labor savings and cost improvement. And again, the human component scores showed a sizable adverse shift.

In all three plants, however, after the short-range improvement in costs, the firm experienced serious and costly consequences. These became painfully evident three to five years after the cost-reduction program was completed. They included such developments as a decrease in productivity (due to a restriction of output), failure to meet delivery dates, a decrease in quality and problems with customers because of lack of quality control, work stoppages, excessive grievances, and other labor relations difficulties.

MEASURING HUMAN COMPONENT CHANGES IN DOLLARS

Some time after the adverse shifts in the attitude of the first plant's personnel had been reported to the plant and division management, a method was developed for computing the value of the change in the productive capability of its personnel in dollars. These computations revealed that worker negativism would increase manufacturing costs by at least $450,000 annually. That is, the cost-reduction program, with its shift toward System 1 management, had produced an immediate annual labor savings of $250,000, but at an unrecognized annual cost of $450,000 because of the less motivated, more hostile, and less productive human component.

The unfavorable developments in this and the other plants in productivity, quality, grievances, work stoppages, and other labor problems in the five years after the cost reduction program was completed confirm the validity of the human component measurements and the dollar estimate of the change in the productivity of the plant's human component.

CONFIRMATION OF RESULTS

An increasing number of chief executive officers of corporations appear to be recognizing that it is highly profitable to build and maintain the human components of their firms. A number of years ago, I told a corporate executive vice president about our findings of the adverse effect on a firm's personnel in the kind of cost-reduction programs described above. He told me his firm had been acquiring smaller companies. In every case, he said, the companies were found to be overstaffed by about 15 to 25 percent according to work standards established by industrial engineers timing the jobs or using standard times for each part of the job. According to him, his corporation was finding it very profitable to send direct orders from the corporate management to the management of the newly acquired firm to reduce personnel by the amount of overstaffing.

About five years after this initial discussion, and after the man had become president and chief officer of his corporation, he surprised me by saying:

"You'll be interested to know how we are handling an overstaffing problem in a firm we recently acquired. The payroll is about $1.5 million more than it should be, based on work standards. In the past, we would have moved immediately to remove this excess by ordering the designated reductions in staff.

"This time, however, we are not going to do that. We have found from previous experience that when corporate headquarters orders a newly acquired firm to cut staff to the level called for by work standards, we encounter numerous serious problems caused by alienated personnel in the five years or so after the reduction in staff. These problems increase costs far above the initial savings we achieved by reducing the staff. We are worse off, not better off, when we cut costs the way we have in the past."

This time, he said, his company intended to improve the management and supervision in the newly acquired firm and gradually move toward a more efficient operation.

This company president is providing help to his divisional and plant managers, including the manager of the new division, to enable them to move closer to System 4. He now sees this as much more profitable than using System 1 pressure-oriented cost-reduction programs. Each organizational unit will increase its productivity and profitability as it moves toward System 4 management. Excessive costs and waste will be reduced.

EXPERIENCES AT IBM

Engineered work standards and low morale. IBM conducted a major research project that yielded conclusions confirming the pattern described above. It found that when engineered work standards were imposed on manufacturing plant managers and supervisors, the employees in these plants resented the pressure and the same kinds of adverse trends followed. It also found that employees whose supervisors were closer to the System 4 style in their behavior showed less resentment of the work standards than employees whose supervisors were closer to the System 1 style. (The IBM investigators did not use the System 1–4 labels, but used measurements that gave similar parameters.)

The reason employees working for supervisors who managed closer to the System 4 style resented the work standards less was that their supervisors actually changed the way the standards were used. If an employee felt a work standard was unreasonable or had another complaint, these supervisors did something about it. They softened the blow. As a result, the impact on the employees was much more favorable than had the supervisors used a System 1 "do it or else" approach. Their responsiveness to complaints made a sizable difference in employee attitudes.

A key factor that kept the pressure-imposed work measurement program from having as much long-range negative impact at IBM as usual was the concern by the firm's top corporate management that high employee morale be maintained. These top managers ". . . started asking questions as to why work measurement generally produced low morale and why something wasn't being done about modifying the program to get higher morale."

High productivity and high morale. Another major finding of the IBM project dealt with a manufacturing plant (Plant A) whose manager had flatly refused to introduce work standards in spite of orders from corporate management and top divisional management to do so. He had tried standards years before and knew of their negative side effects.

This manager used other principles and methods to achieve efficient performance. For example, the plant had been using work simplification for years. It was also making effective plantwide use of procedures that the plant manager had developed for rewarding high production with salary increases and promotions.

In addition, interviews with small samples of employees were conducted regularly. If a problem was revealed, it was promptly and constructively resolved. Group problem solving involving both supervisors and workers was used in setting production and quality goals.

The introduction of work standards in the IBM plants increased productivity, and a much larger proportion of the employees began producing at levels close to standard. But even with these short-run improvements in productivity, the plants using this program failed to exceed Plant A in performance. Plant A still had productivity equal to or greater than that achieved by the best of the work measurement plants. Moreover, employee satisfaction in Plant A was substantially better than in the plants that used work standards.

The Plant A results were highly important. They demonstrated that an IBM plant with a management style that made no use of engineered work measurement achieved higher productivity than any plant using work measurement and had much higher morale besides.

These findings, combined with top management's desire to maintain employee morale (favorable employee attitudes and motivation) at a high level, led to a plan for a change in the way work measurement was used. The control that had been in the hands of the industrial engineers was returned to the manufacturing departments. Each first-line manager was given "the authority to remove any individual from measurement or change any prescribed method if, in his judgment, the standard or the method was inappropriate."

As might be expected, when the management style of the Plant A's manager was measured, the data revealed that, as seen by middle and upper-level managers, he was a System 4 manager.

An important aspect of the behavior of the Plant A manager was his refusal to pass on to his subordinate managers the pressure put on him to use work measurements and to push employees to produce at the level set by standards. He knew from experience that such pressure would yield short-range increases, but result in poorer performance over the long run. He sought to get high productivity over both the short and the long range by holding high performance goals himself, by rewarding high performance, and by using other principles of System 4 management.

This refusal to pass pressure on to their subordinate managers seems to be characteristic of System 4 managers. A recent study of a federal agency revealed that of nine district managers of that agency in the United States, the two managers who were seen by their subordinates as System 4 in their management style did not pass on to their subordinate managers the pressure their chief put on them for high performance. The other managers, especially the five whose management system was closest to System 1, appear to have put on their subordinate managers as much pressure or more of it than the pressure they themselves experienced. The System 4 managers got results without putting direct hierarchical pressure on their organization.

Many other studies have yielded the same findings as those reported here. The introduction of work measurement and the putting of pressure on personnel to produce at the level called for by work standards almost always result in an immediate increase in productivity. Personnel limitations, budget cuts, and requirements to achieve earnings at a specified level are other ways of putting pressure on people to produce. They also yield immediate improvement.

All of these procedures, however, are accompanied by long-range adverse effects. These include less favorable attitudes and covert efforts to defeat the organization in its attempts to obtain high productivity by restriction of output and other evidences of poor labor relations, including slowdowns, excessive grievances, and wildcat and other strikes.

With all of the pressure procedures, there is a shift in management style toward System 1. Investigators have noted that such a shift is accompanied by an increase in productivity. When they compare a System 1 or 2 organization after hierarchical pressure has increased its productivity with an organization that has just started to shift to System 4, they may conclude that System 1 or 2 is more effective than System 4. The rapid short-run increase in productivity that System 1 or 2 can bring about leads to this erroneous conclusion. The longer lasting

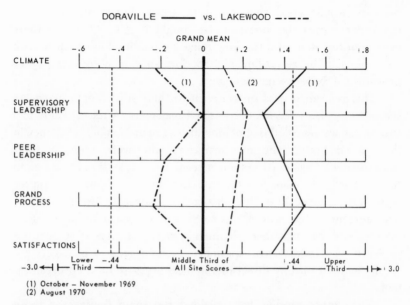

Figure 7–3. Interplant salaried scores compared with ISR grand mean.

productivity improvement of System 4 does not manifest itself immediately. The lag between the introduction of System 4 and an increase in productivity may be one to three years and, in large organizations, even longer.

An example of this lag occurred in an automotive assembly plant. After a substantial improvement in the human component was shown by measurements (Figure 7-3), it took one and a half years for direct labor costs to show an improvement and two and a half years for indirect labor costs to begin improving (Figure 7-4). Costs were still showing an unfavorable trend even after the human component of the plant started to improve.

EVALUATING YOUR FINDINGS

An investigator, therefore, can find evidence that an organization closer to System 1 is more productive than an organization closer to System 4 or the converse, depending on whether or not he ignores the changes in the human component. The results he obtains depend also

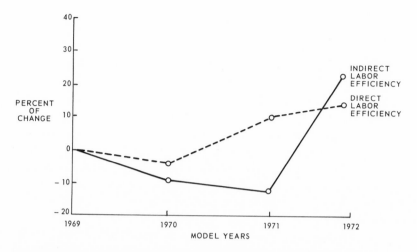

Figure 7–4. Percent of change in operating efficiency at Lakewood.

on whether he picks System 1 or 2 organizations at the peak of their short-run spurt in productivity in response to hierarchical pressure or at their long-run lower productivity level.

Whether the System 4 organizations selected for comparison are at their lower productivity level as their managements are starting to shift to System 4 or at their long-run high productivity level after the system is well established will affect the findings too.

As long as investigators ignore what happens in the productive capability of the human component of an organization when changes are made in the management system, they will reach the wrong conclusions. They will continue to believe that in some situations management systems closer to System 1 yield the best performance and that in others managements closer to System 4 come out ahead. However, if changes in the human component are taken into consideration along with the current data on productivity or earnings, a consistent pattern of findings will emerge. This consistency will also obtain if the long-run shifts in productivity and earnings, and not just the short-run results, are measured.

In assessing different management systems, there are two ways of evaluating the effect of the improvement or deterioration in the human component measurements. One way is to compute in dollars the gain or loss resulting from this improvement or deterioration. The gain or loss is then added to or subtracted from the earnings, costs, or profit-and-loss statement to arrive at a net figure showing total gain or loss.

The second way to take the changes in the human component scores into consideration is to recognize that when these scores have undergone a favorable change, the productivity or financial statement represents an understatement of actual performance. When an unfavorable shift has occurred, the productivity or financial report overstates the true performance. The current productivity or financial statement, consequently, needs to be interpreted in relation to the changes that have occurred in the human component scores. Trends in performance measurements over five or more years often give us some clues to the effect of the changes in the human component upon performance.

Valid conclusions, therefore, cannot be drawn about the relative productivity and superiority of different management systems and leadership styles unless measurements of the changes in the productive capability of the human organization are examined along with the productivity and earnings data.

When the human organizational measurements show an improvement or no change, the productivity and earnings data can be considered to be correct or even an understatement of actual performance.

When the human organizational measurements show a significant adverse shift, the productivity and earnings results overstate true performance and must be discounted by the amount of overstatement. When this methodology is used, consistent findings are obtained on the relative effectiveness of different management systems and leadership styles.

In any specific situation, it obviously is necessary to consider the basic principles or system being used and not just the particular procedures employed. Management systems and leadership principles must always be applied in a culturally relevant manner. That is, in each situation the manager should apply the principles that he or she is seeking to use in ways that fit the work situation and the characteristics, traditions, skills, and expectations of the labor force or work group involved. In comparing performance in one situation with that in another, the focus should be on the principles or management systems being used and how well they fit the culture, traditions, and environment of the organization rather than on the specific procedures alone.

I have examined data from several hundred published and unpublished studies in business, government, schools, hospitals, universities, the military, and voluntary and other kinds of organizations. I am greatly impressed by the extent to which these studies show a consistent pattern of findings when all the relevant organizational variables are taken into account. The studies find the probabilities very high that the closer the management system and leadership style are to System 4, the better the overall performance of the unit is; the closer the management system and leadership behavior are to System 1, the poorer the performance.

Part Two

COMMUNICATION *IS* LEADERSHIP

8

Let's Talk:
Understanding One-to-One
Communication

Edward L. Levine

Are you a good leader? Perhaps the answers to the following brief test will give you some clues:

1. Does your staff freely inform you about their true feelings, opinions, and suggestions for improving operations?
2. Do you become nervous when you communicate orders or suggestions to others?
3. Does your staff typically leave a meeting with you charged with energy and supplied with clear information on how to achieve group goals?
4. Do you often find yourself at a loss for words when you talk to your staff?

From *Supervisory Management*, May 1980.

5. Are you able to gain the commitment of your staff to organizational goals through effective persuasion?

6. Do you choose your communication mediums (telephone, face-to-face communications, or memos) based on their advantages and disadvantages?

7. Do you seek feedback from others on your credibility as a communicator?

8. Are you able to present problems faced by your work group to others in a fashion that fosters cooperation?

9. Is your staff informed on how things are going in your organization and how things look for the future?

As this little test suggests, good leadership and good communication skills are strongly related. People who are viewed as good leaders by their subordinates typically engage in high levels of communication. They keep their staff informed of new policies, changes in procedures, and better ways to do the job. Also, leaders who are most liked are those who engage in high levels of communication.

As a manager or supervisor, you are required to carry out a number of responsibilities that have been closely linked to the management role. The standard list of responsibilities consists of planning, organizing, assembling resources, directing, and controlling. Planning involves the clarification of objectives and the communication of plans to your staff. Organizing concerns the definition of relationships among your staff and the communication of these relationships to the affected individuals. Assembling resources involves the acquisition capital and other resources for your unit, group, or department to allow goal achievement. Effective communication of departmental needs to superiors is an integral component of this management function. Finally, directing and controlling are somewhat related to communication in that they involve giving orders and motivating people to carry them out.

In addition to this standard set of responsibilities, you may become involved in such activities as consulting with others in your organization, meeting important clients or customers, negotiating agreements or contracts, and evaluating the work of others. All these activities are obviously directly linked to effective communication.

One final point can be made to nail down the relationship between good leadership and good communication skills. That is, it has often been demonstrated that the higher you go in the management ranks, the more likely it is that you will be required to spend time communicating. Bass and Ryterband, in their recent book *Organizational Psychology*, report that executives spend 80 percent of their work time talking with others. The importance of communication to management performance is recognized in the high weight given to communication skills when candidates are being screened and selected for management positions. To illustrate this point even more concretely, I would point out that assessment centers are being used more and more frequently in the management screening process. Such assessment centers place a high premium on communication skills in arriving at an assessment rating of a candidate for promotion. Communication is critically important in such standard assessment center exercises as the in-basket, the group presentation, and the leaderless group discussion. And there can be no stronger demonstration of the relationship between good leadership and good communication skills than the notion that you cannot advance in management unless you are a strong communicator.

Communication, then, is a key ingredient in the formula for a good leader.

ONE-TO-ONE COMMUNICATION

During a single day, a supervisor or manager demonstrates his or her communication ability again and again. Of the many forms that communication takes in formal work organizations, perhaps the one most deserving of your attention is one-to-one communication, for it is not only very frequently used but also very important to good supervisor/subordinate relations. Indeed, it has the potential to be the best method available to the supervisor for influencing subordinate behavior.

In this form of communication a single manager and a single subordinate meet to engage in a two-way conversation about some organizationally relevant issue. I am talking about a meeting of at least ten to 15 minutes in duration—not the kind of meeting where the supervisor and subordinate exchange a quick hello or discuss a momentary concern.

I am sure you have encountered the form of communication I am talking about numerous times, not just throughout your career, but this very week. When you get together in peson with a subordinate to solve work-related problems, discuss career goals and career development, provide orientation and training, set production standards, counsel or discipline your subordinate, or get some feedback on how things stand in your operation, then you are engaging in one-to-one communication.

Communicating regularly on a one-to-one basis with subordinates doesn't guarantee that you are a good communicator. That takes training and the proper practice, which includes pre-meeting preparation. If you find it tough to talk to your subordinates about their work, appraise performance and set goals, praise good work, or handle grievances and complaints, devote some time before such sessions preparing for them; don't spend your time fretting about them.

Although some might not think so, one-to-one communication is highly complex. If you don't prepare adequately, you will probably face a communication overload. This overload will definitely make your communication effort less effective.

Needless to say, overpreparation is just as bad as underpreparation. Too much can make the one-to-one communication session seem too formal or artificial. Generally, when getting ready for a meeting with one of your subordinates, aim for that middle ground—somewhere between over- and underpreparation for the session.

THE COMMUNICATION PROCESS

Training and practice are two of the ingredients to becoming an effective communicator. The third ingredient is even more basic: It's an understanding of the communication process. There are barriers to effective communication, but knowledge of what they are—let alone the means to overcome them—is useless unless there is an appreciation of the purpose of communication and what is meant by effective communication. Before you can understand the communication process, you need to understand the reason for organizations and the organization process.

LEADERS, COMMUNICATION, AND ORGANIZATIONS

Organizations are created by people because people believe that they can achieve goals more readily through organizations than through their own unaided, individual efforts. Nowadays, organizations are often regarded as *open systems*. As such, organizations receive inputs of people, information, energy, and materials. The people in the organization process, alter, or transform these inputs in some fashion. This represents the *throughput* that systems analysts talk about and involves the use of energy and information. In the end, *outputs* such as products, services, staff satisfaction, and creative ideas are produced. Organizations as open systems are continually getting feedback on their output and throughput. Adjustments to keep the system going, growing, and developing are made accordingly. Some people have looked at this whole process and decided that basically organizations are inventions of people to process energy and information as effectively as possible.

Where does communication fit in this picture? As I see it, all communication in an organization is part and parcel of the energy/information processing function.

Perhaps an analogy might be helpful to illustrate this point better. Think of an organization as a little like a car battery (even though that "system" may be a little more *closed* than the one we are talking about). All the structures—the terminals, the cables, the electrodes, and the case—may be in place; but the "juice" cannot flow until the proper fluid is put in. The fluid in an organization is communication. Organizations do not really function until communication starts.

Obviously, the function of communication is more elaborate and dynamic than that of the fluid in a car battery. Communication is an ongoing process by which an organization's staff members work together to achieve organizationally relevant goals. To relate this back to the notion of organizations as processors of energy and information, communication within an organization may be thought of as *the exchange of energy and information among organizational staff members*. Let's look more closely at this process.

THE INFORMATION AND ENERGY EXCHANGE

Information refers to the content and meaning of the message sent from one organizational member to another. Energy, on the other hand, is less tangible. Energy refers to the motivational impact of the message.

Information transfer may cover the state of the organization now and in the future, the goals to be achieved, how the goals of an organization may be accomplished, how work tasks are to be carried out, the rewards to be expected with achievement, and the problems that need to be overcome. Energy refers to the choice one makes to devote effort to the achievement of organizational or work group goals, and within that set of goals how energy is to be divided.

From the pattern of communication typically found in organizations, you would probably come to the conclusion very quickly, as I have, that the most important energy and information exchange is conducted between managers and subordinates. This is because "vertical" communication is by far the most frequent type of communication that occurs in organizations. Probably the most important portion of this communication is the exchange of energy and information that takes place when the manager and subordinate meet to confer in person. Thus whatever you can do to improve one-to-one, face-to-face manager/subordinate communication should have a substantial impact on your organization's effectiveness as well as your own, for if an organization's formally designated leaders cannot communicate effectively, informal leaders will take over.

It should be clear from our discussion that I am talking about a two-way as opposed to a one-way exchange. The energy and information flow in communication should move from manager to subordinate and subordinate to manager simultaneously. When your subordinate leaves a communication exchange with you having experienced the satisfaction of his or her needs, and having made an obvious commitment to charge ahead and achieve important work goals, then your energy level and commitment likewise will increase.

A good communication exchange isn't only beneficial to the productivity of subordinates; supervisors also profit from effective communication.

Given their impact on all, communication exchanges should take place as frequently as possible. I can already hear the reaction of some of you to this statement, a reaction based on the idea that people in organizations receive too much communication. However, the fact is that the problem is more likely to be one of too little communication, *particularly too little effective communication*, than too much communication. And before you can determine the right amount of communication, you need to overcome your communication problems and increase your communication effectiveness.

HALLMARKS OF EFFECTIVE COMMUNICATION

What do we mean by effective communication? To answer that question, we need first to look again at the communication process.

Generally, an effective communication process in a one-to-one communication encounter will be characterized by attentiveness, enthusiasm, and a relatively high level of speaking activity on the part of both partners. Communication should be flowing easily in both directions. The amount of eye contact should be high. With respect to the information exchange component of communication, there should be evidence in the form of feedback that each understands the message sent by the other. The information should be timely, accurate, and useful. The amount of information should *not* exceed the partners' capacity to receive, discuss, and absorb it. Thus, if information is on some emotion-laden issue, then the amount should be decreased accordingly, and the message should be repeated to ensure it is understood.

With respect to the energy component, there should be evidence to indicate that each party has accepted the message of the other, and that the message will be translated into effective, goal-oriented behavior.

Secondly, we need to look at the consequences of a communication encounter.

Generally, the behavior of both a manager and a subordinate

should be more effective after a one-to-one communication encounter than it was before. For instance, after a goal setting and progress review session, the subordinate's work output should continue at a high level, or be improved where necessary, and the supervisor should have gained some insights into how to be more helpful to the subordinate. Even in those unpleasant situations where an employee must be disciplined or dismissed, adaptive behavior should follow if communication has been effective. For instance, an employee who has been dismissed should leave the dismissal meeting with a clear understanding of the reasons for the action and his or her rights, if any, to appeal it. The employee would take steps to complete any pending projects or make provisions for someone else to carry them through. The manager should come away from the meeting with an understanding of the consequences of the dismissal to the employee, and would seek to ease those consequences to the extent possible. Certainly, constructive suggestions and possible job leads should be provided to assist the employee in finding a job that is more suited to his or her particular skills, abilities, and interests.

Still another hallmark of effective communication is that the job satisfaction of both supervisor and subordinate should remain at a high level, or increase as a result of the communication encounter. If the communication encounter concerns negative issues such as discipline or dismissal, then the effect of the communication on job satisfaction should be the minimum possible.

Overall, to gauge your one-to-one communication effectiveness, you must take into account the *communication process itself*, and *the consequences of the communication encounter on work productivity and satisfaction*.

Since effective communication is a key ingredient in effective leadership, improvement in your one-to-one communication ability means improvement as a leader. In developing your ability, there are numerous sources to which you can turn. As managers and social scientists continue to explore systematically all the aspects of communication, we will come to know more and more about how to improve ourselves and our organizations. In the meantime, you can mine from the ore of what is already known about one-to-one communication.

9

On-the-Job Communication: Why Isn't It Easier?

Leonard Sayles

Watch two old friends talking to each other. Do they have difficulty communicating? Probably not. They may not even have to use complete sentences—often a single word or a raised eyebrow conveys all the meaning necessary. Since the friends know each other thoroughly, key words or signs are all they need to exchange their ideas.

For the supervisor at work, communicating isn't that easy. In giving a simple order to a subordinate, asking why an assignment wasn't completed on time, or listening to a suggestion from an employee, the supervisor is faced with many communication barriers that almost never exist between close friends.

Let's look at these barriers, along with some specific examples of

From *Leadership on the Job: Guides to Good Supervision* (Rev. Ed.). © 1966 American Management Association, Inc.

how they can impede communication between a supervisor and his subordinates.

The speaker and listener differ in experience and background. A supervisor tells a key person that the company may have to cut back production because some important orders were lost. But the employee hears: "You can expect to be laid off soon." Why? In other companies, lost orders always meant the loss of a job.

Our understanding of what we hear depends largely on our own experience and background. Instead of hearing what people tell us, we may hear what our mind tells us has been said. There is often a vast difference.

Differences in experience often influence the way workers respond to incentive plans. A company offers to give merit increases and higher-paying jobs to superior employees. Some workers fail to respond with enthusiasm—even though they want to earn additional money. Why? It may be that they have never gained anything from being good workers. Perhaps they belong to an ethnic group that is often ignored when better jobs are filled. Perhaps they've worked in companies that "cut the rate" when employees made more money by working harder. Whatever the reason, they hear the company's announcement this way: "Certain workers whom we choose will get benefits by working harder; others will get nothing."

We fail to convey the information the listener needs and can understand. For example, a supervisor may fill a trainee's mind with information the trainee is not ready to grasp. In one survey, cashier trainees in department stores reported that much of their induction training was meaningless to them. The reason: Without any experience on the job, they didn't understand how they could apply the information. It was only after they were on the job handling sales slips that they could have absorbed the knowledge. For this reason, training is more effective when the supervisor can simulate actual on-the-job problems to which the new information can be applied.

It is the supervisor's job, too, to make sure that the information he or she *gets* from subordinates is what is needed. Often, a subordinate is in the dark about what information the boss wants. The boss then complains that the subordinate is failing to keep him informed in vital areas or deluging him with unnecessary information.

Our stereotypes and beliefs influence what we hear. People with a strong prejudice are often confronted by information that contradicts it. But the prejudice may be so powerful that they will twist the information to support it.

For example, let's say a supervisor is convinced that because one worker in the department belongs to a certain ethnic group, he is, therefore, always looking for the easy way out. One day the worker comes up with a carefully worked out, practical shortcut on the job. Instead of praising the employee for the initiative, the supervisor thinks: "Just proves they're all alike—always trying to get away with less work."

Look at how a supervisor can come to three different conclusions about the same situation, depending on his preconceptions. The situation: the supervisor sees a group of employees laughing together.

◇ If the supervisor believes that hard work has to be unpleasant, he decides the employees are wasting time and should be given tougher assignments.

◇ If the supervisor believes that good work and cheerful attitudes go together, he will congratulate himself for being a good manager.

◇ If the supervisor is personally insecure, he may assume that the laughing employees are making jokes about him.

Our emotional state of mind colors what we hear. The worried, fearful employee finds threats in everything he or she hears. Let's say new equipment is being introduced in a department. The employees fear the worst. As a result, everything seen and heard is interpreted as confirmation that they will suffer: "I saw the supervisor looking at the seniority list—it looks as though they're going to lay off half the department after that new machinery comes in."

We're dead set against a speaker's message because we suspect his motivation. The classic example of this particular barrier is to be found in labor-management relations. Many union members are convinced that management is out to weaken their union, and they refuse to believe anything management tells them. Similarly, management may regard all grievances as political maneuvers designed to win union votes. Both sides are sometimes right, of course. But too often this closed-mind attitude makes it impossible for the two sides to reach each other.

The same suspicion can impede communication between supervisors, too. Often one supervisor may reject worthwhile ideas from an associate simply because the supervisor is convinced that the person is trying to show him up.

In dealing with subordinates, the supervisor can be at the receiving end of such disbelief. If an employee is convinced that the boss is trying to manipulate him, all the human relations techniques in the book—no matter how sincerely they are used—will be unsuccessful.

Let's say an employee makes a cost-cutting suggestion to a supervisor. The supervisor says, "Thanks, I'll think about it." If the subordinate believes that the supervisor isn't really interested in developing people, he'll hear this as "Stick to your own job and let me take care of the thinking around here."

On the other hand, if the employee thinks the supervisor genuinely wants to encourage initiative, he'll hear: "I'm pleased that you came up with this suggestion—I'll see if there is some way we can use it."

We fail to evaluate the meaning behind what we hear. Sometimes we go to the opposite extreme—instead of judging what we hear entirely by the speaker's imagined motivation, we completely ignore the possible latent meaning of the words. We forget that most statements are a combination of fact *and* feeling.

An employee comes over to a supervisor and says disgustedly, "This lousy machine is broken again." An alert supervisor will wonder if there isn't more in this complaint than just a maintenance problem. Could the employee be saying, "I don't like this job" or, "I think I'm getting a raw deal"? These possibilities deserve investigation.

We fail to realize that what we're saying has symbolic meaning for our listeners. What we say often has a far greater meaning than it appears to on the surface. That's why we sometimes get a surprisingly strong reaction to what we consider a rather mild statement.

Recently, for example, a production supervisor told workers, "We're going to start using plastic for these parts instead of chrome steel." The supervisor reassured them that they would not lose their jobs and there would be no changes in earnings or working conditions. It was simply an economy move to reduce the cost of this particular component.

Yet the morale of the whole department was shaken. The supervisor didn't realize that the people were proud of the superior appearance and durability of the chrome-steel component. The phrase "chrome steel" was loaded with symbolic meaning: product prestige, a feeling of superiority, a will to be the best even if it cost more.

We forget that words mean different things to different people. Words and phrases often lead to trouble because the speaker and listener interpret them differently. For example, a supervisor spots a dangerous pool of oil on the shop floor near a machinist. The supervisor says, "Get that oil wiped up as soon as you can—it's a real safety hazard." The machinist nods.

Ten minutes later, the supervisor is called back—an inspector has just taken a bad spill on the oil. The supervisor bawls out the machinist for failing to follow his instructions. But the machinist says, "You told me to get it wiped up as soon as I could. I thought you could see that I was working on a delicate cut and had to finish that first."

To the supervisor, "as soon as you can" meant immediately. To the machinist, it meant as soon as the piece on which he was working was finished.

Our reference group often dictates the way we hear a message. The group we identify ourselves with—psychologists call it the reference group—tends to shape our opinions on many matters. The result is often another block to true communication. For example, a night-shift operator found a note left by the day person who runs the same machine: "Don't expect to get any good work from this—I didn't. It needs cleaning and some decent maintenance for a change."

The day operator was just trying to be helpful. But the night operator read the note this way: "Your sloppy maintenance is to blame for my difficulty."

How come? Mainly because of imagined slights, the night operator's reference group—the rest of the night shift—had developed a resentful attitude toward the day shift. Influenced by this attitude, the night operator interpreted the note as an insult.

THE SINGLE MOST IMPORTANT TECHNIQUE

A large group of supervisory trainees listened intently as their instructor gave them elaborate directions on how to arrange five dominoes in a certain pattern. They were not allowed to ask any questions of the instructor. In another room, the same directions were being given, but here the trainees were allowed to ask as many questions as they wanted of the instructor.

The results were startlingly different. In the first room, only three trainees were able to arrange the dominoes correctly. In the second room, only four trainees did *not* arrange them correctly.

This experiment in communication points up what is perhaps the single most important technique in better communicating: feedback. There are other weapons in the supervisor's communications arsenal— and we'll get to these later—but feedback is probably packed with more potential than any of them.

That's because feedback can tell the supervisor *if* he or she is communicating and *what* he or she is communicating to the listener. It turns communication from a shot in the dark that may or may not be hitting the target to a two-way process that leaves both speaker and listener better informed.

Let's look at what feedback is. Actually most of us use this principle constantly without recognizing it. Put simply, it means modifying what we say and how we say it according to the response we get from our listener. This is the same way a thermostat regulates the amount of furnace heat on the basis of feedback, which in this case is the temperature of the room.

A supervisor who uses this method deliberately can develop better ways of learning what is being understood by the listener. Various experiments have revealed that the accuracy of communication increases with the amount of feedback. Limiting the listener to yes or no responses (asking, for example, "Do you understand that?") is less effective than encouraging the listener to ask questions.

NOT THROUGH WORDS ALONE

The first essential for maximum feedback is face-to-face communication. Only then can the communicator find out if the receiver understands, agrees, is sympathetic, indifferent, hostile, or just confused. The feedback comes not only through the listener's words but through nonverbal behavior too. We can watch for expressions of puzzlement, anger, or comprehension that may flicker across the listener's face. Gestures and other physical actions can reveal impatience, animosity, or agreement.

With a facial expression, the movement of an eyebrow, a listener can often tell us more than by hours of talk, because these expressions may indicate attitudes that the listener is reluctant or unable to express in words. For example, a subordinate is understandably unwilling to challenge the orders of the boss. But in the course of an informal, face-to-face discussion, an alert supervisor can detect a lack of enthusiasm in the tone of voice and the facial expressions.

Interpreting feedback is not always easy. What we say may symbolize something to our listeners that is not apparent to us. One such case occurred recently in a large merchandising company. To help her in the preparation of market analysis, a new district sales manager asked her salespeople to compute certain correlation coefficients on the basis of their sales records. The task was not difficult—they simply had to use an easy formula. But they failed to do it. One excuse followed another: The computations were too complicated, it was clerks' work, it wasn't in their job description, the coefficients were really useless anyhow, and so on. Their distaste for this task seemed to be out of all proportion to the difficulty involved.

Why was the modest request greeted with such stubborn resistance? The sales manager came up with the answer after much investigation and interviewing. Three years before, the salespeople had had an authoritarian supervisor whom they thoroughly disliked and who had tried to introduce this same statistical technique. When the new manager brought it up, they immediately rejected it, because to them it had become a symbol of oppressive supervision.

Once the mystery had been solved, the sales manager decided to withdraw the request temporarily. After giving her people time to develop confidence in her, she reintroduced the request and had no trouble getting their cooperation.

OTHER COMMUNICATIONS AIDS

Vital as it is, feedback is only one of a number of aids you can use to improve your communicating. Here are some others.

Projection. Before you communicate something, put yourself in your listener's shoes. How is the listener likely to react to your message, and what should you do to make sure he understands it the way you mean it? For example, you tell an employee he is wanted in the front office. His silent reaction may be, "I'm in for a dressing-down from the big boss." If this isn't the case, you should make it clear. Often there may be a wide gap between the supervisor's experience and that of the listener. The supervisor must try to bridge that gap.

Timing. Once an erroneous belief has been established in employees' minds through rumor and misunderstanding, it is very difficult to dislodge—even with the facts. The answer is to get the facts across *before* misconceptions have a chance to gain a foothold.

Believability. Your words won't mean anything to employees if they're skeptical of your sincerity. Anything you tell them must be supported by your actions. And when something happens that contradicts what you've told them, you should give them a full explanation.

Simplicity. This is an important ingredient of your written communications. Every manager should put his bulletin-board announcements, policy statements, and directives in simple, direct language.

Repetition. Saying something over again often helps to make it stick. This is particularly true when you're giving employees complicated instructions. If they misunderstand what you said the first time, they'll have a chance to catch it the next time around.

Freshness. There are times when you should avoid repetition and find new ways of saying things. Timeworn, overfamiliar phrases will be ignored by your subordinates—they'll figure they've heard it all before. Discussing this problem recently, one worker said, "I know just what the boss is going to say the minute he starts with that line about all of us being one big happy team—so I don't listen."

It's a good idea to review your favorite phrases once in a while and replace them with fresh variations. You'll have a much better chance of gaining the attention of your listeners.

Good communication does not, of course, depend only on these techniques. It must be based as well on a healthy, cooperative relationship between the supervisor and subordinates. The supervisor who has the confidence of subordinates will find it much easier to explain, for example, why there will be no bonuses this year than will the supervisor who hasn't. And using the techniques outlined here will help him or her get the message across to them.

10

Communication . . . or Getting Ideas Across

J. Thomas Miller III

One of the most powerful forces for action is the spoken word. Because of the spoken word, kingdoms have been won or lost. The course of history has been changed by masterful use of language. It creates images, touches emotions, stimulates listeners to action.

It is the manager's job to stimulate action. The manager is a professional communicator just as surely as Walter Cronkite or a writer for the President. Proper communication goes a long way to insure proper action. The truth is, if you cannot write it or you cannot say it, you cannot do it.

Communication is not only a tool but a catalyst. Nothing happens rightly, correctly, or precisely unless the communications are right, correct, precise. One of the frustrating problems with communication, especially the spoken word, is that you never know whether your efforts were successful until after the action that you wanted to happen as a result has indeed happened.

From S.A.M. *Advanced Management Journal,* Summer 1980.

Communication must be appropriate to the business and industrial organization. For our purposes, we define communication as the passing of information and understanding from one person to another for the purpose of changing what they know, think, or do. In the organizational structure, we need communication to be as pragmatic as possible. This means the following must be kept in mind:

1. You encounter another at a particular time and under particular circumstances.
2. That person thinks and acts in an individual way.
3. Your purpose for communication will be to change the way he or she acts. Otherwise why bother?

It will help if you know the level of understanding of the person to whom you are speaking and the circumstances under which the communication is taking place. Each of these has a direct impact on transmission and reception.

"IN THE BEGINNING WAS THE WORD": JOHN 1:1

Only words communicate, nothing else. We use the written word or the spoken word.

What about actions? Let's say you see a baby of preverbal age. The baby is crying. The crying transmits information: "Something is wrong." But you don't know what. In this case it is information but without understanding. To stop the baby from crying, you must use trial and error to find out what is wrong and establish understanding so that proper action can take place.

Too often it is this way in an organization. There is information without understanding, and the trial and error waste time and money. If understanding had been a part of the information, correct action could have been swift and sure.

SHARED MEANINGS

Besides often forgetting that only words communicate, we overlook too frequently the fact that words have different meanings for people.

If you see a picture, you perceive the form it displays but interpret the meaning in your mind by attaching words to it. When you see a picture that you don't understand, you can't describe its meaning because you lack the words to do it. Take this one step further. You see a picture that you do understand, and in your attempt to tell me about it you use words for which I have no meaning, so still no communication takes place. Or you use words for which I have different meanings than you have, and miscommunication takes place.

Words are all you have. If you are to communicate meaningfully, you must know what the other knows and how the other will interpret what you say. You need to know the level of the other's comprehension and speak at that level.

Supervisors often say, "I tell them what I want them to know, and they act like they understand what I'm saying, but then they do something else." People seem to understand what we say, yet later we find they didn't understand the way *we* understood. While words may be all we have, the meaning of the words we use must be the same for both the speaker and the hearer. Words don't mean the same thing to all people. The word "cat" for a child may mean a kitten. To a construction worker it could be a large earth-moving machine. To a lion tamer, it could mean a large jungle animal. The meanings of words are not in the words themselves but in the minds of the people hearing them.

Different people are reared in different environments, developing different attitudes and social values. Their educations are different and their levels of understanding for the same word or term can also be quite different. This was illustrated in a class I conducted for a company not long ago. A supervisor said to one of the employees, "Go out back and pull the stacks of buckets apart." It was at most a 20-minute job. Two hours later, the supervisor found the employee literally tearing the buckets apart. Obviously, for the supervisor "pull apart" meant one thing and to the employee something quite different. They both had a meaning for "pull apart," but they didn't have the same meaning.

IMPROVING COMMUNICATIONS

As a manager, you should ask yourself, "What are some of the things I can do to improve communications in my department?" The barriers to effective communication are many, but applying effective supervisory communication practices can overcome most of them.

1. *Learn variations*. Develop many ways to say the same thing to meet the comprehension level of the hearer.

2. *Reduce the number of levels*. One way to avoid barriers is to reduce the number of times the message must be repeated before it reaches the person it is intended for.

3. *Inform employees*. Make certain that employees know and understand what their jobs are and what is expected of them.

4. *Use staff meetings for communication*. Some organizations have what is called a "tail-gate session" each morning. All employees in the unit are gathered for a stand-up conference and for five minutes tell each other what's going on that day. Regular meetings in which organizational or unit goals are discussed, problems brought forth and solved, gripes and grievances aired, and instructions discussed are vital to good communications.

5. *Daily memo technique*. Another way of keeping employees up to date is a "today" memo written by yourself or someone in your department that briefly summarizes all activities for the day. This should be typed, dictated, or handwritten the first thing in the morning. It is possible to circulate a "today memo" within a few minutes' time. The material remains on written record, providing a daily log that has historical and operational value.

6. *Procedures manual*. Procedures manuals are of tremendous value in communicating policy and procedures. A procedures manual should be located in a convenient place for the employees' use.

7. *Develop your listening skills*. The ability of the manager to learn by listening is vital to communication within an organization. Indeed, government and private organizations spend a great deal of time in training supervisors and managers in the art of listening. Although listening will be discussed in greater detail later, it should be noted here that you can do a great deal by being attentive to the person speaking and questioning points you do not fully understand.

The single most important thing in listening is your attitude. One organization studied the styles of their employment interviewers, who were supposed to be exceptionally skilled. It found that the employment interviewers were talking 60 percent of the time while the person seeking the job was talking 40 percent of the time. Who had the greater opportunity to find out about whom? It's hard to receive information if you do all the talking.

8. *Use the feedback concept.* One of the first things you can do to improve your communication effectiveness is to be sure that any communication of importance has a feedback mechanism tied to it and is used.

9. *Select the proper media.* There are two basic ways to send information. In choosing the media, you must concern yourself with three questions: What do I want to communicate? To whom do I want to communicate? What is the best available media for communicating? The following examples are not all-inclusive but will start your thinking process.

> *Oral*—staff meetings, personal conferences, training sessions, inspection tours, committee meetings, assemblies.
>
> *Written*—manuals, directives, memoranda, reports, educational literature, newsletters, enclosures, attitude surveys, suggestion systems.

EXCHANGING IDEAS

Among the most valuable communications for you as manager are the ideas of your employees. As a general rule, we do not like other employees' ideas. Check this statement for yourself. Make a personal audit of what happens when employees make suggestions. You'll find that the typical reaction is to immediately take the idea apart and show the employee why it will not work. Managers do this by asking aggressive questions or saying things like, "We tried this before," throwing up all kinds of obstacles that interfere with the effective communication of an idea.

An idea is a wonderful thing. It is also easily discouraged. When employees offer an idea, keep yourself from passing judgment on it immediately. Instead, work with them in trying to understand what they are getting at, and help them tell you how the idea can be put into effect. In this way you will find yourself with a valuable possession.

If the idea is not sound, the fact that you listened to the employees and explored the idea with them will make it possible for them to see the weak places in their idea and deal with them. To overcome the weakness of an idea is to make a major contribution to the organization.

What you feel about your employees has a great influence on your ability to understand what they are saying. For instance, we have all had experiences where we expected a particular employee to behave in a predictable way. Because of our expectation, we make ourselves hear words and ideas that suit our preconception, regardless of what the employee is actually saying. Even if we actually hear the words as they are expressed, we interpret them to suit our preconception of what an "employee like that" would probably say. Or we think to ourselves, "That person doesn't mean to say that."

You should show your employees by your actions that you are not defensive but genuinely interested in what they have to say. You must not force them to guard their words. Try to keep from passing judgment on what they are saying for the time being and concentrate on hearing what they believe. In other words, do not think about whether what they are saying is right or wrong because your whole effort at this time should be focused on trying to determine what their point of view is. Once the ideas have been completely stated, you will each be in a better position to judge the merits of those ideas.

During this process of exploring an employee's idea together, note the speaker's mannerisms and motions. Try to determine what the individual's unsaid, or nonverbal, communications are telling you. Employees often tell a lot with a gesture, a shrug of the shoulders, a raising of an eyebrow, and so forth. Think of the varied meanings in a single wink of the eye. To know what each wink means, you have to consider it in the context in which it is presented because it is easy to misunderstand the significance of a single gesture.

Let the speaker know by *your* nonverbal actions that you are interested in what he or she is saying and that you are paying attention. Your nonverbal actions in this instance may simply be looking at the person while he or she talks instead of thumbing through papers, glancing around the room, or continuing to type. Discipline yourself by saying, "I am going to *listen* to what is being said."

Listening is not a natural practice. You must condition yourself to it. When listening, try not to let your mind wander or to get lost in your own thoughts. This is easier said than done because whenever anyone else is speaking, your own internal communication process is at work. You will be surprised at how much you filter out by "talking to yourself."

When you are sure the employee has had a chance to explain what he or she is saying in the best way possible, test your understanding by "feeding back" what you think was said. The employee won't think you are foolish; rather, he or she will be delighted that you got the message. He or she will know you are paying attention.

SETTING AN EXAMPLE

We are not suggesting that you spend your life listening. As a manager, you also have to be able to communicate. But when an employee has an idea or suggestion, or wants to talk, you should practice your listening skills. You set an example.

If you are really to hear what another person is saying, you must do your best to avoid:

Asking questions. The answers to these questions will satisfy your need but will sidetrack the speaker.

Interpreting words or feelings. You can have no idea how the speaker feels. All you can do is tell the person what you think you've been told.

Showing empathy. Being overly sympathetic may be one of the worst things you can do. Excessive expressions of empathy may distract the speaker. However, this is not to say that you must not try to be empathic.

Indicating disapproval. Obviously this will tend to stop communication. Belittling, ridiculing, and arguing are not effective listening traits.

Communication is the core of our ability to coordinate plans and actions to achieve results. It is the essential difference between isolation and concerted effort. Practice it.

11

Unaccustomed
as You Are . . .

Granville B. Jacobs

You are invited to make a speech. You accept—because there's no good reason why you shouldn't and, after all, you're a bit flattered. Later, after thinking it over, you wonder what you've let yourself in for. Misgivings grow in your mind until, when the big day arrives, you're well on the way to wrecking your own nervous system and anesthetizing that of your audience.

It doesn't have to be that way. Your subject is undoubtedly one you understand at least as thoroughly as your listeners. The people you are to address are not hostile; in fact, they picked you out. There is every reason why you should be able to make an effective, forceful talk—if you work and plan to accomplish just that. It doesn't take genius or magic.

Nervousness and discomfort in front of an audience is purely

From *Leadership on the Job: Guides to Good Supervision* (Rev. Ed.). © 1966 American Management Association, Inc.

psychological. Consequently, a person invited to speak before a group should answer only two questions before accepting: "Do I have enough knowledge or experience of the subject to give a worthwhile presentation?" and, "Am I willing to devote the necessary time to getting my thoughts organized and ready for presentation?"

It has been said that the best inspiration is *preparation*. At least 90 percent of the success of a talk before any audience depends upon proper preparation. Here a great many people have difficulty. First, they procrastinate before starting to line up their facts and organize their thinking. The result: The date and the hour for the talk bear down upon them, and they start scrambling around to develop something to get them off the spot.

Some presentations before audiences are read from manuscripts but, nevertheless, are referred to as "talks." This discussion will not cover such presentations, but will deal entirely with the preparation and delivery of an extemporaneous talk.

INFORMAL—BUT NOT IMPROMPTU!

At this point let's clear up the misuse of *extemporaneous*. Many people think of an extemporaneous talk as one delivered on the spur of the moment without advance preparation. Actually, that is an "impromptu" talk. An extemporaneous talk is given without the use of a manuscript but, to be effective, must be thoroughly prepared. Personal experience in the field to be covered, supplemented by research, is probably the best preparation.

After assembling your material in outline form, you must prepare to face your audience. The only realistic way: Get up on your feet and practice *out loud* (in privacy, of course). It takes will power, and many people balk at it. But there's no substitute for such practice. It will, like nothing else, bring your thoughts from the back of the head onto the tip of the tongue, where they're needed.

Nor is once enough. The talk should be run through several times and finally practiced before a mirror. This, of course, is a little embarrassing, even though you're all by yourself. But it is worth a try. You'll see yourself as your audience sees you, and you can decide for yourself which facial expressions or gestures add to or detract from your presentation.

When you accept an invitation to speak, then, start preparing immediately. Get a notebook and carry it around in your pocket. Whenever a fleeting idea flashes across your mind, jot it down before it's lost. When you see something in a newspaper or magazine on your subject, tear it out and add it to the notebook. Since most speaking engagements are arranged at least two months in advance, well ahead of time, you will find that by the end of two weeks you have twice as much material as you need. That is just as it should be.

MAKE AN OUTLINE

Now you are ready to draft a skeleton outline for your talk. You'll find that many ideas you've jotted down aren't so hot after all. Toss them aside. By this process the cream of your ideas will come to the top.

You will do better, in making your outline, not to write complete sentences. The reason is that few people can write the way they talk. When you write speeches in longhand, your ideas are way ahead of the pencil and you lose the thread of your thought. You start fishing for words to finish the sentence. The sparkle is gone. Teddy Roosevelt, in preparing his speeches, dictated them as rapidly as possible to retain a ring of naturalness and spontaneity.

It is true that many people in high positions in business and public life prepare their speeches in manuscript form and read them. They cannot take chances on having one word slip out to be misinterpreted or made into political capital. Most speakers, however, do not have this handicap.

THE OPENING

After the rough outline is developed, you are ready to work on the opening. This is one part of the talk that should be written out in advance. There's a good reason for this—you should know exactly where to start when you get up in front of your audience. The inspiration of the moment when you face the group may cause you to use a different opening; but, if you know definitely where you plan to start, you will have greater confidence and poise.

The moment for getting favorable attention is at the very beginning. If you depend on the inspiration of the moment for your opening you will almost certainly fumble for words. You will get a negative reaction from the audience—at the crucial period so important to the success of his talk. Remember, the first 20 words and the first 20 seconds can be decisive: They can put you over—or put you under.

Now forget the body of your talk, temporarily, and plan your closing. Apply the same principle as for the opening: Write out the last sentence so that, when it comes time to finish, you have a definite doorway through which to exit. We've all heard speakers who hit the climax only to ruin it by taking on their second wind and continuing. This often occurs when the speaker doesn't know in advance how he or she is going to bring his talk to a close.

Let's take an overall view of the skeleton you are building. The outline of your talk should consist of four main sections. First, the opening sentence—which will be an attention getter, sweeping into the consciousness of your listeners like a man on a swift-swinging trapeze. The next section should quickly justify your subject in the mind of the audience. The third section, the body of the talk, should be filled not only with ideas but with supporting examples to illustrate and back up the points. And the fourth section is the close. At this stage it is always well to summarize—but *briefly* summarize—the points covered, repeating each one for emphasis. Then bring in the closing sentence you have planned, give your audience a nod, smile, and sit down. It is not an act of discourtesy *not* to thank your audience. In fact, a "thank you" weakens your talk by seeming to apologize to an audience that should appreciate the message you have given them.

PLANNING A TYPICAL TALK

Let us illustrate the development of a talk according to these suggestions.

Imagine you have accepted an invitation to speak on "Human Relations in Industry" before a diversified group of business and professional people. In the group there will be bankers, lawyers, doctors, operators of small retail establishments, a school superintendent with faculty members, and advertising and real estate people. What kind of opening will you use to get the favorable attention of this diversified group?

First, pause a few seconds after being introduced. With a pleasant expression, glance around at your audience and give the people a chance to settle down and refocus their attention—on you. Incidentally, if some people haven't stopped their little private confabs, nothing will get them to clam up more quickly than for you to remain quiet for a few seconds. This has the effect of turning a spotlight on them. The pause will also inspire the audience's confidence in you, because it is the mark of an experienced speaker.

Of course, don't appear lackadaisical to your audience. Step up in an alert manner; but, after you get into position, square yourself around and look out over the audience. Survey it, looking to the left and to the right. Look directly at some individual, rather than at the group as a whole. If you spot a genial countenance, give it a smile whether you know the person or not. The entire audience will establish contact with you mentally as a result of your demonstrating interest in it.

You are now ready for the opening. Don't make it stiff—make it casual. Turn to the person who introduced you and say, "Thank you, Mr. Chairman," or, "Thank you, Mrs. Smith," depending upon the occasion. Turning to your audience, again without rushing into your words, say, "Good evening, everyone," or, "Good evening, members of the XYZ group." Then say something that will spark these people's interest in your subject. Quickly show how it relates to them. For example:

> There is no group of business and professional people in any community in the United States that is more alert to the importance of maintaining good human relations in industry than are the members of this group. Even though you may be a member of the legal or the medical profession and may not be an employer yourself, you are vitally concerned with industrial peace in this community, and you yourself can exercise an important influence toward maintaining it.

By these two sentences you have built a bridge from your attention-getting opening to the interest of your audience. You have tactfully reminded the people of their vital interest in the subject. They say to themselves, "This sounds as if it may be worth listening to. When I came to the meeting tonight, I didn't think this would apply to me, but I see now that it does."

Then swing quickly into the main body of your talk. Develop the points you want to make and be sure to make them in terms of your audience's interests.

Now you are ready for your close. It may be no more complicated than a direct, positive statement such as this: "You men and women of Smithville know the value of good industrial relations to this community. By supporting the kind of program we have been discussing, you can help improve them." Finally you nod to your audience, *smile*, turn, and walk to your chair. Remember, *no* "thank you."

NERVOUSNESS CAN BE AN ASSET

There. The job is done; you've given your audience a simple, direct message about a topic in which, as you've shown, they have an interest. They've liked it; and, more important, you've gotten them thinking about something you want them to act on. And nothing terrible has happened to you in the process. In fact, you enjoyed it.

If you were concerned about nervousness, that's forgotten now. For remember, nervousness is a *good* indication. Nervousness is the difference between a race horse and a rhinoceros. Horses that are lethargic don't ordinarily win races.

Every speaker needs nervous energy to put his message over effectively. To stabilize that energy, take a couple of deep breaths before you get up to speak. Then let yourself go, putting your entire body behind your message, using gestures to emphasize your points. After the first few sentences you will have forgotten all about the tingle in your spinal column.

KEY POINTS TO REMEMBER

It's as easy as that. So, if you have to make a speech, remember these keypoints:

◊ Know your subject—collect ideas and material on it. Proper preparation is 90 percent of effective speaking.

◊ Make an outline.

◊ Write out the opening and closing statements.

◊ Practice *out loud*—but do not try to memorize the talk word for word.

◊ When you get on the platform, calmly survey your audience before you start to talk.

◊ Use an attention-getting opening.

◊ Close with a brief summary—and without any "thank you."

12

Cut Those Rumors
Down to Size

Keith Davis

Wild rumors can sweep through an organization with the speed and destructiveness of a summer storm. Nearly every organization occasionally experiences such an onslaught. Morale at one large company hit a new low when a rumor went around that the credit authorization department was closing and 50 workers were being transferred to the equivalent of Siberia.

Another company, where variable product demand requires an occasional small layoff, suffers an 8 percent productivity decline whenever an impending layoff is rumored. The employees appear to be working as hard as ever—but the rumor affects their will to produce up to their capability. And this small decline makes the difference between an adequate profit and a marginal one.

Rumor is a natural result of human interaction. Supervisors need

From *Supervisory Management*, June 1975.

not be alarmed every time a breeze rustles the grapevine, since most rumors turn out to be harmless speculations that die off by themselves. Only rarely are rumors serious enough to require action; but when rumors do seem to threaten the organization, something has to be done.

There are essentially two ways to cope with rumor in an organization. The first is to try to prevent it. How can wild rumors be prevented? First, a supervisor has to recognize that rumors are not haphazard developments; they arise from definite causes. If those causes can be controlled, there is much less probability that rumors will develop.

LACK OF INFORMATION

A major cause of rumor is lack of information about things important to employees. When they do not know what is happening in their world, they are likely to speculate about the situation—and thus a rumor is born. Employees who observe an unscheduled disassembly of a machine, for example, may speculate that machines are being transferred to another plant and workers will be laid off. If they had known that the machine was being replaced by a newer model, the rumor would never have gotten started. Their supervisor unwisely left a gap in the workers' information, and they took the normal, human approach of trying to figure out what's happening—to make sense of changes in their surroundings.

INSECURITY

Another basic cause of rumor is insecurity and the anxiety that goes with it. Insecure, anxious employees are more likely than others to perceive events negatively, and they are better motivated to tell others about their worries. It is easy for insecure workers to imagine the worst in almost any situation. The remedy? To give employees emotional and economic security by providing stable employment and fair wages. In countless ways, day by day, over months and years, supervisors should try to build trust and keep communication open. As employees feel more secure, wild rumors are less likely to arise.

EMOTIONAL CONFLICT

Emotional conflict can also lead to rumor. Rumors thrive in such emotion-laden situations as a disagreement between a hard-driving union and an uncompromising supervisor, or cutthroat competition between two departments. Personality conflicts too can activate rumors. Sometimes, malicious lies enable one person to gain advantage over the other. In other instances, there is no maliciousness—one person is merely so biased in favor of his own viewpoint that he interprets real events in unreal or untrue ways. Strong emotions almost always distort perceptions.

An obvious remedy for the rumor that arises from conflict is cooperative teamwork among various special-interest groups in an organization. Each group should feel that it is part of a larger whole, that the goals of the whole are paramount, and that its own success depends on the success of the whole. People who feel that they are on the same team are not likely to make incorrect or malicious assumptions about each other. As the saying goes, "The people in the same boat with you are not likely to bore a hole in it."

HOW THE RUMOR MILL OPERATES

Whether a rumor starts because of job insecurity, emotional conflict, or an information gap, each person receives and transmits it in terms of his or her own biases. The general theme of the rumor is usually maintained, but not its details. Any oral communication is subject to "filtering"—a process of reducing the story to a few basic details that can be remembered conveniently and passed on to others. Generally, each person chooses the details in a rumor that fit his particular perception of reality and passes these on.

People also add new details to a rumor, frequently making it worse, in order to reflect their own strong feelings and reasoning. This is known as "elaboration." If, for example, a rumor about an employee injury arises, someone who does not like his supervisor may add the notion that the supervisor's failure to provide proper machine maintenance caused the accident. By the time a rumor has undergone both filtering and elaboration, it often bears only a faint resemblance to the original story.

In spite of all the efforts a supervisor makes to prevent rumors, some will still arise. Most rumors that flow through the work area do not cause serious harm, and in any event they soon die a natural death. It would be a waste of effort to try to stop them. Some rumors may even provide certain benefits—such as giving people a way to release pent-up emotions. They may even help maintain employee contacts and add interest to the work.

SERIOUS RUMORS

A few rumors, however, may be serious enough to require attention. It is these rumors that a supervisor will want to restrain or subdue—the second method of dealing with rumors.

If productivity is affected, or community relations suffer, or interdepartmental cooperation is hampered, a supervisor must do something. The most effective approach is to vanquish the rumor with the truth. When the true story is released, the information gap is filled and the rumor dies. Even when the truth has negative implications, it is less destructive than rumors that feed on fear of the unknown. Although the truth may sometimes sound farfetched, it is more likely to be accepted than any story a supervisor could concoct. A reputation for honesty in management will also do much to ensure employee confidence in and loyalty to the organization. The great advantage of truth is that it stands the test of time.

HOW TO REFUTE A RUMOR

In refuting a rumor, never repeat the rumor or refer to it directly. Why? Because if the rumor is repeated during the refutation, some people may hear or read only the rumor, which will thus be reinforced in their minds. Here's an example of how a rumor was refuted simply with the truth—without reference to the rumor itself. According to the rumor, which arose in a plant, an employee had lost a hand in a machine accident. To refute the rumor, the general foreman released a "weekly accident report" stating that there had been no lost-time accidents during the week.

In restraining a rumor, a supervisor should release the truth as quickly as possible; the more a rumor is repeated, the more people tend to believe it. If a rumor is not quashed quickly, people will interpret later events in light of the rumor. In the injury example just given, if employees had heard an ambulance siren outside the plant, they would have been even more convinced that the employee had been seriously injured. In the case of a rumored layoff, an employee noticing two personnel men conferring with his supervisor might see this event as reinforcement of the rumor. Then, too, rumor spreads very quickly throughout an organization—so the quicker it can be refuted, the fewer people will hear it and the less damage will be caused.

THE HORSE'S MOUTH

Communication of the truth behind a rumor is more effective if it comes from a source considered reliable by the receivers. If the rumor concerns future plans, for example, the appropriate person in higher management should be the one to respond. If it concerns an accident, the medical department might respond; if it concerns a technical problem, someone with respected technical knowledge should respond; and if it concerns a supervisor's practices, then that supervisor should respond. In many cases, the public relations department is not the best source for a response, because employees all too often consider it to be simply a mouthpiece for management's viewpoint.

Face-to-face release of the truth is a particularly effective way to deal with rumor. This method has the advantage of speed, particularly in clearing up specific misunderstandings on the part of each individual. It allows each person to be approached in terms of his own personality and outlook. The face-to-face approach can be followed up by a written statement to reinforce the facts.

Management sometimes seeks the help of the union in combating rumor. Although the union does not control the rumor mill any more than management does, it has some influence. Since rumors can be particularly unfavorable when management and labor are in conflict, any reduction of conflict should reduce rumors. Marked improvement frequently results in a department when the supervisor gains the union steward's cooperation in combating rumor—especially when the steward is also an informal leader.

LISTENING TO FEELINGS

When a supervisor hears a rumor, he or she can profit by listening carefully, even though the rumor may be blatantly untrue. Rumors do provide important information about employee feelings and misunderstandings. They can indicate where gaps exist in employee information. And even when a story is untrue, it does show what is worrying employees. During a strike, for example, a supervisor listened carefully to what the workers said management was going to do even though he knew that their statements were rumors because management had not yet decided what to do. He listened because the rumors gave him insight into worker attitudes toward management and the kinds of issues that concerned them.

Supervisors can sometimes understand rumors better if they search for the message behind them. Some rumors are symbolic expressions of feelings that are not really offered by their communicators as fact or truth. If, for example, a worker starts a rumor that shows how unfair his supervisor is, he reasons along this line: "I think the supervisor is an unjust tyrant, and I'm going to let everybody know by telling them a story to illustrate how unjust he really is. It's okay to make it up, because he *would* do what I'm saying if he had the opportunity." The difficulty is that others along the rumor chain accept the story as fact.

Although you may never quell all the rumors in your department, you can materially reduce the causes of rumor by providing subordinates with a sense of security and with all necessary information. And you can even profit from the rumors that do go around by listening for common employee fears, misconceptions, or gripes. Rumors need not defeat you as long as you rely on the ultimate weapon—the truth.

Part Three

**HUMAN RESOURCES: THE KEY
TO MANAGERIAL SUCCESS**

13

Job Engineering for Effective Leadership: A New Approach

Fred E. Fiedler

What makes a good leader? Who has not asked himself this important question when trying to fill a key job in his organization? For many executives, a quick look in the mirror provides one attractive answer: After all, how else could you have reached the top? But even if you could hire carbon copies of yourself, the problem still might not be solved.

Every management text tells us that an outstanding leader in one situation may be quite unimpressive in another. Henry Ford might not have been a very successful elementary school principal or chairman of a book review club; and Freud, the charismatic leader of a scientific circle, would probably have been an unsuccessful president of General Motors or of General Electric.

From *Management Review,* September 1977.

A leader's personality by itself does not determine effectiveness. Rather, it is determined by the way in which his or her personality meets the needs of a particular leadership situation. Thus the secret of improving leadership effectiveness lies in matching the leader and the situation, or in changing the leadership situation so that it fits the leader's personality.

A theory of leadership, the contingency model, suggests how leadership situations can be changed. This theory holds that the performance of a leader depends on two interrelated factors: (1) the degree to which the situation gives the leader control and influence— that is, the likelihood that he can successfully accomplish the job; and (2) the leader's basic motivation—that is, whether his self-esteem depends primarily on accomplishing the task or on having close supportive relations with others.

Whether a person is basically motivated by task accomplishment or having close supportive interpersonal relations can be measured by asking the individual to describe the one person with whom he or she can work least well. Those who strongly reject people because they are poor co-workers tend to be task-motivated; those who see even their least preferred co-workers in a more dispassionate way tend to be relationship-oriented.

It is very important to remember that one type of personality is not better than another. Both are effective, but under different conditions, and both tend to be equally well liked by their subordinates and colleagues. Remember also that we are talking about the basic needs that motivate people, not the way they necessarily behave. Different behaviors may result from the same motivation, and the same behaviors may be the result of different motivations. That's why most people find it very difficult to guess the leadership type to which they belong.

There are many conditions under which task-motivated leaders are quite considerate and concerned with interpersonal relations. Likewise, there are conditions under which relationship-motivated leaders worry primarily about the task. But the priorities of these two types of people differ. For the task-motivated leader, it's "business before pleasure." The relationship-motivated leader, on the other hand, sees good relations as the key to getting the job done.

Studies have shown that the task-motivated manager performs

best in situations in which he has a very high degree of control or else relatively little control. The relationship-motivated manager performs best in situations that give him moderate control and influence.

The degree to which a leadership situation provides high, moderate, or low control can be determined rather easily by three scales that measure whether the leader's relations with group members are good or poor, whether the task is highly structured and defined or relatively vague and unstructured, and whether the power position of the leader is relatively strong or weak.

A well-liked construction foreman usually has high situational control: His relations with his subordinates are good; his task is very highly structured, since he must follow a blueprint and clearly spelled out instructions and material specifications; and his position power is strong since he has a good deal to say about work assignments. A chairman of a board in conflict with other board members, on the other hand, has little situational control. His fellow board members do not accept his leadership; the task of policy and decision making is very unstructured; and as a rule, he cannot reward or punish fellow directors.

Generally, a well-liked board chairman or director of an R&D laboratory (situations typified by good leader-member relations, an unstructured task, and low position power) and a disliked manager of a production department (one operating in a high-task structure with high power position but poor leader-member relations) have moderate situational control. Note that these moderate-control situations require tact and personal sensitivity. Hence the relationship-motivated leader performs best in them. He is able to stroke delicate egos, negotiate bruised sensibilities, and work with people who would just as soon get rid of him. Conditions of high control in which the group is harmonious and simply waiting to get its marching orders do not provide him with enough challenge, while conditions of low control or high stress make him so anxious for close relations that he neglects the task. It is in these situations that the task-motivated leader performs best. He is perfectly willing to accept poor relations with his group as long as the task gets done.

Figure 13-1 is a schematic representation of the contingency model. The leader's situational control is shown on the horizontal axis and the group's performance on the vertical. The effectiveness of the

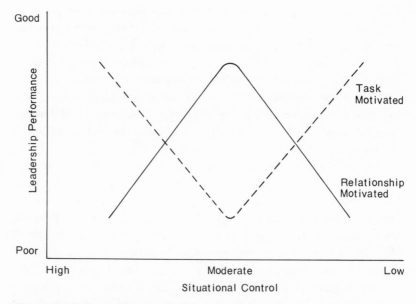

Figure 13–1. Contingency model of task-motivated versus relationship-motivated managers.

relationship-motivated leader is indicated by the solid line and that of the task-motivated leader by the broken one.

Three important points are illustrated. First, as mentioned before, task-motivated leaders perform best in high- and low-control situations. Second, provided they are technically qualified to handle the job, most people will be successful leaders in at least some situations. This means that we cannot really speak of a good or a poor leader, but only of a leader who is likely to be good in one situation and poor in another. Third, and perhaps most important, the performance of the leader will change as his situational control changes.

For example, as some people become more experienced on a job, their control increases and their performance improves. They learn how to handle conflict with their associates and how to spot crises before they become full grown. For others, however, increasing experience and control result in poorer performance. The job no longer challenges them, and they become bored or stale. They then have to be given a job that provides less situational control—that is, a more challenging job.

I could easily cite examples from history to prove that inexperienced leaders can perform better than their more experienced colleagues. But perhaps even more convincing is the evidence around us. A quick look tells us that managers who have been in their jobs longest or who have MBAs and have completed innumerable training courses do not necessarily perform better than those with considerably less leadership training or experience. In fact, don't we talk of people who are "overtrained"?

How can the principles and the findings of the contingency model be applied to improve managerial performance?

I believe the answer is, first, by teaching leaders how to engineer their own leadership situation so that it matches their own personalities, and, second, by teaching them how to match the situations of subordinate leaders to their personality pattern. This is certainly a more viable approach than trying to put round pegs into round holes and square pegs into square holes in the hope that this will permanently solve the personnel problem. After all, any organization that is alive is in an almost constant state of flux. And its pegs and holes, too, are in a constant state of change.

The contingency approach to improving leadership effectiveness has been incorporated in a self-study program called "Leader Match" (F. E. Fiedler, M. M. Chemers, and L. Mahar, *Improving Leadership Effectiveness: The Leader Match Concept*, John Wiley & Sons, 1976). The program, which takes four to seven hours to complete, begins by having the manager determine his basic motivational pattern by identifying his least preferred co-worker. He then learns how to determine his situational control by studying scales that measure leader-member relations, task structure, and position power. Finally, the program shows the leader various methods for modifying his own leadership control and the situational control of his subordinate leaders. For example, he can take such simple steps as making himself more accessible or less accessible to subordinates; asking for detailed instructions and clearly defined goals or suggesting to his boss that he be allowed to decide on the method himself; carefully planning the job prior to his presenting it to his subordinates or encouraging them to participate in the planning; or making the most of his rank and status or trying to be just one of the gang.

The program has been formally tested in four civilian and four military organizations. In each instance, trained and untrained leaders or managers were randomly selected and were evaluated two to six months after completion of the training. In every case, the trained leaders and managers received substantially better performance ratings from their superiors than did those who were untrained. Moreover, the trained leaders and managers attributed much of their success to their application of at least some of the methods suggested for modifying their leadership situation as well as the leadership situations of their subordinates.

The studies show that leaders can be taught to modify their leadership situation to fit their particular personality type in order to increase their performance. Of almost equal importance, these studies prove that there are ways that organizations can make more effective use of personnel. For those businesses that in the past have had to discard employees or relegate them to jobs that did not fully utilize their talents because they did not measure up in previous positions, the "leader match" concept opens up an avenue of new opportunities.

14

The Importance of Knowing Your Employee's Needs

Arthur Sondak

Management—and the true test of leadership—is getting people to *want* to do what's needed, not just go through the motions. This isn't easy, for it means that managers must influence the behavior of their subordinates.

Some managers try to do this by utilizing their authority, the "gold badge" of management. But the "gold badge" proves only something that the subordinates already know—that is, that their boss has power. And their attitude toward the work remains the same.

How, then, can a manager hope to change or improve an employee's attitude toward the job? The answer is simple—present the job so that it works to satisfy the employee's needs.

If you want to do this, you must first *identify* your employee's

From *Supervisory Management*, May 1980.

needs. People are different, seek different goals, and behave in different ways to achieve those goals. And when it comes to taking direction, they will react based on how the resulting behavior will carry them toward or away from their personal goals.

Many managers have found, much to their surprise and puzzlement, that they cannot use the same technique of direction with each of their subordinates. What is accepted by one may be summarily rejected by another. Thus the best method of getting a job done is less a matter of what is right and more a matter of what is appropriate, with appropriateness measured by two varying factors—the individual and the situation.

Behaviorial science studies have contributed heavily to the identification of individual personalities and the needs that direct behavior. Utilizing that knowledge, a manager can adjust work assignments to satisfy the needs of a person and influence him or her to perform a job willingly, even eagerly. This is the key to motivation—using work to satisfy needs. The manager creates a psychological climate that will encourage employees to view their jobs as a means to fulfilling their needs. As Maslow said, it is an unsatisfied need that directs behavior; a satisfied need no longer motivates.

Maslow places human behavior and the needs driving it in a hierarchy with levels of priority. The implication is that observed behavior may have more than one need or motive behind it. If effective direction is to be applied, a manager must know his or her people well enough by observing their behavior to be able to identify the need level that each employee is at. Remember, the human being is perpetually wanting. He does not live by bread alone—provided he has bread!

The hierarchy of needs as described by Maslow is:

1. *Physiological.* The need for food, air, water, and sleep—those items essential to physical survival and well-being.

2. *Safety and security.* With survival reasonably assured, behavior develops to protect the individual from danger, either physical or psychological. For example, infants cry and seek protection from the unknown, thunder, or darkness. Adult behavior is directed toward making certain that physiological needs continue to be met, or that the means to retain them are not threatened. In other words, one holds onto a job because its salary pays for food, clothing, and shelter. People find security in order, schedule, routine, and predictability. They hold

a preference for the familiar. Job duties that provide these satisfactions are welcome; abrupt changes and managerial tyranny that might affect their job security are certain to produce protective, defensive behavior.

3. *Social: belonging and affection*. After safety and security are reasonably taken care of, social needs take over. Behavior is directed outwardly, toward family, friends, and business groups. The objective is to be accepted and wanted by others—to give and receive acceptance and affection.

4. *Esteem and recognition*. Next on the ladder is the need for esteem—by others and for oneself. It is the need to be useful and necessary and to get attention and recognition from others for being so.

5. *Self-fulfillment*. The top rung on the needs ladder is to be the best that one can be. It is behavior that is beyond ego or esteem—what one *can* be, one *must* be.

IDENTIFYING EMPLOYEES' NEEDS

While it is easy to identify by personality the position of someone, even yourself, on the needs ladder, it is not so easy to determine people's needs levels by situation. Situational behavior can move a person up or down the ladder. An insecure person, one who normally looks for safety and security, can be in a situation where his or her own particular interests, knowledge, or ability results in an increase in self-confidence that produces self-fulfilling behavior. Conversely, someone high on the ladder can drop down suddenly and dramatically. For example, someone can lose a job unexpectedly, and the need for a new job to provide a means to pay for food, clothing, and shelter takes on top priority.

All around us, we see situational behavior in action. Eating or drinking is not done just to satisfy hunger or thirst. Business objectives, for ego or self-fulfillment, might be achieved through lunch, dinner, cocktails, or all three. Joining a group at a restaurant might be done to gain group acceptance. Thanksgiving dinner is an occasion for love and togetherness; some people even feel a direct relationship between the reason and the actual consumption of food and drink.

On the job, an understanding of situational behavior is necessary.

The wise manager will get to know his or her people well, for understanding a person—recognizing his or her behavior and the needs behind it—points the way to effective and productive leadership.

To meet the organization's needs through the efforts of others, the effective manager has to recognize and meet the changing needs of each of his or her people. A tall order? Of course. It takes perception, awareness, and continuing, conscious efforts—in other words, good management skills. Between continuing and ever changing work pressures and the moods of people, calling effective management a challenge has to rank as an understatement alongside the observation of one of Noah's neighbors that it looked like rain. But knowing the needs hierarchy developed by Maslow is a big step toward meeting that challenge.

When people's needs are not met, frustration sets in, and their behavior shows it. Resistance; inflexibility; absenteeism; lateness; accidents; reduced productivity; increased waste of materials, money, and time; apathy; sulking; and arguing—these all tell a manager that something is wrong. That's their purpose—to demonstrate frustration in an attempt to get it alleviated.

The manager's objective is simple—to prevent frustration from developing. When he or she fails and it does develop, the error in handling it is often just as basic. Action is taken on the behavior, not the cause, although the behavior is only the symptom. The real problem lies in why an employee's behavior takes a turn for the worse. To find that answer, the manager must discover what needs of the employee are not being met. This is where knowing the needs hierarchy will help.

Let's reexamine the needs hierarchy to see what behavior is typical at each level. Then we will see what the manager can do to show the employee at that level how the job can satisfy his or her needs.

Need: Safety and Security

How does a person behave?
1. Precise, orderly, and systematic in business and personal life.
2. Conscientious; intent on doing a good job.

3. Tactful and diplomatic; cooperative and accommodating; consciously trying to avoid antagonizing others.
4. Attentive to keeping an orderly workplace.
5. Interested and concerned over the organization's security programs and types and level of benefits.

Typically, this type of behavior is found in people new on the job.

What does this person want?
1. Avoidance of anything that will threaten security.
2. No abrupt changes without warning or careful preparation.
3. A sharing of responsibility.
4. Clear job duties and clear means to meet them.
5. Predictable behavior by the manager.
6. Supportive leadership that will show the way to get the job done.
7. Reassurance that what's being done is what's wanted.

What should the manager do?
1. Make sure that the way to do the job is clear by providing careful instructions.
2. Encourage the person; build confidence.
3. Give reassurance through periodic praise for accomplishment.
4. Be available for and provide support, especially when things seem to get difficult.
5. Condition the person carefully before making any changes.

Because the individual in need of security is wary of any changes made in the work schedule or routine, it is important that changes be explained to him or her well in advance of their implementation. Take the time to answer any questions the employee may have, and detail how the change will affect the individual.

Need: Belonging and Affection

How does a person behave?
1. Friendly and outgoing; the individual wants to make friends.
2. Close to family and to groups both on and off the job.
3. Cooperative and willing; anxious to please.
4. A good team member and worker.

What does this person want?

1. To be wanted and accepted; to belong, both professionally and personally.
2. A feeling of accomplishment and evidence of appreciation for his or her efforts, since this conveys acceptance and belonging—having "made it."
3. Sincerity in relations with others. Phoniness or manipulation will be spotted for what it is and will demotivate the employee.
4. No abrupt changes, particularly without warning. Preparation for change is seen as synonymous with concern for the person as an individual.

What should the manager do?

1. Show a sincere interest in the person as an individual.
2. Give periodic reassurance and praise for accomplishments.
3. When appropriate, give tangible rewards or awards. Even a lunch on the boss will go a long way in making an employee feel accepted.
4. Show ways that will make it easier to get the job done; it shows you care and that the person has been accepted.
5. Involve the person in group efforts, particularly a capable group. Teamwork will be the product.
6. Give forewarning and explanation of change; even solicit input, where possible, before instituting changes.

Need: Esteem and Recognition

How does a person behave?

1. Sociable, friendly, and outgoing; not only makes friends easily but takes the initiative and acts socially aggressive.
2. Poised, confident, and personable; at ease in almost any kind of situation and with different kinds of people; able to deal with new situations; even welcomes them.
3. Interested in a variety of activities.
4. Fits in easily with others and usually works well with them.
5. Often seeks to take the lead in both work and social situations.
6. May seek to be the center of attention.

What does this person want?
1. Recognition, status, popularity, and attention from others.
2. Variety in work and outside involvement.
3. Self-respect and respect from others for ability, knowledge, and accomplishment.
4. Heavy involvement with people. This is an opportunity for achievement from which recognition from others will come.
5. Close identity with a group or an organization.
6. Because of the need to display ability, regimentation, close control, and heavy detail or procedure are not welcome. They reduce the opportunity to show "can do!"

What should the manager do?
1. Provide opportunities for group work.
2. Look for opportunities to provide variety in work assignments; special projects are particularly welcome.
3. Give opportunities to show accomplishment and receive recognition.

Because of the active nature of this type of individual, there are several things that a manager must take into consideration when dealing with this type of employee. First, due to the employee's dislike of regimentation, the manager must work out limitations that give the employee room for independence, yet maintain safeguards regarding approval and authority.

Second, these limits should be followed up periodically with meetings between subordinate and manager, rather than the manager continually keeping "an eye" on the employee.

Third, this employee will welcome change in the work operation. In fact, the employee may enjoy change so much that he or she tends to overdo it. Review the objectives of the job regularly to see if change is needed, and be sure to have the employee get your approval before making any major changes in operation.

Need: Self-Fulfillment and Growth

How does a person behave?
1. Keeps technically up to date in an occupation or profession.
2. Looks for problems to solve.

3. Questions the existing, trying to make things better.
4. Approaches questions and problems analytically; keeps looking for "why."
5. Looks for change to make sense and adapts easily when it does. Otherwise, it is questioned.
6. Displays a minimum of emotion or emotional shifts—attention is to fact and objectivity.

What does this person want?
1. Challenge and stimulation.
2. New assignments and problems to solve.
3. The opportunity to do something worthwhile, to learn and grow.

What should the manager do?
1. Provide exposure to new knowledge and new work assignments. Present problems to solve and research to conduct. Special projects and creative assignments are particularly welcome opportunities.
2. Consult before instituting changes; the insights and analysis will probably improve the plan. Where possible, turn over examination of the need for change to the individual; the results will be even better.
3. Give help toward improvement. Share relevant knowledge and provide coaching for job development.
4. Make it possible for further self-development to take place, on and off the job. Identify sources and, if possible, provide resources.
5. Provide opportunities on the job for the employee to apply the results of the self-development effort.

Despite individual personalities people can behave at different needs levels in different situations. For example, even the most aggressive individual will become agreeable and bending when starting a new job in a new company. No doubt you can identify your own behavior in different situations and recognize the accompanying needs. As a supervisor, you need to be aware of and understand as well the behavior and needs of others.

There is no substitute for knowing your people as individuals if you are to understand their behavior. Knowledge of their likes and dislikes on the job, and their interests and activities off the job, are strong needs indicators. It can make easier the difficult job of moving your people up the needs ladder, and as people progress from safety toward self-fulfillment, they become increasingly capable and productive. As they progress, the job you are responsible for will show better results, things will run more smoothly, and your own sense of well-being will improve.

You may not be able to get all your people to self-fulfillment. Some of them may not be geared to do so. Others may not stay in your operation long enough—you may well see them move up the organizational ladder.

In fact, you might not even be there to see it happen. Your improvement of your people will be evident. Your capability to get the job done and your reputation as a "people grower" will have you moving up the organizational ladder.

After all, you've got needs, too.

15

Treat Your Employees as Customers

Sandra A. Vavra

As a marketing person, I have been trained to look for trends in the marketplace. An interesting one of late has been the very strenuous effort of American industry to prove that it is concerned with various media, to such reminders of corporate concern as: Have It *Your* Way, We Try Harder, and We Do It All for *You*.

From hamburgers to financial services, in new industries and more established ones, the "in" thing is to prove to consumers that their needs can be happily satisfied by the big-brother figure otherwise known as "the American corporation." In fact, one implication that we are supposed to draw from these instances of corporate altruism is that the bigger the corporation, the more human it is! Sometimes I can't help but visualize the rather bizarre image of a consumer skipping, schoolgirl fashion, down a road and holding the hand of a smiling, gleaming glass corporate headquarters building, as they both sing "Follow the Yellow Brick Road."

From *Supervisory Management*, April 1978.

WHAT BUSINESS IS DOING

At more lucid times, however, I begin to sense what it is that big business is trying to do. As a marketing person, I know that the giant corporations have researched, polled, and analyzed statistics—all to answer the question: What does the public want?

Another thing I know is that the big corporations have been trying to adapt their public images and concerns to fit the growing demand of consumers to be treated well, fairly, and with respect. So basically it seems that big business has come to the realization that consumerism is more than a passing fad and that being consumer-oriented is a matter of survival.

But I think there's an equally critical "market" that management has usually overlooked because of its very closeness to business: employees.

Why should business concern itself with satisfying the needs of employees? In the first place, a contented employee is likely to provide better service to the company's customers, thereby maximizing results. But also important is the fact that a contented employee stays longer with a business, thus holding down training and turnover costs.

It seems that until very recently, employees have been relegated to the status of white rats in a behavioral psychologist's laboratory. In fact, from Frederick W. Taylor to Douglas McGregor, the concern of managerial experts and behavioral scientists has been to find even more subtle and sophisticated ways to manipulate—or even coerce—employees into increasing output, thereby maximizing profits.

But has this single-minded pursuit been all that successful? Or has this cold, scientific attitude toward employees actually decreased results because of lost customers and increased labor costs?

WHAT THE FIGURES SAY

One way to answer these questions is by taking a closer look at some of the relevant financial figures of a specific industry—the savings and loan associations, for example. In my industry, there is an annual loss factor in savings customers of 10 percent. In monetary terms, the average investment loss per customer works out this way:

Cost of advertising and other promotional enticements to get one customer *in the door*	$25
Cost of signing up customer for one industry service (includes employee time, materials, and computer time)	15
Cost of providing customer information (includes mailings, lobby displays, stuffers, and other cross-selling efforts)	25
Cost of closing out account, purging files, and adjusting records	5
Total lost investment per customer	$70

Now we can get an idea of the magnitude of lost investment—and lost profits—in the industry because of customer dissatisfaction. In a savings and loan association of 200,000 customers, a 10 percent annual customer loss at $70 per customer adds up to an enormous $1,400,000 in lost funds! No wonder the industry has been putting increased emphasis on trying to discover what the customer really needs and then to satisfy those needs. Of course, it's a sure bet that the loss of many customers can be directly attributed to undertrained or disgruntled employees. But there are other, even more distressing costs associated with unhappy employees and high turnover. Consider the investment lost on each new employee who leaves or is terminated at the end of one year:

Average cost of hiring and terminating one employee (includes record keeping, management time, and advertisements)	$ 100
Average cost of on-the-job training or special training classes	1,000
Average employee's annual salary	8,400
Average cost of employee benefits (includes insurance, medical reimbursements, and paid holidays)	2,520
Total cost to hire, train, and compensate average employee for one year	$12,020

Since the average turnover rate of employees in the savings and loan industry is about 30 percent annually, and since approximately

1,000 employees are needed to service the previously mentioned 200,000 customers, this would mean an approximate turnover of 300 employees for a savings and loan association of this size. And the investment loss for these 300 employees would be an incredible $3,606,000! Even the manager who is unconcerned with employee development must respond to this figure.

GOLDEN RULE FOR EMPLOYEES

What can employers do to reduce such a large drain on potential earnings? The picture is not all gloomy. The figures used above are, after all, approximate and assume that the employee has done nothing productive in his or her year on duty—which is itself a suspect assumption. These figures are meant only to delineate the problem of dissatisfied employees on business earnings. And once the problem has been delineated, the problem solving can begin.

A number of renowned behaviorists have tackled just this problem and come up with a rather simple solution for employers: "Treat your employees as they would have themselves be treated." Or even more to the point: "Treat your employees as you would treat your customers." This paraphrasing of the Golden Rule is based on the realization that taking care of employees is essential for maintaining customer loyalty and, hence, staying profitable. And it doesn't take a managerial expert to see that many of the current creative and nontraditional approaches to managing subordinates have a practical monetary dimension as well as a humanistic one.

Where I work, we have discovered that a few managerial guidelines, when practiced consistently, can yield substantial benefits in terms of more responsive employees, more satisfied and loyal customers, and an improved profit picture. These guidelines are:

◊ Realize that workers operate in a social system. As Karl Albrecht, the management consultant, once wrote, "At best, all that managers can do is to strategically intervene in the lives of their employees." In other words, don't try to control your employees. Rather, the emphasis of your managerial strategy should be on creating nourishing environments for them. How? By asking for and using employees' ideas on projects; by informing them of contemplated changes *before* implementation and asking for their input; by talking spontaneously with employees at times other than crises; by letting employees make their own mistakes; by offering suggestions as a means of guiding, rather than commanding, employees (except, of course, in emergency situations); by giving positive "strokes" (such as complimenting an employee on a successful project in front of his or her peers); and by demonstrating that you are just as willing to hear bad news as good.

◇ Distinguish between those factors that truly motivate employees (such as job control, recognition, opportunity for advancement) and those factors that are considered merely necessities of life (job pay and working conditions). Once you realize the difference between the two kinds of factors, you're in a position to manage more productively.

◇ Identify those employee behaviors you consider valuable (good judgment, dependability, cooperation) and those you believe to be costly (absenteeism, poor quality work, discourteousness to customers), so that you have a target for your solutions.

◇ Develop yourself as a manager. Recognize your strengths and weaknesses and take both into account when determining your style. Deal from a position of strength, but allow your employees to develop a sense of strength and autonomy themselves.

◇ Give your employees a vision to follow in attempting to do a job successfully. Do this by first encouraging them to mentally rehearse the job *before* they attempt it. This technique works especially well in preparing employees for customer-contact situations. Practice role-playing with your employees before they deal with actual customers.

◇ Think of yourself as an orchestrator—one who blends the disparate personalities and styles of a number of employees into a harmonious team. Then let your employees do their work on their own terms.

◇ Don't use any behavioral technique exclusively. Each is merely a tool, and the specific tool must be right for the specific situation. Try hard to avoid what I call the "oh-no-she's-been-to-another-management-seminar" syndrome.

◇ Realize that your industry, job, and lifestyle are in a constant state of change. Engage your people periodically to creative exercises such as "imagineering." And develop your ability to manage change by helping your employees accept the changes they themselves are going through.

◇ When appropriate, consider implementing such nontraditional work techniques as: flexible working hours; management by consensus; periodic sabbaticals for employees; and Japanese-style management (that is, working in the midst of your employees, rather than always in an office).

◇ As you move into higher management positions, remember to "water the garden" periodically by socializing with employees. And even at a lower management level, it's not a bad idea to tactfully encourage upper management to become more involved with employees.

◇ Remind yourself to see the world as an environment of continuing opportunity rather than one of frustrating dead ends. Realize that, by being a positive Pygmalion, you can help create any number of successful employees. Encourage your employees to continue their education—whether in the form of seminars, classes, books, or professional association participation—as a means of retarding hardening of the attitudes. Then take the same advice yourself.

◇ Most of all, realize that all the fancy academic models really boil down to a common-sense attitude of appreciation for your fellow workers. This appreciation can take an infinite number of forms—from giving a smile to giving the responsibility for completing a project. What the appreciation shows is an attitude of sincere caring for employees and an honest desire that their needs be satisfied.

16

The Manager
as Coach

Margaret V. Higginson
Thomas L. Quick

"Coaching" refers to discussions between a manager and subordinate that contribute to the latter's improvement and higher effectiveness. It is probably one of the most important activities of a manager in upgrading his or her resources, yet it is often neglected.

In many cases, the reason for this neglect is one that an executive would prefer not to face. That phrase "growth and development" sounds great when it is applied to the executive—but to her subordinates? Why should she help them grow out of her department? Why should she develop someone who may then get ambitions to take over her job?

But a manager who ignores her coaching responsibilities limits her

From *The Ambitious Woman's Guide to a Successful Career*, by Margaret V. Higginson and Thomas L. Quick. © 1980 AMACOM, a division of American Management Associations.

own job and pays a penalty for doing so. Whatever her actual title, she reduces her role, in the eyes of her subordinates, to one of mere supervision. She rejects a chance to initiate change in favor of merely reacting to it if it occurs. Most important, she deprives herself of employees' talents and capabilities that could contribute to her own success as leader of a team and that could enhance her own managerial reputation.

The manager who accepts her coaching responsibilities and who sees the possible advantages to herself inherent in them may nonetheless have some problems in working out a course of action. Even in organizations that have formal periodic performance appraisals that involve some coaching, she may not get much benefit from those occasional interviews. Frequently the framework for the interview is prescribed by top management, and all the emphasis is put on getting the information needed to fill in a narrowly focused evaluation form. Questions that aren't on the form just don't get asked. Moreover, the amount of time allotted for the interviews may be too short for the manager to update her knowledge of what the employees really need in order to grow in their jobs. As was mentioned earlier, such formal interviews need to be supplemented with informal ones.

Informal talks with each subordinate are only a preliminary, however, to the formulation of a growth and development program that brings results. For that, a systematic approach is necessary with equal emphasis on three points:

1. *Set up your own "data bank."* Take notes immediately after your conversation with each subordinate. Otherwise you will probably forget some of the areas you've covered. Also, if something was said or hinted at that alerted you to a quality you never knew the person had, add it immediately to your notes—that will give you still more to build on. And make a note to yourself to follow up each interview at a specific time in the future, to ensure the continuation of the program.

2. *Present specific guidelines.* "Growth and development" is in itself an amorphous phrase, which may be another reason managers have difficulty in coming to grips with it. Giving shape to a growth and development program is a task that requires managerial imagination and precision. Subsequent discussions with the subordinate should point to specific developmental experiences, such as further training or

education, a field trip, servicing a key account, temporary duty in another department, or a new assignment. And these suggestions, too, should be added to your notes.

Aside from the benefits to the employees, working within this framework gives you a reason to keep in touch with them. And this is important, not only because it will keep the growth and development program alive (and structured) but because it makes your concern and your expectations convincing to subordinates.

3. *Touch all bases.* A good growth and development plan should include everyone in the department. (Keeping a record for each employee is a way of making sure there is full coverage.) This is not just a matter of fairness, although that can be useful in maintaining morale: it is also a way to avoid the pitfall of depending on "indispensable" people who may fall ill, take early retirement, or quit. There may be other "indispensables" in your department that you will discover through your talks with them.

The validity of a development plan rests on how it suits each individual, and that requires checking back. What struck you as an ideal developmental experience may have left the employee cold. You may need to offer another suggestion or to probe more closely into the employee's aspirations and capabilities as he or she sees them.

It's wise to keep in mind that people change, even though outwardly they may seem the same. Thus, an employee who states that she has "no interest" in going into management may later regret her flat negative and may not know how to retract it unless given an opportunity to do so. Or she may have been talking without knowing what management opportunities were available or what they involved.

Conducting informal interviews in a way that the manager knows is regular but that seems casual to employees—and hence does not produce tension—offers her a chance to bring her own perceptions of the people in her department up to date. And she can use these occasions to help them broaden their own thinking as well.

17

Improving Productivity: Ways to Get People Started

Curtis E. Dobbs

In the press for increased productivity, the attendant fanfare over quotas, indexes, and slogans sometimes diverts attention from the one really essential element of productivity: people. It is people, after all, who make plans work or fail. To get people back into the limelight when productivity plans are being made, managers may need to refocus on a few things. How do people affect productivity? What about people cost in productivity? What about the responsibility of supervisors for people and productivity?

First, let's look at the meaning of productivity. Productivity measures what is produced in relation to what is consumed in order to produce it. What kinds of things are consumed? Money, for one, and materials and wear and tear on plant and equipment and—of course—

From *Supervisory Management,* March 1976.

the time and effort of people. But people affect productivity not only in terms of their time and effort (which has a dollar cost measured in salary and benefits), but also in terms of the problems they create (which can also be measured in dollars, though much less precisely). Later, we'll take a look at the kinds of people problems that affect productivity.

To improve productivity, an organization must get more out of what it has—get more output from its consumption or input of resources and expenditures—or change the kinds or amounts of inputs involved to get relatively greater output. Can a department produce more reports, for example, by purchasing new equipment? Or can it produce the same number of reports with fewer people doing the work? In these examples, resources are changed to improve the productivity measure. But management may also be able to improve productivity simply by improving techniques to increase output (by using form paragraphs in reports, for example) without altering resources.

POTENTIAL EFFECTS ON EMPLOYEES

In thinking about new programs and techniques for improving productivity, management needs to be aware of the potential effects on employees—because negative effects may stimulate employees to create problems. Although this is only common sense, it is often overlooked—especially when times are bad and an organization's financial position is shaky. Particularly important are the effects on production employees, clerical employees, and supervisors. These people do the day-to-day work, so most productivity programs are logically aimed at them. But such programs are fruitless if employees resist improvement efforts—and they have been known to do so strenuously enough to reduce productivity.

Let's look at two potential effects commonly occurring. An important one is the triggering of resistance to change. Many employees do tend to resist change—even those who claim to accept it readily. There are many reasons for this, but let's look at just one: fear.

Yes, the prospect of change often scares people. They may naturally fear:

◊ Job loss—"Maybe this change will eliminate my job."
◊ A speed-up—"They want me to do my job faster, but I can't!"
◊ Relocation—"Hey, could this new program cause me to transfer to a new department?"
◊ The unknown—"Hold it! I don't understand! What about my friends? Will I get a new boss? New responsibilities? I just don't know what might happen!"

Another effect is typified by the question, "What's in it for me?" The point is perhaps debatable—and has been debated—but it does seem that most people do not work for the pleasure of working. Most of us, and most of our subordinates, work to provide for our needs and obligations and those of our families. It's natural that an employee faced with new approaches like productivity programs will begin to think (consciously or subconsciously) about "What's in it for me?" Can he or she expect problems or "good things" like more pay or better working conditions?

THE PEOPLE COSTS INVOLVED

Now let's take a brief look at people costs as they affect productivity. The obvious ones are salary and benefits and an obvious way to decrease these is to reduce the number of employees. As we mentioned, however, there are other people costs to be taken into consideration—and although they are not so obvious, reducing them can improve productivity.

Turnover and absenteeism, for example, create many problems—especially for the manager or supervisor trying to increase productivity. Although the costs involved are hard to measure precisely, they take the form of late work, duplicated work, mistakes, additional administrative effort, lost time, and so forth. Management often places too little emphasis on the costing and control of these factors.

It is not too difficult to identify such turnover costs as those for recruiting, selection, placement, and training. Almost any organization can calculate the cost of recruiters, recruiting material, employment tests, medical examinations, and employee orientation programs; indeed, many organizations have formalized training budgets. But there are additional factors such as lowered morale and decreased company loyalty that lead to increased production costs, errors, and lower productivity. The dollar cost of turnover is difficult to assess in any organization, but may range from $300 for a production worker to $7,000 and more for a manager. These are significant costs.

Putting dollar figures on employee absence is more difficult. A key cost factor here is that of lost production. Even if management institutes cross-training programs to offset production loss during employee absences, there is an added training cost. And, of course, there is also the cost of various sick-pay programs, as well as other intangible costs.

The point is that the people cost—as a key factor in calculating productivity—is made up from more than simply salaries and benefits. The rate of turnover, absenteeism, tardiness, and the like can increase or decrease people cost and thus increase or decrease productivity. Managers who address themselves to these costs—that is, concern themselves with their people—have a significant opportunity to affect productivity.

SOME USEFUL APPROACHES

Following are some approaches that can help increase productivity through concentration on the people who do the producing. These are not all new ideas—some, in fact, are a little old-fashioned—but they point up the availability of a variety of ways to increase productivity through people. (Note that an organization doesn't have to have a fancy or even formal program to get a better job done. Many of the following steps can be taken by individual managers in their own departments.)

1. *Make a diagnosis of on-the-job problems.* This should be a careful examination of what is going on in the workplace, not an intuitive assessment. Don't let an abundance of problems pressure you into unplanned solutions. Set priorities for solving them and proceed accordingly.

One tool that can be used in both diagnosis and priority setting is a series of candid interviews with each hourly employee and any subordinate supervisor involved. These interviews often yield much information—some useful and some not—but by putting it all together, management can establish a meaningful pattern of concerns and problems. Upon analyzing such interview responses, managers have been surprised to see how well employees know the problems, can define them, and can set priorities.

When this diagnostic approach is part of a broad management undertaking, assistance may be required from outside the department. However, an individual manager or supervisor can make his own diagnosis if he is willing to be objective. To increase his or her objectivity, the manager can discuss the situation with another manager or get assistance from the personnel department.

2. *Don't forget training.* Sound, well-thought-out, formal (at least outlined in writing) training is a productive investment. Many companies have training budgets and full-time training directors. The meaningful content of this training, however, must come from first-line supervision and middle management. If your organization has formal training programs, make sure the content is good. If it is not, suggest changes. If there is no formal training, you might outline one or two basic programs and recommend them to the appropriate superiors.

3. *Involve your subordinates.* Supervisors should not forget that subordinates have knowledge about their work that can help. Let employees have input to productivity programs. Inform them of problems and goals. Anticipate with them the results of the new programs.

The need for effective communication and employee involvement cannot be overemphasized in productivity improvement programs. Meetings provide an excellent way to accomplish this. Depending on the scope and structure of the program, the meetings may be organizational, departmental, team (one team may consist of all managerial staff, another of all employees at a certain level, and so forth), or one-to-one. To be useful, however, any meeting must be specifically planned to facilitate the exchange of information on productivity plans and progress among all team members.

Attitude or opinion surveys and suggestion systems are con-sidered by some to be old-fashioned, but they are nevertheless useful. When designed to elicit the proper response, they can open up communication on problems that block progress, establish manage-ment's credibility, and involve employees. A word of warning, however: Don't ask for ideas or suggestions unless you plan to respond to them. Inaction will destroy management's credibility in short order.

Many organizations use newsletters effectively to communicate with employees. Effective ones are not simply propaganda sheets, but include information meaningful to employees in terms of what they do, what they care about, and what affects them.

4. *Make use of performance appraisals and objectives.* Performance appraisal *is* important to the employee. He or she really does want to know "How am I doing?" Day-to-day compliments and constructive advice are most important—but the annual or semi-annual written appraisal is quite significant. A written appraisal lets the employee know his boss is willing to stand by his comments by putting them in writing. Giving the employee a copy of the appraisal will assure him that there are no secrets concerning appraisal of his performance. More and more organizations are building objectives into such appraisals. These objectives can be set jointly with employees and then measured and reset at each formal appraisal session. It is still true that if employees know what is expected of them, they usually perform better and more productively.

5. *Don't overlook training for subordinate supervisors—or for yourself.* Remember that you and any subordinate supervisors you have may also stand in need of further training and education to keep abreast of change. More and more supervisors are taking advantage of training sessions offered by management organizations and colleges on such supervisory techniques as performance appraisal, employee relations, communication, and the like. Training is important both for new supervisors and for "old pros."

All the ideas discussed are people-oriented approaches to productivity improvement. Remember that the people doing the work are the hourly people—not management. Don't forget that they know the work and have ideas about how it can be accomplished more efficiently. Managers who want to improve productivity will use these ideas, establish credibility by acting on them, and get meaningful participation from employees.

18

Evaluating Subordinates: How Subjective Are You?

Robert R. Bell

One of the most important areas of employee relations is concerned with rewarding the worker for his or her contribution and, on the basis of this, deciding on promotability. One of the key elements of this process is the performance appraisal. Yet in many cases, the appraisal is a very subjective interpretation of the employee's performance by the supervisor. As managers, we must be aware of the type of performance appraisal techniques being used in our organizations and the potential personal and technical biases we bring into the performance appraisal process.

THE CONCEPT OF MERIT RATING

Employee rating is perhaps one of the oldest management practices. Its primary goal is an evaluative one, designed to assess the employee's potential for future success and promotability since, as Arch Patton

From *Advanced Management Journal*, Winter 1979.

suggest, "past and present performance is the most reliable key to future performance."

There are, of course, many types of performance rating systems, and there are probably hundreds of labels associated with each type. For purposes of simplicity, we will group all systems into two categories—"objective" and "subjective"—which we will discuss briefly.

Objective Performance Evaluation

The most obvious method of evaluating the performance of an individual is by analyzing his or her work output.

When the output is measurable, such as the number of sales made or units produced, performance evaluation becomes simply a matter of maintaining proper records, determining the measure of productivity, and comparing the measure with the standard. A number of benefits are derived from the utilization of specific (objective) standards:

1. Measurable standards give both the employee and the supervisor a common referral point in appraisal sessions. And compensation can be based on solid evidence of performance.
2. Employees who are aware of the level of performance expected can continuously evaluate how well they are doing. The employee does not have to ask for an assessment of performance and, if needed, can initiate corrective changes in performance without waiting for the supervisor. (Peter Drucker calls this the "self-control" process.)
3. Since job objectives are clarified by performance standards, the employee and the supervisor can agree on goals for employee development and training.
4. Measurable objectives give an incentive for improvement.
5. The supervisor has the chance to compare the performance of several subordinates on the basis of common criteria.
6. Performance criteria give the supervisor a way to measure his own effectiveness as a leader.

Subjective Performance Appraisal

Even with the benefits associated with objective appraisals, many companies and many managers still wholly or partly use subjective rating methods. There are several rather obvious reasons for this. First, tasks and relationships in certain jobs are ill-defined, and production output is the "synergistic" result of combined worker productivity. Objective indices of individual worker productivity are fairly difficult to define. Other jobs, such as those of university professors, have very abstract productivity criteria associated with them. Is a professor's productivity defined by the number of students he teaches or the number of times he has been published? What is the trade-off between quantity and quality? Other managers point out that, whether we like it or not, organizations are social systems and totally quantitative measures of performance and potential are simply not realistic.

TECHNIQUES FOR PERFORMANCE EVALUATION

The organization trying to design a performance appraisal system has a number of techniques from which to choose. Table 1 gives an overview of several appraisal methods and some of the factors affecting the choice of one over the other.

Graphic rating scale. This technique is among the oldest known performance appraisal methods and is very easy to use. Typically, the evaluator is given a chart or graph and is expectd to rate the employee on a number of qualities such as job knowledge, dependability, motivation, and caliber of work. The scale usually ranges from excellent or outstanding to satisfactory and then to unsatisfactory.

Ranking. Using a ranking technique, the evaluator is asked to rank each employee relative to the other employees in a unit, usually with respect to several criteria such as quality of output and motivation. Obviously, this technique forces the manager to decide which employees within the work group are better than others. This is not the case with the graphic rating scale, where all employees can end up with a "very satisfactory" rating.

Paired comparison. The paired-comparison technique is an application of a specific type of ranking. The evaluator compares each person being evaluated with each other person being evaluated. For each pair of evaluations, the rater chooses the person who ranks better in the pair. The number of times each person is "preferred" is

Table 1. Performance evaluation techniques.

Technique	Ease of Use by Evaluators	Criterion of Use					
		Developmental Costs	Usage Costs	Useful in Promotions	Useful in Decisions	Useful in Personnel Development
Graphic rating scale	Easy	Moderate	Low	Yes	Yes	Moderately
Ranking	Easy	Low	Low	Yes	Not easily	No
Paired comparison	Easy	Low	Low	Yes	Not easily	No
Weighted checklist	Easy	Low	Low	Yes	Yes	No
Critical incident	Easy	High	Moderate	Yes	Moderately	Yes
Forced choice	Moderately difficult	High	Low	Moderately	Moderately	Yes
Forced distribution	Difficult	High	Moderate	Not easily	Not easily	Moderately

Source: Adapted from William Glueck, *Personnel: A Diagnostic Approach,* Business Publications, Inc., 1974, p. 302.

calculated, and a ranking is made on the basis of this preference frequency.

Weighted checklist. This method involves a great deal of technical work to prepare the rating scales. First, personnel specialists and experienced managers develop a series of descriptions associated with different kinds of behaviors. Weights are given to each statement in rank order, and evaluators mark the extent to which each statement describes the person being evaluated. The employee is rated on the basis of the average weight of the evaluators' choices.

Critical incident. The critical incident technique uses a series of categories to rate the subordinate. These categories may involve specific management functions—planning, communicating, developing subordinates, and so on—or other aspects of the job. The evaluator keeps a log of behaviors, noting for each employee "critical incidents" in each category. The log of the critical incidents for a particular performance appraisal period then serves as the basis for an evaluative description of each employee's performance in each category.

Forced choice. The forced-choice method is also quite complicated. It involves a series of groups of statements (two positive and two negative), developed by personnel specialists. One statement in each group is a discriminator: It statistically differentiates ineffective performance in the organization. The manager doing the evaluation is asked to choose the positive statement that describes the employee *best*, and the negative statement that describes the employee *least* accurately.

Forced distribution. This technique "forces" the manager to group his evaluations around some fixed distribution—for example, 20 percent above average, 60 percent average, and 20 percent below average. A larger distribution (10 percent outstanding, 20 percent above average, 40 percent average, 20 percent below average, and 10 percent very unsatisfactory) across several criteria (motivation, work output, promotability) can generate a variety of performance appraisals.

Essay evaluation. This approach is much more flexible (and much more susceptible to bias) than the others. The manager is asked to write an essay concerning the strong and weak points of each employee. The difficulty, from a performance appraisal standpoint, is that the technique usually results in essays that are hard to compare, and thus evaluations for compensation or promotion purposes are hindered.

RATER BIASES

The problem inherent in most subjective appraisal systems is rater bias, and all of the rating systems described above carry some degree of subjectivity. Management literature contains many discussions of the types of rater biases. Perhaps the most common tendency leading to bias is the so-called "halo effect," in which the tendency is to rate the individual based on a general impression of one specific trait. A person's performance may be rated highly, for example, because the supervisor perceives the individual as dynamic and aggressive as a result of his hyperactivity around the office. This hyperactivity is sometimes referred to as the "faster than a speeding bullet" syndrome. The halo created by this superhuman activity may disguise the fact that the person is really an ineffective worker.

"Severity" and "leniency" tendencies also lead to bias. In these cases, the manager's performance criteria are so high or so low that he fails to discriminate among workers. All workers are judged as "below average" or "above average," and all of the ratings fall at one end of the rating continuum. Ratings made as a result of these biases provide little basis for realistically compensating employees and are of no help in deciding which employees are most qualified for advancement.

THEORIES OF INTERPERSONAL ATTRACTION

In addition to the familiar biases mentioned above, findings in interpersonal attraction research suggest that several other factors may contribute to a manager's bias in giving subjective ratings.

Similarity of Attitudes and Values

In his article "The Psychological Studies of Values," F. W. Dukes suggested that the grades students receive are significantly related to the similarity of values between student and instructor. On the basis of these findings, Dukes said, one might suspect that vocational success is significantly related to the congruence of values among employees and employers or managers-owners. This implies that in addition to the familiar biases previously mentioned, we may be able to identify certain psychological variables that affect the individual's performance ratings. Since interpersonal attraction or the "liking" of another person would imply a favorable disposition on the part of the rater, the variables that influence interpersonal attraction may contribute to our understanding of biases in the rating process.

Figure 18-1 illustrates some aspects of the theory. According to Dukes, we seek to keep our mental make-up in balance or in a condition of equilibrium. In the figure, P represents some person (say, ourselves), O represents another person, and X represents some object about which we both share some attitudes and beliefs. A plus $(+)$ indicates a favorable attitude, and a minus $(-)$ a negative one. In situation a, person P has some positive attitude toward the object. P perceives that the other person (O) also has a favorable attitude toward the object. Because P perceives that O thinks similarly, he should also have a favorable attitude or an attraction toward O.

If we perceive that O has an opposite feeling about some important object, then to maintain a "balanced" mental image of ourselves, the theory suggests that we would not have an attraction toward O. Situations b and c represent possible examples of this case. Situation d represents another case in which both P and O have similar attitudes toward X (in this case, both hold negative feelings toward X). Again, P and O should be attracted to each other if they perceive that they have similar feelings toward the object. (We tend to be attracted to people who reinforce our feelings or attitudes.)

If we view the supervisor as P and the subordinate as O, then in situations a and d the supervisor would have a tendency to like or be attracted to the subordinate. Conversely, in situations b and c where the supervisor and subordinate have different values or attitudes, the tendency would be for them not to be particularly attracted to each other. If we accept Dukes' contention that the schoolroom situation (another type of performance or appraisal) also applies to the work situation, then we have another potential bias in performance ap-praisal—the attitude similarities between superior and subordinate.

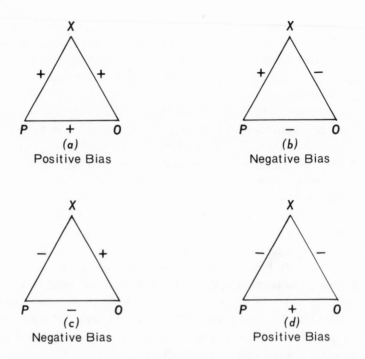

Figure 18–1. Possible attraction relationships and their effect on perform-ance appraisal.

Propinquity

Research has shown that physical nearness increases the probability that persons will be attracted to each other. In their classic study of housing projects in 1950, Festinger, Schacter, and Back showed that location was a primary determinant of friendship choice. T. H. Newcomb's study of college men in *The Acquaintance Process* gave further support to the hypothesis that proximity promotes attraction, but he also added a caveat.

Newcomb wrote: "We assume that proximity promotes readiness of communication, as a result of which individuals have an opportunity to discover each other's common attitudes. Such discovery may—or may not—lead to reciprocated high attraction, in the long run, depending upon what common attitudes of importance are to be discovered."

Other persons have noted that physical proximity allows the

participants, in addition to gaining increased information about each other, to experience rewards and punishments meted out by their role partners. What does this suggest? That supervisors who work closely with subordinates may make bias evaluations (either positively or negatively) as a result of physical nearness.

Need Complimentarity

The voluminous research on marital-partner selection has provided much data supporting the idea that we are attracted to those who can fulfill our needs and whose needs we in turn can satisfy. An argument can be made for the existence of the need-complementary-attraction relationship in industry. It can be argued, for example, that the formation of labor unions takes place because of perceived complementarity on the part of the union and the worker. Similarly, a supervisor may not be inclined to give a subordinate a lower performance rating if that subordinate has a skill needed by the supervisor (regardless of how that skill contributes to the "formal" accomplishments of the employee).

Pleasant or Agreeable Characteristics

Generally speaking, research supports the idea that we are more attracted to pleasant than to unpleasant persons. Our "balanced" world is not disturbed when we interact with people who are agreeable. In the job situation, for example, it is obvious that a person who is gregarious will be attractive to many workers, and this individual has a good chance of developing friendly relationships and little chance of developing unfriendly ones. Gregariousness, then, may increase the attraction between a manager and subordinate and may also bias performance evaluation.

Being Liked

A supervisor may be hesitant about giving a poor evaluation to an employee from whom he or she receives respect and admiration. The positive relationship between liking by others and attraction has just been explained in several ways. Liking is probably a reward when considered just by itself but it often isn't. Perhaps the best operational analogy can be derived from the concept of ingratiation—the act of giving esteem to another with the view in mind of obtaining rewards and/or benefits from the recipient.

The factors that affect interpersonal liking should cause the manager to evaluate carefully the performance appraisal process currently in use in his or her organization. In cases where very subjective measures of performance are necessary, the manager should be aware of the particular sources of bias that affect the process. All of us are susceptible to biases like the halo effect, and all of us have certain tendencies toward leniency and/or severity. As we develop an understanding of the factors that influence our performance evaluations, we also develop increased knowledge about the appraisal process—and this should be of considerable help to us in evaluating subordinates.

19

Motivating the New Breed

Lauren Hite Jackson
Mark G. Mindell

In today's organization, it is no longer enough for an employee simply to perform in a dependable manner—changes in organizational technologies increasingly require a highly motivated employee who can display creative and innovative behaviors based on technical learning. It must be remembered that modern technology is no longer synonymous with automation. On the contrary, instead of creating mass production techniques that lead to a loss of jobs, current technologies demand increased numbers of employees with increasingly specialized and complex knowledge. The problem posed is to motivate such employees in new ways so that they will perform effectively in jobs that cannot be easily supervised. The "carrot-and-stick" approach is inadequate, even irrelevant.

Environmental changes have added to the need for new approaches in motivating employees. The increased unionization of white-collar workers, the rise in foreign and domestic competition, the

From *Personnel*, March–April 1980.

increased number and jurisdiction of government agencies, and the power of citizens' lobbies all accent the need to utilize employee resources effectively and efficiently.

The most important changes affecting motivation, however, are those in the values of the workforce. Whereas pay was traditionally a basic motivator, for instance, other values such as self-worth, leisure time, and more communication from management have recently become primary concerns among employees. But why should something as intangible as values have an appreciable impact on job performance?

Behavioral scientists have pointed out that employee job satisfaction is determined by the way an employee perceives the job situation in relation to his own values—that satisfaction increases with the similarity between various aspects of their jobs and their job-related values. Not only is this relationship between job satisfaction and work-related values important in determining employee motivation—at a more basic level it becomes critical because it directly impacts productivity and profitability. Obviously, identification of critical work-related employee values could help organizations in their efforts to increase productivity.

TRADITIONAL AND CONTEMPORARY VALUES

What values appear to be most important to employees? No more than ten years ago, the workforce generally held the following values about the organization:

⋄ Strong loyalty to the company.
⋄ Strong desire for money and status.
⋄ Strong desire for promotions up the management hierarchy.
⋄ Critical concerns about job security and stability.
⋄ Strong employee identification with work roles rather than personal roles.

Many of these values were shaped by environmental factors. Years ago, employees learned their skills at the company's expense and planned their careers around that company. The training and promotions offered by the company forged strong employee ties to the organization. This relationship, however, is changing.

A majority of employees today acquire their skills and specialized knowledge independently of the company and consequently are not as loyal. Furthermore, it is no longer the norm for an employee to enter the company and work his or her way up. On the contrary, employees increasingly are entering organizations at higher levels than those of employees who have worked in the company for long periods of time.

Values characterizing this contemporary employee may be described as follows:

◇ Low loyalty or commitment to the organization.
◇ A need for rewards geared to accomplishments.
◇ A need for organizational recognition of his or her contributions.
◇ Decreasing concern for job security and stability.
◇ A view of leisure as being more important than work.
◇ A need to perform work that is challenging and worthwhile.
◇ A need to participate in decisions that ultimately affect him.
◇ Stronger employee identification with his personal role than with his work role.
◇ A need for communication from management regarding what's going on in the company.
◇ A need to rise above the routine and approach tasks creatively.
◇ A need for personal growth opportunities on the job.

This new breed of employee wants recognition for accomplishments and the freedom to find new and better ways of approaching problems. Such employees do not depend on their jobs for feelings of self-esteem, but they do desire to be recognized as persons. That is, they prefer to think of themselves as individuals and not as members of a highly structured organizational hierarchy.

IDENTIFICATION OF EMPLOYEE VALUES

There are substantial differences between traditional values and contemporary values, but the values of individual employees are rarely at either extreme. Managers who want to be more effective in devising

Figure 19-1. Excerpts from the Employee Value Inventory.

---

1. "How important is it for you to have a management that recognizes the importance of both work and family?"

   Extremely unimportant 1 2 3 4 5 6 7 *Extremely important*

2. "How important is it for you to get credit for your ideas when they are used?"

   Extremely unimportant 1 2 3 4 5 6 7 *Extremely important*

3. "It is important to me to feel proud of the company I work for."

   Strongly disagree 1 2 3 4 5 6 7 *Strongly agree*

4. "How important is it for you to have frequent communication from your supervisor about work goals?"

   Extremely unimportant 1 2 3 4 5 6 7 *Extremely important*

5. "I would rather solve problems myself than have my supervisor provide the solutions for me."

   Strongly disagree 1 2 3 4 5 6 7 *Strongly agree*

---

and using motivational techniques need a way of accurately identifying the degree to which particular values come into play between an employee and his manager. The next step would be to develop profiles of group values as a way of working toward a successful complement between employees and managers. Upon the achievement of such a match, the organization could expect significant increases in bottom-line results.

METHODS FOR IDENTIFYING VALUES

A way of assessing employee values has been developed: the Employee Value Inventory. This instrument measures nine critical factors that differentiate between traditional values and contemporary values. The 81 survey items ask the employee to indicate the importance of various job-related characteristics. Sample items from the Employee Value Inventory are shown in Figure 19-1.

As employees complete this Inventory, a personal profile emerges that characterizes the employee on the traditional/contemporary continuum for each of the nine values. Figures 19-2 and 19-3 illustrate profiles that characterize "typical" traditional and contemporary em-

Figure 19-2. Value profile of a "contemporary" employee.

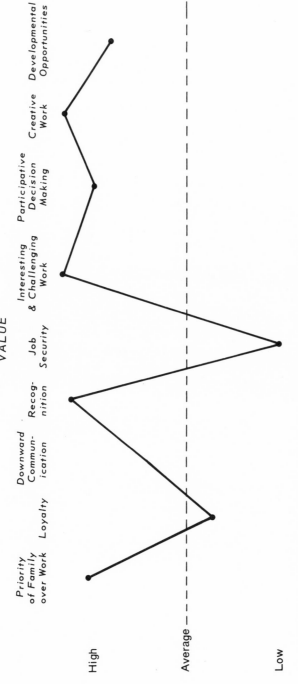

This employee places a much higher priority on his family role than on his work role, has high recognition needs, desires job duties that are varied and nonrepetitive, and likes to identify job related problems and develop solutions to those problems independently. This individual does not value job security or place a high priority on company loyalty.

Figure 19–3. Value profile of a "traditional" employee.

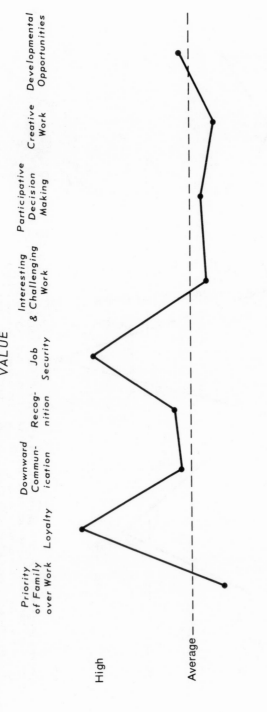

This employee places a much higher priority on his work role than on his family role and has high needs for job security. Further, this employee is extremely loyal to his or her organization. Of less importance are identifying problems and developing solutions to work-related problems himself, having different kinds of things to do on his job, and taking part in decisions affecting him or his work.

ployees. Examination of an employee's personal value profile might reveal, for example, an employee who has both a strong sense of loyalty toward the organization (a traditional value) and high contemporary values of personal recognition and a desire to do creative work. Results, in other words, could help managers develop motivation strategies that best meet the productivity goals of the organization and the needs and values of employees.

Employee value profiles are most meaningful, however, when they are used to work toward an optimal match between employees and managers—an effort that requires a poll of managerial values as well. A device developed for this purpose—the Management Style Inventory—measures five critical values that managers need for successful motivation of subordinates with differing values. These critical values are labeled locus of control, self-esteem, tolerance of ambiguity, social judgment, and risk taking. Let's look at each of these:

◊ *Locus of control*. A manager with high locus of control feels that there is a strong relationship between his managerial efforts and the organization's success. This manager also believes that advancement depends on achievement and that he or she has a great deal of control over subordinates' behavior.

◊ *Self-esteem*. A high score here indicates that the manager considers his or her ideas to be creative, understood, and accepted. Such a manager would place high priority on employee feedback.

◊ *Tolerance of ambiguity*. This refers to the degree to which managers are capable of functioning in unstructured, ambiguous situations.

◊ *Social judgment*. A high score on this scale characterizes a manager as one with social perceptiveness, sensitivity, and a belief in the importance of good interpersonal relationships.

◊ *Risk taking*. Those who score high on this scale tend to seek excitement and change rather than cautiously stick with the status quo.

Figure 19-4 shows some sample items in the Mangement Style Inventory. No manger, of course, holds exclusively contemporary values or exclusively traditional values, but each has a value orientation that strongly influences his or her managerial behavior. Although both

Figure 19-4. Excerpts from the Management Style Inventory.

---

1. Organizational success is usually due more to chance than systematic planning.
   Strongly disagree 1 2 3 4 5 6 7 *Strongly agree*

2. My ideas are rarely well understood by others in the company.
   Strongly disagree 1 2 3 4 5 6 7 *Strongly agree*

3. There is no such thing as "one right way" of doing things.
   Strongly disagree 1 2 3 4 5 6 7 *Strongly agree*

4. I often worry about what my job will be in five years.
   Strongly disagree 1 2 3 4 5 6 7 *Strongly agree*

5. Most people work in an organization because they have to, not because they want to.
   Strongly disagree 1 2 3 4 5 6 7 *Strongly agree*

---

traditional and contemporary managers should regard high locus of control and self-esteem as desirable, they would differ significantly in their view of the importance of tolerance of ambiguity, social judgment, and risk taking. The Management Style Inventory produces a personal profile for each manager, characterizing his or her style on the traditional/contemporary continuum. Typical profiles of traditional and contemporry managers are illustratred in Figure 19-5.

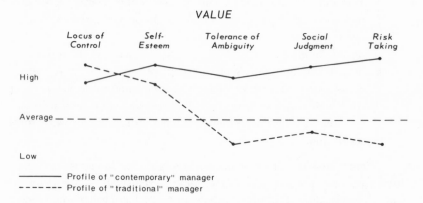

Figure 19–5. Profiles of "contemporary" and "traditional" managers.

USES OF VALUE INVENTORIES

Used together, the Employee Value Inventory and Management Style Inventory can serve a number of useful purposes. First, they can be used in making personnel decisions. When recruiting or making interdepartmental changes, an examination of the candidate's values can help determine the suitability of an individual employee for a given position.

Consider, for example, a case in which two candidates are being considered for a managerial position that makes the incumbent responsible for the operations of a large department. From the Employee Value Inventory shown in Figure 19-6, it is evident that the group with whom the prospective manager will be dealing is contemporary, with high needs for participative decision making and recognition. Further, this group prefers to work in rather unstructured situations in which more than one way of approaching a task is acceptable. These employees also desire a great deal of communication from management regarding what's going on in the department and the company, and they prefer a variety of tasks in their job duties.

An examination of Management Style Inventory profiles (see Figure 19-7) shows that both candidates for the manager's job score high on the locus of control scale—so they both feel that they can control events through their decisions. They also feel that they have a great deal of influence over the behavior of their subordinates. Similarly, both candidates score high on the self-esteem scale—so both have the capacity to recognize employee accomplishments by providing employee feedback. Managers who are able to exercise self-control, who feel that their ideas are creative and understood, and who deem employee feedback important tend to score high on this scale.

Candidate 1, however, scored much higher on the tolerance of ambiguity scale, so is more likely to function well in unstructured situations than Candidate 2 is. He also believes that there is more than one right way of doing things and likes to experiment with a variety of ideas.

The candidates' scores also differ on the social judgment scale. Because contemporary employees value good interpersonal relationships and personal recognition based on accomplishment, it is important for them to work for a manager who displays high concern for

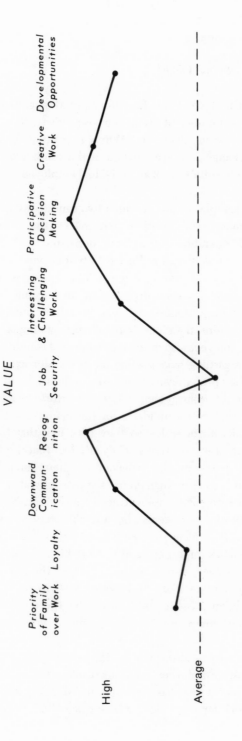

Figure 19–6. Employee group profile.

VALUE

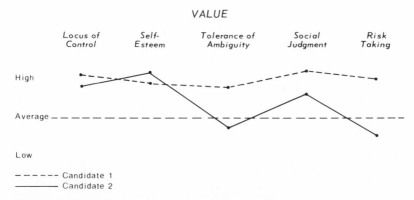

Figure 19–7. Value profiles of managerial candidates.

these values. The more contemporary manager (Candidate 1) exhibits a greater sensitivity and social perceptiveness than does a traditional manager and seeks to create a working environment in which people work because they want to; he is also more apt to use positive rewards to motivate people and allow worker feelings to contribute to task accomplishment.

Candidate 1 also scored higher on the risk-taking scale, so he is more likely to take risks in making decisions instead of being highly conservative and cautious. This high score complements the group's high score on the creative work scale. In this instance, Candidate 1 would obviously be the better candidate to manage this department of employees.

Identifying the values of both employees and managers is useful in other areas, too. In training and development, for example, it is important to acquaint high-potential employees and prospective managers with the variety of values held by employees and the impact that these values have on the use of incentives and successful management. Identification of a prospective manager's values can make him aware of his own management style and motivate him to learn how to use alternative management styles if he is to work with employees who have values different from his own.

20

Getting Ready for the Appraisal Interview

Dan H. Nix

One of your subordinates is due for a performance appraisal. Are you ready for the meeting? You may have all the documentation you'll need and you may have prepared all the forms you're required to use, but have you prepared yourself?

Giving performance appraisals is probably one of the least palatable aspects of a supervisor's job. Organizations provide their supervisors with evaluation instruments, forms, or guides to aid them, but most supervisors are still uncomfortable about this awkward and often ineffectual process.

When questioned about the difficulties encountered in the evaluation process, supervisors find it hard to explain why they feel uneasy about the appraisal. One problem may be that a great many of them have had little, if any, training in conducting an evaluation interview. And even those who have been exposed to appraisal dos and

From *Supervisory Management*, July 1980.

don'ts still feel uncomfortable about taking on the responsibility of judging another person—and what's worse, *discussing* their judgment with that individual. They worry about the effect that interview may have on future relations with the subordinate. This seems particularly to be a problem where the supervisor was promoted from within his or her work group and now is in the position of having to evaluate former peers.

FEELINGS

How does one go about conducting an appraisal interview or, perhaps more importantly, how does one *prepare* to conduct such a meeting?

Much has been written about the need for communication, the clear articulation of work goals and department objectives, and a positive climate during the interview. Equally important to the interview's success, however, is the supervisor's awareness of his or her own feelings about the session. After all, the evaluation process requires a two-way dialogue. The supervisor must be aware of how his or her feelings will affect the outcome of the interview. Those feelings stem from two concerns of the supervisor, namely, the past performance of the individual and the perceived impact—positive, neutral, or negative—that the interview might have on the supervisor/subordinate relationship. It is a rare individual who can evaluate and/or criticize another and not wonder what effect there will be on their future relationship.

In order to help supervisors put their feelings in the proper perspective, we have developed "Pre-interview gut-level scales." These scales can provide a supervisor with an understanding of his or her fears about the upcoming interview. Even more important, though, they are a planning tool that the supervisor can use to prepare for the session.

The scales are tied to a series of questions, shown in Figure 20-1, that the interviewer must answer in his or her own mind prior to the actual interview. It is best to answer the questions about each subordinate before tackling your organization's standard appraisal form.

The first step is for the supervisor to answer each of the first four

---

Pre-Interview

First ask yourself questions one through four, then mark the scales in questions five and six.
1. How do I *really* feel about evaluating this person? (Gut-level reaction only!)
2. Why do I feel this way (either good or bad)?
3. What is the worst possible outcome of this evaluation interview? (Let your deepest fears decide this.)
4. What is the best possible outcome of this evaluation interview? (Be positive here.)
5. Indicate on the scale the likelihood of the occurrence of either number three or number four, whichever you feel is most likely.

Worst   Best
Possible   No Change   Possible

6. Indicate on the scale the overall performance rating you think you will assign this person.

Unsatisfactory   Average   Outstanding

Figure 20–1. Pre-interview questions for interviewers.

questions with the soon-to-be-appraised subordinate in mind. The questions must be answered, not necessarily in writing, but honestly, candidly, and with some serious thought. (Remember, the perform-ance review is serious business; another person's career can depend on it.) The supervisor then complies with items 5 and 6 by approximating responses on the continua. The scales labeled A, B, C, and D in Figure 20–2 are next marked. The numbers are then transferred to the score profile shown in Figure 20–3. To develop the profile, straight lines are drawn connecting each score. The final step is the determination from

A. Past Relationship Scale

B. Past Performance Scale

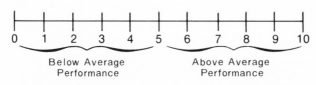

C. Future Relationship Scale

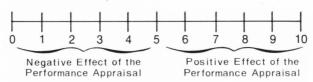

D. Anticipated Future Performance Scale

Figure 20–2. Performance/relations scales.

the profile of the position the employee would occupy on the planning matrix (Figure 20–4).

PLANNING MATRIX

The matrix contains nine boxes, each one signifying a different performance/relationship level. Identifying from the profile the position the employee will occupy on the planning matrix can help the supervisor plan the actual interview and enable him or her to determine developmental needs, the future focus and objectives of the supervisor/subordinate relationship, and the impact that the appraisal will have on performance.

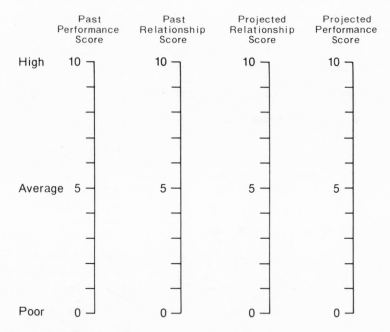

Figure 20–3. Score profile.

Let's look at each of the boxes in the matrix to see how a supervisor should respond during the performance appraisal interview in each instance.

◊ *Position #1*. Low future relationship, low future performance. Of all the positions, this is obviously the least desirable. In this

Planning Matrix			
	Projected Future Performance		
	Low	Average	High
Low	1	2	3
Projected **Future Relationship** Average	4	5	6
High	7	8	9

Figure 20–4. Planning matrix.

instance, the supervisor should plan on conveying concern about performance. The subordinate's shortcomings, dysfunctional behavior, lack of knowledge, and so forth need to be dealt with in an open, candid interview. Needless to say, this position requires the most careful planning and preparation on the part of the supervisor.

◇ *Position #2*. Low future relationship, average future performance. In this situation, the supervisor should stress specifics about how performance can be improved and examine the reasons behind the negative relationship. Here, the supervisor must be concerned with his or her own relating skills and should take the lead in attempting to improve the relationship.

◇ *Position #3*. Low future relationship, high future performance. The concern here obviously should be with the supervisor/subordinate relationship. Performance may be high now, but a poor relationship can change that. The first steps in improving the relationship may need to be taken by the supervisor, and the appraisal interview is a good time to begin.

◇ *Position #4*. Average future relationship, low future performance. In this case, the supervisor's goal is to improve performance while maintaining or improving the relationship. This might be approached best from the performance side, discussing specifics about performance weaknesses accompanied by positives about the relationship.

◇ *Position #5*. Average future relationship, average future performance. This employee has the potential for going either way and must be encouraged in a positive manner so as to enhance both performance and relationship.

◇ *Position #6*. Average future relationship, high future performance. The employee shows much promise. In fact, he or she might have the potential to be a supervisor one day. In this instance, the manager needs to emphasize performance while attempting to nurture the relationship. Again, this nurturing is the responsibility of the supervisor.

◇ *Position #7*. High future relationship, low future performance. The supervisor has a good relationship with the subordinate, yet the subordinate demonstrates a low level of productivity. The supervisor and employee need to re-examine their roles, responsibilities, and relationship. The supervisor must take the lead in such a situation.

◇ *Position #8*. High future relationship, average future performance. This employee relates positively with the supervisor and does adequate work. The potential for improvement is a plus factor, and the supervisor should attempt to build on that while maintaining the high relationship.

◇ *Position #9*. High future relationship, high future performance. This is the ideal position. It is possible that this subordinate is a key employee, and he or she should be given appropriate recognition. This type of employee can contribute significantly to the achievement of the organization's objectives as well as to overall group cohesiveness.

PREPARATION MAKES THE DIFFERENCE

The performance appraisal is indeed an often poorly executed supervisory responsibility. Recognizing the fact that preparation, planning, and thought are vital to the process is the first step to meaningful, productive evaluations. By following the steps outlined here, a supervisor can better prepare himself or herself to constructively discuss performance with the subordinate and improve their relationship. One interesting side benefit to the supervisor of the process is the opportunity to analyze objectively the information gathered to determine patterns in performance or relationships within the department. The supervisor may gain as much insight from this process about his or her management style as may be learned about how to conduct a performance appraisal. At the very least, the supervisor will approach the session more secure. Coupling the "getting-ready" system with the organization's appraisal system, the supervisor should find that he or she is better prepared and more comfortable about the task to be faced.

Part Four

MANAGING YOUR JOB

21

How to Manage Your Boss

Peter F. Drucker

If there's one problem most of us talk about, grumble about, but do nothing about, it's the boss. Every manager I know find's managing the boss the most difficult task he has. Very few even try.

How you handle the problem of your boss can be quite revealing. For example, it is one of the few indicators we can rely on to tell which of the younger people in an organization are going to go places and which are going nowhere. Those who only talk about how incompetent and impossible the boss is and complain about how much they suffer are not going anyplace. On the other hand, you can spot the comers because they do something about managing the boss—and I don't necessarily mean buttering him up or polishing the apple. It's really quite simple. What you do almost depends on the boss himself.

The first thing to recognize is that the boss is neither a monster nor an angel; he's a human being who insists on behaving like one. Bosses, therefore, have to be treated like human beings, like

From *Management Review*, May 1977.

individuals. So for some bosses, then, you do polish the apple; for others, that's the worst thing you can do.

The second thing to know is that no matter how able and competent the boss is, he is not a mind reader. You have to make sure he understands what you're trying to do.

The third thing to remember is that although he does not give you enough of his time, he gives more, as a rule, than he should—more than he has to give. So it's up to you to manage that time and to ensure that it's productive time.

Finally, remember that it's more dangerous to underrate the boss than to overrate him. The most serious mistake you can make is to underrate the boss and be caught doing it.

WHAT MAKES THE BOSS TICK

I'm always amazed that almost nobody ever seems to recognize that bosses, like most people, can be divided into "readers" and "listeners," the same way people can be divided into right-handers and left-handers. So the first thing you do is figure out whether your boss is one or·the other.

If you have a reader for a boss—like an Eisenhower or a Kennedy—don't just go into his office and talk to him about a problem or a project. Write it up first, make sure you have something for him to read; then you can start to talk.

If you have a listener—someone like Franklin Roosevelt or Harry Truman—don't send in a memorandum. Go in and talk about it first; then you can leave the memo.

If your boss likes a little reassurance, a little flattery, or if he wants facts and figures or a page of recommendations, then that's what he should get. Give him 150 pages out of a statistical abstract. Accept the fact that he's a human being, that he's set in his ways and unlikely to be changed by you, and that it's up to you to get him to respond to your need. Those who want to manage the boss should first find out who it is they want to manage. In the final analysis, however, one doesn't really manage a boss; you work with a human being. And if you learn to do this, your batting average is going to be a great deal better than if you don't.

WORD MAGIC

Now this may strike you as trivial, but be sure to learn about word magic. That is, know which are good words and which are bad words when talking with your boss. One of the ablest men I ever worked with—an engineer who was also an autocrat and a pedant—couldn't stand the word "control." Instead of control, we had to learn to say "measurement." The rule was never say "control." If you did say it, his mind snapped shut, and for the next six weeks, he delivered sermons on why "control" was a bad, bad word.

In any case, it's your job to work with the boss—he's your resource. Resources have to be worked the way they are, not the way you want them to be. Now that may sound manipulative, but it's manipulation in the sense of adapting yourself to the way an individual is put together.

NO SURPRISES

Many people assume their bosses are mind readers. That's only natural—children assume it about their parents, parents about their children, teachers about their students, and students about their teachers. Apparently, a very difficult thing to accept is the first insight of modern psychology, which started around 1880 with the startling discovery that *what is obvious to me, nobody else can see at all*. Very few people accept this, particularly in dealing with the boss. But you'd better keep it in mind.

It's your job to make sure the boss knows what you are trying to do, what you need, what you expect from him. If you just blithely go ahead, assuming that what you're doing is so obvious that any fool can see it, why then does everybody wonder just what is it you are doing?

Think through what you're trying to do, including those things you'd rather the boss didn't know about. Then make certain that the fellow on whom you depend so heavily—the fellow in that office next door, the boss—understands. Maybe not necessarily approves, but understands so that he isn't surprised. There's really no such thing as a pleasant surprise.

Don't baffle the boss. Go to him, or write a memo, saying: "This is what I am going to do." Or, "This is what I'm not going to do." Let him know that you are aware, say, of that problem with the branch office in England, but that you're not going to tackle it now because you think that if you leave it alone, they'll work it out. Of course, you say, you'll keep checking it, and if London doesn't solve the problem in six months, then you'll come down on them like a ton of bricks.

The idea is not to let him wonder why *you* don't seem aware of the mess in the London office. Let him know you have made a decision—that you are giving London another six months to straighten out, and if they don't, you'll have to tackle it.

That's a decision. But don't make the mistake of thinking it's obvious. It isn't. Mind readers exist only in science fiction novels. You won't find them in executive offices.

NEVER HIDE AN ELEPHANT

In many instances, then, you don't have to tell the boss what you're going to do; you tell him what your objectives are and how you're proposing to achieve those objectives. But how you handle it really depends on the boss. With some bosses, you tell them exactly what you're going to do—others you ask for their advice. It depends on how the boss works, not on what you like.

One thing you never do is hide problems. Never try to brush an elephant under the rug. Hiding problems is unfair to the boss. It's also very unfair to you.

I wish every young man or woman could have the same good fortune I had in my early twenties when a wise old man, a senior partner in the firm I worked for, called me in and said:

"Mr. Drucker, you've been an awful fool again. You've been hiding a problem. You've done it twice, and if you do it a third time, I'll make damn sure that you go to work for the competition."

I never did it again. But I needed to be spanked hard. I was a conceited pup and needed rough treatment—and I got it. It was a lesson most young people still need to learn. Their instinctive reaction to a problem is to hide it because, they think, maybe it will go away. Well, maybe it will, maybe it won't, and if it won't, you're in trouble.

Better to handle the situation by thinking through how to warn the boss of an impending problem. Anyone working for me had better come in and tell me what he plans to do about a problem. On the other hand, anyone working for a certain friend of mine had better go in to him and say something like this: "There's a cloud on the horizon, but I think I know how to deal with it. If it gets any bigger, I'll let you know."

My friend doesn't want to know how you propose to do your job; he feels that's your business—and he may be right. But other bosses want to be part of the problem, so you say to them: "Look, I see this coming, and I thought I might impose on your time to get your advice." The boss in this kind of situation is a person who believes that a superior should be a coach, a problem-shooter.

So look at the individual. It isn't important whether you crow about successes or try to minimize mistakes. They are fairly unimportant. Again, what is terribly important is the rule: no surprises. It's your job to make sure that your boss is never going to be surprised. He has a boss, too, you know—someone who probably takes a dim view of being hit by a storm that's been brewing for six months without anyone telling him about it—until he learns of it from the outside.

Take a situation where an account, say an old customer, is having trouble, perhaps going delinquent. It may well be that you can repair the situation. But if you can't, and six months later you've had an acrimonious correspondence filling several file folders, it's *your* fault if the relationship is destroyed.

But if you see your boss promptly and tell him what's happening, he might be able to straighten things out then if you can't. And if necessary, he can mobilize his boss in time to help repair any damage. But if you wait six months, *you* have lost that account. Indeed, you have.

MANAGING THE BOSS'S TIME

Many things are kept from bosses because their subordinates know how busy they are and mistakenly hesitate to impose on them. You've got to balance conflicting demands; you shouldn't monopolize the boss's time. At the same time, however, you are entitled to his advice.

A wise, old German peasant proverb says, "Don't go near your prince unless he calls for you at least twice." There's something to be said for not being too much in the limelight. On the other hand, almost every manager complains that his boss doesn't have enough time for him and that his own subordinates take too much of his time. He's right on both counts.

The responsible and intelligent manager thinks through how to use the boss's time. Again, look at the boss as a human being, not as an abstraction. Remember that you're looking at a person—a man, a woman.

One boss may work by sitting down with a subordinate (though very rarely) for three full hours. In between sessions, he may not want to see anybody. Another boss may prefer ten-minute ad hoc meetings (which some people, by the way, consider a total waste of time). You have to adjust to the way a boss manages, or mismanages, his time. There's very little you can do about how he manages.

DO YOUR HOMEWORK

Never go into the manager's office unless you have done your homework. There's a sound old rule: It takes ten minutes of preparation for each minute of interview time.

There's no need to overdo this advance work, however. It's impossible to have every fact and figure. It's more important to know what you are going in for, to think through what you expect to come out with. Do you want a decision? Advice? Do you want to advise the boss that down the line you might come to him with this or that? Be sure he understands.

The military has some good advice for this kind of situation: The first rule of warfare is to control the battlefield. This means that *you* must set the stage by doing your homework. But at the same time take into account that the boss already is complaining that his subordinates take too much of his time. That's why you must make your occasion with him productive—for him and yourself.

Follow-up is important. Sit down afterward and tell the boss in writing, "This is what happened in our meeting this morning . . ." Remind him that he decided that Carter should be pulled off his present assignment and put on the redesign of the water cooler as soon as he returns from his trip, and that you'll let him know when Carter is being reassigned. This ensures that there will be no doubt later about what was decided.

Doing this gives him a chance—since people are not infallible—to remember prior commitments that may conflict with any promises he made to somebody else. For example, he may look at the memo and say, "Oh, my god, I forgot that only the day before yesterday, I promised the president that he can have Carter for that meeting in Washington." Or the big boss may call him and ask when Carter is coming back from that trip to the Near East—"I want to put him right to work on a study of that question we discussed at the last board meeting." Your memo keeps the boss from going too far out onto thin ice.

WHEN TO ABANDON SHIP

Rating the boss is a function of your own native intelligence, not of your relationship with him. It's just stupid to underrate the boss, yet very bright young people do it all the time.

You risk nothing, as a rule, by overrating a superior. And if it turns out that you haven't overrated him at all, then you have an ally, a supporter. The worst that can happen is that you've been too pushy.

But if you systematically lose because you overestimate the boss, get out. One of the first things to learn about managing anything is when to abandon it—even a boss. There's no better prescription for success than to have a boss who is going places, and there is no more certain prescription for frustration and failure than to work for an incompetent.

Another time to change jobs is when the boss is corrupt. He doesn't have to have his hand in the till—that's only one form of corruption. A more serious form of corruption is when the boss has values and standards that are ethically and morally unacceptable to you. Never work for a boss whose standards demean you—you become corrupt yourself, you become contemptuous of yourself, you begin to loathe yourself.

When it becomes obvious that you are working for an incompetent or corrupt boss, I think you have to say, "All right, I like the company, but this isn't going to work out." Abandon the job and look for something else—within the company or outside it.

You also have a problem if the boss is a paragon. It's possible to stay too long with a paragon or near-paragon for the good of your career. Staying makes it too easy to become just an "assistant to" rather than your own man.

There's still a great deal of fear—though less now than ten years ago—of becoming the organization man, someone whom the organization uses as a servant. There has never been enough emphasis on the opposite, however; that is, looking upon the organization as *your* tool.

Size up your job from two viewpoints: (1) What can I contribute to it? and (2) What can it contribute to me? Also ask yourself, "What has it done for me lately?" and "What is it likely to do for me in the future?"

If you are in a position where you have gotten as much out of the job, the boss, and the company as they will ever give you and if you are still below late middle age and have given all you are likely to give, then it's time to move on. Don't move out too often, however, and don't rush. Remember there is a time limit, and keep in mind that a person moves out because of success as much as failure.

ACCOUNTABILITY

In today's society, everybody has a boss. Even the company president and the chief executive officer are accountable to stockholders and to outside regulatory and other agencies just as a hospital administrator is accountable to the community and the president of the United States to the voters and to the Congress.

You don't have to like and admire your boss, nor do you have to hate him. You do have to manage him, however, so that he becomes your resource for achievement, accomplishment, and—let's be candid about it—personal success as well.

22

Speaking with Authority: How to Give Directions

Beverly A. Potter

Much of our waking life is perceived through the medium of words. Radio and television entertain with words; books transmit messages with words; teachers guide with words; interactions with family, friends, and colleagues are dominated by words—even our solitude is invaded by an endless stream of words. Perhaps it is only in dreams (and in the movies) that words assume a secondary place to images.

Yet despite the importance of words, it is likely that you seldom think about language and its impact on virtually every aspect of life. When things go wrong—when you are confused, worried, or depressed; when social or business affairs don't work out; when you see yourself making blunders in personal or work matters—you blame many things for these difficulties. Sometimes you may blame your physical health or nerves, other times you may blame the establishment or world events. If the problem involves an interaction with

From *Supervisory Management*, March 1980.

other people, you may blame their attitudes or lack of ability. Even when you suspect that there is a problem in communications, you will probably neglect to investigate your specific words as a possible source of the trouble.

It is hard to believe that thinking about language is so limited when its uses and effects are so extensive. But few understand the relationship between the specific words used and their effectiveness in supervising others. It is easy to believe that the basic message to be communicated is more important than the words themselves. It is assumed that once the idea is straight, the words will just fall into place. But the words you use are as important as the ideas they express. Your words influence the way subordinates feel about you as well as the way you feel about yourself.

DEVELOPING AN AUTHORITARIAN STYLE OF SPEECH

The language you use is one of the best indicators of your position in an organization. Not only can the use of a less prestigious form of speech cost you status and authority, it can limit your advancement as well.

That speech can be a social barrier is well illustrated in George Bernard Shaw's *Pygmalion*, the play on which the musical comedy *My Fair Lady* was based. The Cockney flower girl, Eliza, can be installed in a West London apartment, clothed fashionably, and taught socially sophisticated behaviors, but she will still be a Cockney as long as she speaks like one. Her social status will change only when her speech changes. Likewise, a person making a vertical move in the corporation is confronted with subtle but real speech barriers. This is particularly evident in the case of the person entering management for the first time: The new manager must drop deferential speech and adopt authoritative speech—the language of management—with subordinates. The more he or she does this, the more positively that person will be viewed. The individual will be seen as more competent and more in control of himself or herself and the situation and will be allotted greater respect and authority.

Generally, in the world of commerce, people who express their opinions strongly and forcefully are taken more seriously than those who state their views tentatively, for stronger means of expression suggest confidence in one's assertions. Consider these examples:

Gosh, John, you've lost two good people in the last month! And both left in a huff, didn't they? Maybe I'm an alarmist, but this could lead to serious morale problems, couldn't it? Perhaps I'm wrong, but it could be indicative of some kind of communication problem. Next week the company is sponsoring a seminar in communications. It may surprise you, but I've gone to a couple of these in-house seminars, and they gave me a lot of ideas. Won't you please attend this one?

Hell, John, you've lost two good people in the last month! And both of them left in a huff. This kind of thing could lead to serious morale problems. And it could be indicative of some kind of communication problem. Next week the company is sponsoring a seminar in communications. I've gone to a couple of these in-house seminars myself, and they gave me a lot of ideas. I want you to attend this one.

There is a marked difference in the feeling of confidence conveyed by the two managers in the example. The first, Manager A, sounds apologetic and almost embarrassed by the discussion, comes across as being uncertain, and makes attending the seminar sound optional. John could easily challenge manager A and refuse to attend the seminar, saying, "There's no communication problem here. Both of those guys were freeloaders, and the whole company knew they were. I told them to shape up or get out. They got out."

Manager A has placed himself (or herself) in a position where he might have to defend his opinion and eventually resort to threats and ultimatums. He has created a potential problem for himself with his own words. Manager B, on the other hand, sounds confident in his analysis of John's problem and there is no doubt as to what action is expected of John. The difference lies in small but important changes in speech patterns.

Linguist Robin Lakoff has identified several speech patterns that decrease a manager's credibility when giving directives: weak expletives, tag-questions, disqualifying prefaces, and directives stated as requests. Let's look at each of these.

WEAK EXPLETIVES

Consider the following statements:

Good grief, sales have dropped ten percent.
Hell, sales have dropped ten percent.

Dear me, I'll never find a replacement.
Christ, I'll never find a replacement.

Oh fudge, I've lost the quarterly report.
Damn, I've lost the quarterly report.

Although the specific information transmitted in each pair is identical, the implied importance varies dramatically with the expletive. The expletive is meaningful only insofar as it conveys that the speaker has an emotional reaction to the information contained in the remainder of the statement. The force of the speaker's feeling is implied by the strength of the expletive: "Hell" is more forceful than "good grief," for example. Of course, the speaker who says, "Good grief, sales have dropped ten percent," might in fact feel more strongly than the one who says, "Hell," but "good grief" is a weak expletive.

According to Lakoff, weaker expletives tend to trivialize the statement that follows. Because words influence the listener's perceptions, it is easy for the listener to conclude that the topic is trivial. Moreover, speakers who use weak expletives frequently find that their credibility drops. Because swear words are often used to express anger, it is not surprising that they make stronger expletives.

Some weak expletives: Oh fudge, dear me, golly, gosh, gosh darn, drat, goodness, gracious me.

Some strong expletives: Damn, hell, and some stronger expressions.

I don't want to suggest that you take up swearing to increase your credibility and authority, but if you catch yourself frequently using weak expletives, it would be wise to practice making such statements without any expletive at all. Or use one of the more acceptable strong expletives—such as "damn"—to express strong feeling.

TAG-QUESTIONS

An authority person projects an air of confidence, and conversely the person who conveys confidence is perceived as having more authority. That is, confident-sounding people are listened to more carefully, and what they say is more likely to be heeded. On the other hand, people who express their opinions in a tentative way project an air of uncertainty and are not listened to as carefully, nor are their statements taken as seriously.

Suppose a supervisor said to a typist: "This report has to be retyped, doesn't it?" The fact that the statement is phrased as a question suggests that the supervisor is unsure whether the report needs retyping. Or you might think the supervisor believes the report needs retyping but is asking for the typist's confirmation. In either case, asking for confirmation still implies uncertainty. Thus the supervisor has diluted his or her authority with the tag-question. On the other hand, had the supervisor said, "This report needs to be retyped," that would have conveyed confidence in the assertion.

There are times, of course, when a tag-question is useful and appropriate. If for example you want to initiate small talk on the elevator, you might say, "Elevator's slow, isn't it?" Here the tag-question conveys friendliness and elicits talking on a subject common to both people. At other times you might actively seek confirmation to check out your understanding of what the other person has said. A manager might confirm an assistant's opinion by saying, "You think this is a good idea, don't you?" Finally, asking for confirmation can be used as a way of getting a commitment for some action: "You'll complete the sales report before you leave today, won't you?" Here the request for confirmation actually reaffirms the manager's authority because the manager is confirming another person's promised actions.

But, in general, the tag-question is inappropriate in a supervisory situation when you as the manager are stating your opinion or making an assertion to your subordinate. In such a situation you lose credibility if you ask the subordinate to confirm your opinions. Fortunately, the tag-question is easy to eliminate from your speech. If you become aware that you are using tag-questions frequently, simply drop the tag and use instead a declarative statement.

DISQUALIFYING PREFACES

In a staff meeting I observed a novice manager pose a suggestion with the preface: "This may sound like a silly idea, but . . . ." Not unexpectedly, no one in the meeting looked at the speaker or made any response to the suggestion. Undaunted, the novice persisted with several other suggestions prefaced with disqualifiers such as, "Perhaps you have already tried this, but I think . . . ." Each suggestion was either rejected abruptly or simply ignored. The suggestions themselves, while not earth-shattering, were as reasonable as any of those presented by others, but the implicit message was, "Don't listen to my ideas—they aren't any good." The group heard and accepted the implicit message, and nobody listened.

Attaching a disqualifying preface to a statement not only instructs listeners to dismiss the statement in question as unimportant but influences their general impression of the speaker and of his or her future statements. The person who uses disqualifying prefaces sounds unsure and even incompetent; in fact, the speaker is explicitly stating his or her doubt about that particular statement.

Certainly, if you are going to go to the trouble of thinking of an idea and stating it, you want the idea to be considered. Disqualifying prefaces defeat your purpose. People generally believe what you say about yourself. If you tell people that what you are about to say is without value, then those listening will probably believe you and will not continue to listen. Once you have set this cycle into motion, it becomes difficult to get an audience, and your ideas fall on deaf ears.

Obviously, if you want what you say to be taken seriously, then it is wise to drop the disqualifiers. Some people use the preface as a way of gaining the listener's attention. Unfortunately, the disqualifier often has the opposite result.

If you feel you must preface your suggestions in order to get an attending audience or simply to build up momentum, then you should practice more assertive prefaces. For example, you can gain the attention of a listener with assertive prefaces such as: "I have a suggestion. Perhaps we could . . . ," or "I want to make a suggestion. If you. . . ," or "Have you considered . . . ?" Of course, the preface is not necessary; you can simply state your suggestion or directive.

In a group situation, if the others continue to speak, then begin again and speak louder.

DIRECTIVES STATED AS REQUESTS

A manager is responsible for seeing that specific company objectives are met, and those being supervised are by and large employed to perform tasks that ultimately result in achieving these objectives. In most cases the manager does not hand over to the subordinates the authority to decide who should perform these tasks, yet many managers feel uncomfortable giving directives—they feel it is impolite.

When you want someone to do something and at the same time wish to be polite, you could probably make a request or suggestion. Both requests and suggestions allow the addressee to decide whether to comply. The implication is that the action you are requesting is a favor. But this is appropriate only in a social situation or a work situation with a peer. Framing a subordinate's required tasks as a favor is inappropriate and can cause you problems.

Consider the following directives stated as requests:

1. Please retype this report.
2. Will you retype this report?
3. Will you please retype this report?
4. Won't you retype this report?
5. Won't you please retype this report?

Examples 2, 3, 4, and 5, can be translated into "Are you willing to retype this report?" If in fact the typist has an option (if another typist can do the typing, for example), then such a request would be appropriate. But if there is no option involved, the speaker is undercutting his or her authority by stating the directive as a request, and anybody who makes such requests too frequently will lose credibility in the eyes of subordinates by being put in the awkward position of repeatedly having to ask them to do tasks that are part of their required work. In extreme cases, the supervisor might even end up doing the work!

Although the use of "please" in example 1 also converts the directive to a request, it is an effective form to use when you want to soften the directive. But if you feel compelled to preface all directives by "please," then you are probably having trouble asserting your authority.

Of course, you do not want to be seen as an insensitive autocrat who does nothing but give orders; it is a matter of degree and timing. An occasional directive stated as a request can be effective in establishing rapport with a subordinate. In short, as a manager you ought to be able to give a directive comfortably and to rely on the request form only when you feel it is particularly politic to do so.

If you feel compelled to be polite at all times with subordinates, and if you hear yourself giving many of your directives as requests, practice the "please" formation in example 1 until you can do so comfortably. Then practice giving directives with no preface.

PUTTING IT ALL TOGETHER

In my workshops on authoritative directives, many students object to the idea of telling an employee directly to do something. They know that they must give directives, yet they want to be liked and not be seen as aggressive, pushy, or authoritarian. Some students make the point that few people like to be told what to do, even though they are in a system in which they are being paid to perform tasks under the direction of someone else. They say people like to "feel" that they have an option. Others point out that softening a directive with qualifiers or framing it as a request gives employees the feeling that they are being considered as people. Certainly these objectives are valid—it is important that managers be sensitive and considerate of employees. Nevertheless, the goal of business is to get the job done. Managers who set up a false dichotomy between treating employees humanely and getting work done have a problem on their hands.

Some managers go to the opposite extreme—giving directives with no consideration for the employees. Many employees have excellent ideas; in fact, they may have more expertise about their particular job than the supervisor does. It is a foolish manager who doesn't seek out such ideas or who overrides suggestions without consideration. Such a person can be seen as a despot. Certainly this is not conducive to cooperation, rapport, and productivity. And although at first glance such people may seem confident, upon closer observation they are often revealed to have an abrasive facade covering a lack of confidence. Such a person is not respected but feared. Managers who have genuine confidence reserve decisions until they have carefully evaluated the situation. Part of a careful evaluation includes eliciting the opinions and suggestions of the employees involved. The confident manager will give a directive only when there is a high probability that it is the most appropriate one. Nothing is more damaging than leaping into a situation without adequate information and giving orders that will have to be retracted later.

There is a way that managers can give directives while eliciting the opinions or suggestions of the employees involved. The acronym DAD stands for the three important steps in the process: Describe, Ask for clarification, and Direct. Describe the problem situation objectively to your subordinate, ask how that person feels about the situation and what suggestions he or she might have, then give the directive. The DAD components provide a guideline for giving a directive with authority.

You begin the directive process by describing to your subordinate the situation or the problem in question. Be objective and specific and, whenever possible, describe observable behaviors. Also, avoid judgmental and emotional statements such as, "Betty, that feasibility report was the dumbest thing you've ever done." A better way would be to say, "Betty, that feasibility study was vague and confusing in several places. It left me with a lot of questions." Then, too, avoid vague terms such as, "You have a bad attitude." Use simple, concrete terms: "You have made a number of negative remarks about the company."

Next, ask employees how they feel about the situation and find out what suggestions they might have. If an employee is new to your unit or if asking for clarification is new to you, then you'll need to work a little at this step. Employees at first may not believe that you are sincerely interested in their ideas and feelings and may dismiss the question as patronizing. Over time, however, they will come to understand that by asking for clarification, you are demonstrating your concern and interest in their ideas.

Once you have clarified an employee's position, you are ready to direct. You now know how the employee feels and what that person thinks ought to be done. Frequently, an employee's suggestions will be exactly the same as the directive you would have given had you not used the DAD method. Great! All you have to do, then, is to agree that this suggestion is the best course of action! At other times, the employee's feelings or suggestions will differ from what you have anticipated. Sometimes the suggestion will be one you hadn't considered; sometimes the suggestion will be one you must reject. Here, of course, you hold the final authority, but whatever directive you give, the employee will be much more likely to be cooperative in following it.

Remember to state the directive as a simple declarative sentence. Avoid the disqualifying prefaces, the weak expletives, the tag-questions, and the request formation. You'll get the best results if you use simple, concrete terms and avoid vague generalities: The clearer the directive, the less opportunity for confusion and error. Whenever there is any possibility of confusion, ask for clarification a second time to determine whether or not the directive was understood.

A CASE IN POINT

Let's look at an example of a poor directive.

> *Manager*: This grant application has got to be typed immediately. You've got to get on it right away.
>
> *Typist*: But I can't, I just can't. You're not the only person I work for, you know. Everyone around here thinks their stuff is so important. Well, I've had it—I just can't do it!
>
> *Manager*: Look, this grant means a quarter of a million bucks. Part of that money pays your salary! Get on this report now!

It's pretty easy to guess what will happen here. If the typist doesn't quit or get fired, the manager will probably find all kinds of typos, incorrect spellings, and deletions in the final copy. Furthermore, neither the typist nor the manager will forget the argument. By giving a directive too soon, this manager has created a problem.

Let's see how it would sound with the use of DAD principles.

> *Describe*: I'm really in a bind. This grant application must be postmarked by midnight tomorrow. It means a quarter of a million bucks to the company.
>
> *Ask for clarification*: What's your workload like today and tomorrow?
>
> *Typist*: Gee, I have several reports for Williams due and then that marketing prospective for you. Oh yes, transcripts for Montgomery. He said it's urgent.
>
> *Ask for clarification*: Do you think you can squeeze this grant in?
>
> *Typist*: I can delay on everything but Montgomery's transcripts. You know how he is!
>
> *Direct*: Look, I can handle Montgomery—don't worry about that. Just get on this grant right away. Can you do that?
>
> *Typist*: Well, as long as you talk to Montgomery, I think I can get it done. If not, I'll stay late tomorrow.

The typist was overloaded with work and probably not too receptive to an additional job. The DAD process, however, helped to obtain willing cooperation. The describe step enabled the typist to understand the manager's predicament and the importance of getting the grant application completed as soon as possible. The ask for clarification step conveyed the manager's concern and elicited the problem with Montgomery's transcripts. Thus, it was easy for the manager to give the directive. The typist was cooperative and even volunteered to work late to complete the grant.

As you can see, the DAD process can be a useful guideline for giving a directive. It enables you to convey to employees the problem situation, to elicit their reaction and suggestions, and to give a directive in such a way that it maximizes the possibility that the employees will follow the directive cooperatively.

23

Five Mistakes You Can't Afford to Make

O. A. Battista

Making mistakes is an inevitable part of life, inside and outside the office. The danger in making mistakes lies in not owning up to them or trying to learn from them. An error does not really become a mistake until you refuse to correct it!

Several mistakes commonly made by managers are easily avoidable if you are aware of them. Following are five mistakes that, if they go uncorrected, can topple any otherwise able manager.

1. *Stealing the credit.* One manager with a reputation for being able to get out of tight spots proved in the end to be too smart for his own good. He made the fatal mistake of ignoring this time-tested advice: The most important mistakes to correct are those you feel sure you can get away with.

This manager's troubles began when he made the mistake of claiming full credit for an invention he had overheard a subordinate

From *Supervisory Management*, January 1977.

describe. The subordinate, a man without formal training, was unaware of the value of his idea. The supervisor, however, was sure that the company could make hundreds of thousands of dollars by promoting the invention. He saw it as the chance of a lifetime, and he deliberately set out to sell management on "his" idea. He figured that once the profits came rolling in, he would be set for life.

Soon after he advanced his claim to the invention, the supervisor began to have qualms. But by this time the company had filed a patent application in the name of the plagiarist-inventor. The supervisor thought that he had gone too far to turn back, so he began piling one lie on top of another. He stole a model of the invention constructed by the true inventor long enough to copy it and he faked notebook entries in an effort to predate his records.

His stomach began churning at the mere thought of his precarious situation. His cigarette consumption soared, and he could barely face the true inventor long enough to say, "Hello."

Only after suffering a severe nervous breakdown was he able, with the guidance and counsel of the company psychiatrist, to admit his lie. He eventually recovered his health, but his reputation was shattered. The company had to engage in lengthy legal proceedings to invalidate the illegitimate patent application and file an amended application in the name of the true inventor.

No manager can get away with stealing credit over an extended period of time. The truth will certainly become known eventually—by way of a guilty conscience or otherwise.

2. *Slandering others*. Deliberate malice aside, it is all too easy in gossiping about the misfortunes or misdeeds of others to "stretch" a point here and there to make a more interesting story. Such mistakes have destroyed friendships, ruined marriages, and cost many a manager his job and future. Indeed, rumors started in this way have destroyed big corporations and driven famous people to suicide.

Deliberate slander can wreak havoc more quickly—and it can also backfire. Let's look at a case in point.

A bright young man—we'll call him Hal—was singled out for a big promotion. When he first joined the company, he worked for a department manager who felt threatened by Hal's aggressiveness, intense enthusiasm, and youthful drive. The department head himself was a genius in his technical field, but he was a dud when it came to supervising. He had used underhanded tactics to achieve his position, and he guarded his post tenaciously.

After working for this manager for about three months, Hal had pretty well sized up the situation. Seeing no other way to avoid a real clash with his supervisor, he asked for a transfer; the department manager, understandably, did everything he could to help Hal get it.

Hal's new boss was quite different. He saw that there was a good future in the company not only for Hal, but for both of them. When Hal got a promotion, his former supervisor began to get worried. He felt the "young upstart" was moving ahead too fast, so he started planting stories about him here and there: "Hal's too cocky," "Hal can't be trusted," "He's radical," "He has paranoid tendencies."

Hal began to feel the effects. He was puzzled by the cold way in which some associates were suddenly treating him—as though he had acquired a contagious disease. Before long, the only person sticking by him was his new boss, a man who refused to entertain the gossip that reached his ears. His boss knew from firsthand knowledge that these accusations about Hal were not true.

Fortunately, Hal enjoyed his work so much that he was able to ignore the momentum building up against him. He didn't know it, but he was turned down for one good opening at a higher level simply because of the reservation voiced by his previous supervisor at management meetings when promotions were discussed.

In the end, Hal fared far better than the man who maliciously tried to block his career. Hal was so involved in his work that he was oblivious to the gossip and unfriendly behavior around him. When his boss was promoted to the position of vice-president over the heads of senior candidates, he brought Hal along as his second-in-command. After this demonstration of confidence (enhanced by his boss's increased power), the tide of opinion throughout the company turned in Hal's favor.

Hal's former supervisor redoubled his efforts to discredit Hal— but to no avail because the vice-president was in a position to refute them. In fact, he discovered what was going on and made life on the job so difficult for the malicious supervisor that he had to resign.

3. *Rumor-mongering.* Rumor-mongering is common in organizations where promotions are obtained through political maneuvering.

But although helping to spread a rumor isn't as bad a mistake as initiating one, this too can lead to a manager's downfall. Many enlightened managements today move to weed out poisonous grapevines.

The best way to avoid mistakes 2 and 3 is to be careful about saying derogatory things about others. if you can't say something good about another employee, the wise course usually is to say nothing about him or her.

4. *Letting power go to your head.* Jim had been quite a capable manager with no interpersonal problems until he was promoted to a top managerial spot. Soon afterward, Jim started throwing his weight around instead of pulling his own load. He was all humility in dealing with superiors, but his dealings with subordinates were another story indeed. He began gruffly calling his first-name buddies by their surnames. He concluded staff conferences with a windup of conclusions that he had railroaded through the meeting. His two approaches to subordinates were to (1) clobber them with his power or (2) become facetious with them. He avoided lunching with anyone earning less than $20,000.

Within six months, Jim had lost the willing cooperation of his subordinates, and the efficiency of his operation deteriorated. Morale plummeted. Jim's boss began to regret having promoted him. Finally, he gave Jim thirty days to relocate—after stripping him of every vestige of authority.

5. *Treating everyone the same way.* Although we know that no two people are alike, we often make the human mistake of treating them as though they are. Some people are much more serious than others; some don't think clowns are at all funny on the job. A practical joke laughed off by one person may cause serious complications when tried on another.

Sizing up a person's temperament is a crucial aspect of good judgment on the job. Once you have done this, you are not likely to make such mistakes as saying the wrong thing to or taking the wrong tone with someone else. Let's see what happens when such mistakes are made.

Charlie, a sales manager in the head office of a Chicago firm, had been quite friendly with the firm's previous president. And the past president had been congenial and friendly to everyone. Charlie had joked with him on several occasions and twice had gotten big laughs when he stopped the president in the hall and told him funny stories.

The new president of the firm had a completely different temperament from his predecessor. A deeply religious man, he did not particularly enjoy off-color jokes, and he was a strict disciplinarian who expected his employees to treat him respectfully.

Light-hearted and light-headed, Charlie continued on his merry way to make the serious mistake of trying to treat the new president with the same informality he had the previous one. Stepping out of the elevator one morning Charlie ran into the president, who was obviously just coming into the office—over an hour past starting time. Wagging a finger at him, Charlie said, "You're just in time for coffee break!" Barely glancing at him, the president hurried on.

On another occasion, Charlie stopped the president in the hallway as they were walking in opposite directions. A more sensitive person would have sensed at once that the president was preoccupied and in a hurry. But not Charlie! As he launched into one of his jokes, the president stopped him and, in a chilly tone, remarked that he had no time to waste. Fortunately, Charlie "wised up" after that and after a sustained effort managed to regain a measure of his employer's confidence.

Everyone makes mistakes, but a good manager learns from his mistakes and becomes wiser than he was before. Again, the most important point to remember about them is this: *No error really becomes a mistake unless you refuse to correct it!*

24

Delegation: There's More to It Than Letting Someone Else Do It!

Marion E. Haynes

I'd like you to meet Mary Ryan. The manager of a medium-size accounting department, Mary heads one of the company's most efficient, most well-run operations. Openings on her staff are sought after by young people eager for advancement because she is known throughout the company as a developer of management talent.

What's different about Mary? Her subordinates say she never makes a decision for them; she views mistakes as learning opportunities; and she fully backs them when they have developed a feasible course of action.

Does this make her a soft or a tough manager? Ask any subordinate who has gone to her to get a problem solved, and you'll find out how tough she can be as you sit there sweating out your own

From *Supervisory Management*, January 1980.

solution under her guidance. No matter how hard you try, you just can't get her to make your decision for you. She will help you, but only one time.

Does this make her task- or employee-oriented? Ask subordinates what her reaction was to their first mistake—they've all made at least one. Mary feels that making a mistake—within limits, of course—is the greatest learning opportunity available, even better than most management training courses. She sits down with you, congratulates you for making a decision and taking a risk, then goes over the situation with you. In the course of the conversation, you discuss what went wrong with your plan and decide how to do it right the next time. In the meantime, she is guiding you through the analysis and encouraging you to learn from your mistake.

You may be wondering how Mary spends her time. If she's not using it to make the operating decisions for her department, what is she doing?

Mary spends her time in three major activity areas—that is, the time left over from what she calls staff-development time. First, she does a lot of planning. She sees herself as solely responsible for the future of her department. She has at her fingertips staffing and equipment requirements to operate the department for one-, two-, and five-year intervals. Second, she represents her department in the company. This means being involved in a number of management decisions as well as keeping in touch with how her department's services are viewed by its customers. Finally, she reads a lot. Mary feels that by keeping up to date in relevant areas, she is better equipped to tell if subordinates' proposals are likely to work out and to guide them in the analysis of problems they come up against.

So, what's different about Mary? She delegates! Each of her subordinates has a clear set of performance objectives that Mary had an active hand in negotiating. And there are control systems that let everyone know, on a timely basis, how each of the five sections under her direction is doing in relation to its objectives.

That's Mary's system. You do not need to install a total system for a department; the principles of delegating can be learned and practiced while working with as few as one subordinate.

To delegate or not to delegate is never the question. To get things done, and to get somewhere yourself, you must learn to make effective use of this tool. It is the only way to broaden your span of influence beyond your own ability to personally do the work. Delegation may well be the most difficult aspect of the art of good management. Yet the ability to delegate is one of the most important tools you have as a manager to get the work for which you are responsible done efficiently and effectively.

WHY SOME DON'T DELEGATE

Why do managers hesitate to use this proven tool? Some who are, or at least feel they are, less competent than their staff fear the consequences of being outperformed. Others simply believe that the work won't be done properly unless they do it themselves. These managers are so sure of themselves that they automatically assume no one can do the job as well as they can—and no one ever gets a chance to prove them wrong.

While it is necessary to recognize that attitudes like these exist, they probably represent a small portion of the real problem.

There are more common reasons for lack of delegation. The manager may simply enjoy doing a task to the extent that he or she is reluctant to let someone else do it. This is especially true when the person was promoted within the same department and is now expected to manage work previously performed. Some managers do not delegate because they do not fully understand their job as a manager. Others endorse delegation in principle but do not delegate because they mistakenly see delegation as an all-or-nothing arrangement. It's a bit unfair, however, to assume that the nondelegating manager is always at fault. Sometimes the superior expects the manager to know every detail of a project, and this makes it difficult, if not impossible, for the individual to delegate. Or the staff may resist accepting more responsibility because of its own insecurities or lack of motivation.

DEGREES OF DELEGATION

There are degrees of delegation ranging from fact finding to decision making. As a manager, you decide which degree is appropriate by considering the nature of the task, the ability of the person doing the work, the amount of top management interest, and the time available for task completion.

Management experts have identified five degrees of delegation. The authorities list:

1. *Investigate and report back*. The staff member investigates and brings you the facts. You make the decision and take appropriate action.
2. *Investigate and recommend action*. The staff member investigates and recommends a course of action to be taken. You evaluate the recommendation, make the decision, and take action.
3. *Investigate and advise on action planned*. The staff member investigates and decides on a course of action. You evaluate the decision made by your staff member and approve or disapprove.
4. *Investigate and take action; advise on action taken*. The staff member decides and takes action, then advises you so you have a firm handle on what's going on.
5. *Investigate and take action*. The staff member is turned loose. This is full delegation and displays complete faith in the individual's ability.

Under most circumstances, full delegation should be your goal. This means the staff member is given an area of decision making and the decisions are accepted. To reach this level, you must be willing to give up a portion of your authority. You must support decisions after they have been made whether you feel they are the best ones or not. You must be willing to gamble that your staff can do a better job when left on its own than when closely supervised. If you play it safe and avoid risk by not delegating, you merely make your staff an extension of yourself rather than the separate, competent individuals they are capable of becoming.

HOW TO DELEGATE

Delegation is both personal and individual. As such, it depends to a large extent on the relationship between you and each member of your staff as well as each staff member's ability and interest. Still, there are some general guidelines to follow:

◇ Delegate by results expected—not by the method to be used in performing the task.
◇ Set performance standards to measure accomplishment against results.
◇ Give the staff member all of the relevant information you have about the task.
◇ Delegate only to qualified members of your staff. (This may mean that you will have to train some of your staff in preparation for further delegation.)
◇ Establish controls that will alert you to exceptions to normal operations.

You don't cut your staff loose and say, "Okay, you're on your own. Go to it." You have to provide standards and guidelines. That's where objectives are helpful. If you let people know what they are to accomplish but leave the questions of how to accomplish it open for them to decide, you are moving in the right direction.

Next, you establish controls that let you know what is going on. Controls provide you with the opportunity to examine actual performance against standards or objectives and to undertake whatever corrective action is called for. The following should give you some ideas for controlling operations:

Personal inspection. When a tangible product or service is the output of your group, you can assess the group's effectiveness through periodic personal inspections. Such visits, however, should be unannounced in order to be most effective.

Visual displays. Graphs and charts can be maintained to compare actual to forecast. This works particularly well for sales, production, and expense control.

Computer printouts. When the volume of activity increases, computers can be used to summarize data and compare them to forecast. The computer can be further programmed to single out areas requiring particular attention such as expenses over budget or sales below forecast.

Status reports. Staff members can each be asked to provide, either orally or in writing, periodic reports of results.

Staff meetings. Your staff can get together to discuss the results of the department against standards or objectives. This approach is particularly appropriate when sections must work together to achieve results.

Throughout, you cannot abdicate responsibility. Delegating does not mean letting an aggressive, although capable, subordinate take over the operation. You can delegate without fear as long as you remain in charge. Staff members must understand that their authority derives from you, and it can be recalled as quickly as it was delegated, if they begin to overreach. A point for both you and your staff to understand and respect is that while you can delegate authority and responsibility, you cannot pass on accountability. In the famous words of Harry Truman, "The buck stops here."

The first thing to do if you're interested in delegating is to analyze your own involvement in the work of your department. In this analysis, you should categorize all of the work you now perform into three groups:

1. Work that can only be done by you, the manager.
2. Work that can be delegated as soon as someone is ready to take it on.
3. Work that can be delegated immediately.

The next thing to do is to evaluate each staff member's readiness for delegation. Two things must be considered: ability to do the work and interest in doing it well. Has the person done this type of work before? If so, what was the outcome? Were quality, quantity, cost, and timeliness all up to standard?

Work that only you can perform includes your leadership role and your duties as coordinator. Other duties in this category are those you may not be authorized to delegate, such as personnel and cash-disbursement responsibilities. On the other hand, you should delegate all of the routine work of your job. As manager, you should confine yourself as much as possible to the nonroutine—to doing things the first time.

When you have identified work that can be delegated but that no one is capable of performing, you have identified training and development needs to be accomplished by you or other appropriate persons. Once someone has been prepared to take over these duties, you can proceed to delegate by degree until full delegation has been achieved. If there is lack of interest, provide work assignments with clear performance expectations, then follow up with feedback on performance.

Work you are now performing that can be delegated immediately should be assigned to staff members in accordance with the currently appropriate degree of delegation. Then, as you acquire confidence in your staff's abilities, you can increase the delegation until you have accomplished as near-complete delegation as possible.

Delegating has been characterized as giving staff members plenty of rope but making sure they do not hang themselves. This means not only training them but providing the kind of environment where they feel at ease coming to you when the going gets tough or a decision has failed. They need also to understand that they must keep you informed—because of your mutual interest in what's going on, not because you're the boss peering over their shoulders.

BENEFITS OF DELEGATION

When you pick up any business-oriented periodical today, you probably will be exposed to someone's urgent appeal for employee involvement. Much of the meaning has been taken out of jobs, according to observers of the business scene. Employee talents, skills, and abilities lie fallow because of the constraints of bureaucracy. Involvement in decision making is often proposed as a means of increasing both productivity and employee satisfaction. How can involvement be attained? Through delegation!

One of the most marked effects of delegation is the feeling of self-respect it gives staff members. When you give people a task to perform, and let them make their own decisions as to how it should be done, you make it plain by your actions that they are capable, and they gain in importance and self-confidence. Further, giving employees the authority to make decisions gives them a vested interest in the results produced. There is no greater motivating force than to put someone in charge of a portion of a department's work, to delegate the authority required to make decisions that spell success or failure, and then to provide rewards commensurate with accomplishments.

An employee working for a manager who delegates as much as

possible has an excellent opportunity to learn, for it is well accepted that people learn best by doing. For example, the best way to prepare for a position that requires decision making is to have delegated responsibility now for making decisions. Further, the training thus acquired can be instrumental in helping the person grow within the organization.

As manager, you also receive benefits from delegating. The most obvious benefit is the time that is freed for managing—more time for planning the future of your department, for coordinating the efforts of your staff, for developing new and better techniques to do the work, and for establishing better relationships with those with whom you deal in your day-to-day contacts. When your staff is properly trained and performing the duties assigned, you will have a well-managed and smoothly operating organization.

What better recommendation could you receive for a more responsible managerial position than that you are an excellent manager and that you motivate your staff to peak performance?

HOW DO YOU SCORE AS A DELEGATOR?

The following quiz will tell you how you score as a delegator. If you want an even better reading on how well you delegate, have your staff complete the quiz on you and compare the results with your own. If they agree, you are on the right track—if not, you'll be able to pinpoint some areas for improvement. Begin by checking the appropriate column on the right.

Yes No

1. Do you make sure your employees are trained and able to handle an assignment before giving them responsibility for it?   — —

2. Do you carefully define the limits of your staff's authority and responsibility and make sure they are fully understood?   — —

3. Do you give your staff the responsibility for making certain decisions, then overrule those decisions when you think you can do it better?   — —

4. Do you trust your employees and work to instill in them the confidence they need to handle emergency situations on their own? — —

5. Do you make sure your staff gets all the information you have on a project when making job assignments? — —

6. When staff members' decisions turn out wrong, do you let them take the blame, even though final accountability rests with you? — —

7. Do you have a system of follow-up that lets you know how smoothly things are going without constantly peering over shoulders? — —

8. When members of your staff make a wrong decision, do you criticize them rather than help them figure out what went wrong, then help them correct it? — —

9. When members of your staff find it difficult to make a decision, do you help them work it out rather than just give them the answer? — —

10. If staff members make a mistake, do you show your trust by giving them a second chance? — —

Answers: 3, 6, and 8 "No"; all others "Yes."

25

Have the Confidence to Train Your "Replacement"

Marion Farrant

If an accident or sudden illness causes your absence from work for an extended period, is someone trained to take over your job?

You might think, "Nothing'll happen to me." Let's hope you're right. But supposing something *does* happen . . . are you prepared?

Your mind will be at ease if you know someone is fully trained to step into your spot and manage the work. You will be pleased that you had the foresight to protect your job, not only for your own sake, but for management's as well. Work flow and production won't cease because of your absence.

RELUCTANCE TO TRAIN

A few supervisors and managers are unwilling to teach all segments of their jobs. Lacking confidence, they fear that providing complete

From *Supervisory Management*, August 1980.

knowledge to someone else might be detrimental to their own positions.

Take the case of Joe Nichols, for example. Joe, a head draftsman, is responsible for preparing important daily records on the work done by his group. At the end of each day, Joe *hides* the records so no one else can find them. Childish, to be sure, but there are so many "Joes" (and "Janes," too) in the business world who lack confidence in their ability to retain their supervisory positions if they share their knowledge with others. If they do have an assistant, they've limited that person's responsibility so that individual is merely a "go-for."

The person, either on his or her own or with the help of the supervisor, has become familiar with the overall functions of the department. He or she may even have been trained to step in, when necessary, to direct the work, perhaps during the boss's vacation. But the staff knows that that is the extent of the assistant's authority. Knowing he or she is in charge only for a short duration, it delays important questions and problems until the boss's return. It's not necessary for me to describe what can happen in the interim or the often insurmountable problems the supervisor faces on return.

This does not happen if a supervisor trains an assistant thoroughly, imparting full knowledge of specific duties connected with his or her management job and making the staff aware of the assistant's responsibility. During the training period the assistant should be given trial runs of managing the department while the supervisor is on the job. Then, and only then, can the assistant take over as a replacement and receive full recognition from his or her co-workers as "boss" of the unit.

PREPARING YOUR ASSISTANT

A few suggestions might help in training your assistant:

Interviewing. If part of your responsibility is to interview applicants for jobs in your unit or department, insist that your assistant be present at all interviews. Your assistant will not only become aware of how to question applicants but also learn to follow your lead in assessing qualifications for hiring. If at a future time the assistant does interviewing, he or she will be well grounded.

Training subordinates. Perhaps you have a regular training program for new employees. If so, let your assistant handle it. New employees will readily accept the assistant as a "boss," and it will be an excellent opportunity for you to observe from a distance how well your assistant performs.

Purchasing supplies. When requesting supplies for your section, familiarize your assistant with methods of ordering. No doubt you make requests through a stockroom or purchasing department, but certain procedures have to be followed. Also, the assistant needs to know how far in advance ordering is necessary. Some supplies disappear fast and to find stock depleted can mean disaster to the work flow. Your helper's acquired knowledge might mean a vast difference in production.

Discipline. It is not advised that you permit your assistant to discipline subordinates. That's your job—unfortunately. You can, however, acquaint the person assisting you with personnel problems and how you solve them. This part of your job is difficult to teach someone else, for problems have a habit of always being different. Still, let the assistant *observe* how you settle disputes.

Work procedures. No matter how long you have been on the job, new procedures will be introduced that have to be put into effect. At meetings to bring employees up to date on changes, let your assistant occasionally preside so subordinates (especially old-timers) will recognize that authority has been given to a specific person to act for you.

OTHER DUTIES

To this partial list of suggestions, you might want to add other duties that relate to your particular job. Do you rotate employees from time to time so they'll learn other jobs? If so, fully instruct your assistant, giving personal opinions as to the capabilities of subordinates who could handle more difficult work.

Peruse your personal files. Don't say, "No use discussing this problem. It'll never happen again!" You may be right, but just hearing about your methods of handling different cases could be beneficial to the assistant in future resolutions of problems that arise.

Above all, train a *replacement,* one who has complete knowledge of everything you do. And select one qualified to take over. Don't be afraid of losing your job—*you* are the leading member of a team. If you have any qualms, dismiss them. In training someone else to take over and in delegating authority, you are protecting your job and functioning as a *real* manager.

26

Making Decisions: Individual or Group?

John J. Sherwood
Florence M. Hoylman

A well-known joke belittling the effectiveness of groups says, "The camel is a horse designed by a committee." This statement reflects the attitude that groups often fail to use common sense in accomplishing their tasks. Nevertheless, from corporate boards of directors to fraternity membership committees, groups are used for problem solving and decision making by almost all organizations.

Although the use of groups is frequent and the dissatisfaction with the products of group efforts is widespread, managers often lack clear and explicit criteria by which to decide when to assign a problem to a group for solution and when to assign it to an individual. The purpose of this article is to provide such a straightforward set of criteria for determining whether a group or an individual is likely to produce

From *Supervisory Management*, April 1978.

better results on a given task. In addition, for those instances when the task is referred to a group, we offer some guidelines on how to manage the group for the most effective outcomes.

CHOOSING BETWEEN A GROUP AND AN INDIVIDUAL

There are five factors to consider whenever one is faced with deciding whether to assign a particular task to an individual for solution or to a group of people for their joint consideration: The nature of the task itself; the importance of general acceptance of, or commitment to, a solution for its implementation; the value placed on the quality of the decision; the competence, investment, and role in implementation of each person involved; and the anticipated operating effectiveness of the group, especially its leadership.

The Nature of the Problem or Task

The nature of the task itself is the first and most important criterion for any manager to consider when deciding what to do with a problem. Research tells us that individuals are more effective than groups as idea generators and as creative problem solvers. In other words, individuals working separately are more creative than individuals working together in groups. (The one exception to this is when individuals get together for a brainstorming session. When brainstorming, a group becomes a collection of noninteracting individuals following an established procedure. Under these conditions, groups generate more ideas than individuals working alone.) Let's examine the best approach to several categories of tasks in terms of these research findings.

Creative tasks. When the task calls for a creative solution—that is, a new alternative or a heretofore unconsidered option—an individual is a better choice than a group. For example, individuals do better than groups at creating or constructing an original crossword puzzle, designing a technical component, or writing a computer program. When seeking a creative outcome, one would do better to find an expert in the area of concern rather than to assemble a number of people.

Convergent or integrative tasks. When the problem requires that various bits of information be brought together to produce a solution—such as developing a business strategy, evaluating a new product, or solving a crossword puzzle—groups can offer superior outcomes. The *proviso* here is, of course, that the group of people is capable of working together effectively. The operating effectiveness of the group is a key factor and will be discussed in detail below.

Independent tasks. Sometimes in our eagerness to establish more teamwork, persons whose jobs are for the most part independent of one another are encouraged to work as a team. When interaction with others is required to get the job done—because of the flow of the work process, the necessity to share information or skills, or other forms of task interdependency—then frequent or occasional work together as a group may be very useful. One way, however, to assure *un*satisfactory work-group meetings is to insist that people whose jobs are in the main independent of one another work together as a team. Effective managers understand which of their subordinates need to work together to get their jobs done and which do not.

Goal setting. The lesson of management by objectives (MBO) is that persons should be involved in determining the goals that are designed to guide their behavior and against which they will be evaluated. When goal setting is done in relevant groupings of managers and their subordinates, more commitment to individual objectives can be expected. This discussion leads us to consider the question of commitment, which is the second factor to consider in deciding whether a particular matter is better suited for a group or an individual.

The Importance of Acceptance of a Solution

Research has shown that when people participate in the process of reaching a decision, they have more commitment to that decision—that is, they feel more ownership over the outcome. Therefore, they are likely to have greater interest in it and to work harder to ensure the satisfactory implementation of the outcome.

On the other hand, when an individual solves a problem or makes a decision, two tasks still remain for him or her. First, others must be persuaded that the particular outcome is the best or at least is a desirable course to follow. Second, others must agree to act on this decision and carry it out. The principle here is that participation in the decision-making process increases ownership of the outcome and, therefore, reduces the problems of surveillance, monitoring, and follow-up in its implementation.

Not all solutions to problems depend on the support of other people for effective implementation. Therefore, a manager needs to be aware of those issues requiring commitment by others in order for a solution to work and convene those people who will be critical to a solution's effective implementation. Clearly, all decisions are not so dependent on others that they should be addressed by group action. In some cases, a manager may be willing to make a decision he or she knows to be unpopular or to assign a problem to an individual expert for solution, with the knowledge that additional resources will need to be invested in monitoring its implementation.

The Value Placed on the Quality of the Decision

The best managers are aware when they are making trade-offs between the quality of the outcomes of a decision and the anticipated difficulties in seeing that the decision is carried out fully and in a timely manner.

If a manager is sufficiently concerned with distributing responsibility to ensure that a solution will be carried out completely and with dispatch, he or she may accept a solution of somewhat lower quality because it has widespread acceptance rather than insisting on a solution of somewhat higher quality that lacks acceptability to those persons on whom the manager must depend for its implementation.

The quality of a group product, in contrast to one produced by an individual expert in the field, varies depending on the competencies of group members and information available to them, plus how effectively they are able to work together as a group.

The Characteristics of Individual Group Members

When assembling a group of people to solve a problem or make a decision, a manager needs to consider each possible member of the group with three guidelines in mind: the expertise each individual will bring to the particular problem under consideration, the stake each person would have in the outcome, and the role each is likely to play in implementing any decision—that is, how dependent others will be on each member's support of the overall group solution. Keeping these factors in mind, it is obvious that managers will probably not wish to convene the same collection of individuals to address every issue.

There is an additional characteristic of the members of a group that deserves consideration, and this is how effectively they are able to work together. This is the fifth criterion to use in deciding whether to assign a problem to a group or to an individual:

The Operating Effectiveness of the Group

A question that needs to be raised each time a new group is assembled is: How effective will this collection of people be in working together to produce a solution of merit? It may be a better choice to ask an individual to solve a problem or make a decision, rather than to call several people together who will have great difficulty in working effectively as a group.

The skills of the leader of the group are particularly important, because the leader can do more than any other person both to enhance and to block the effectiveness of group efforts. Key leadership issues are discussed below, along with a set of guidelines for productive work in groups.

In summary, the five variables that should be considered in deciding whether a group or an individual is the better locus for addressing a particular problem are: whether the task is creative or integrative in nature, how important acceptance of the decision or commitment to the solution is for implementation by those who must carry it out, the value placed on the quality of the decision and any trade-offs that appear to be necessary to assure acceptance, the competency and investment of each person involved and the role each person plays in implementing the decision, and, last, the anticipated operating effectiveness of the group, taking into account the critical role of the group leadership.

It is to the operating effectiveness of groups that we now turn our attention. First, we will consider what it is that groups have to offer— that is, the *assets* of groups. Then we will offer a discussion of the reasons why groups often fail to meet our expectations for performance—that is, the *liabilities* of groups. The final section of the paper deals with various considerations of leadership.

ASSETS OF GROUPS

Greater total knowledge and information. Even where one person (for example, the boss or a technical expert) knows much more than anyone else, the limited and unique information of others can fill important gaps. There is simply more information, experience, and competencies in a group as a whole than in any one of its members. The issue, therefore, becomes how to make this expanded pool available and utilize it effectively.

Greater variety of approaches. Each person brings a somewhat different perspective to a problem, and these different ways of viewing the world can open avenues of consideration that are outside the awareness of any single individual. In addition, we all get into ruts in our thinking or into patterned ways of defining problems and approaching issues. Assembling a number of people expands the potential ways a particular problem can be approached.

Increased acceptance. When individuals have an active part in the decision-making process, each individual's ownership of the outcome is increased. The responsibility people feel for making the solution work is thereby enhanced. As we mentioned earlier, when an individual solves a problem, two additional problems remain: persuading others both to accept the solution and to carry it out.

Reduced communication problems. The implementation of a decision is likely to be smoother and to require less surveillance when people possess full knowledge of the goals and obstacles, the alternatives that were considered but rejected, and the facts, opinions, and projections leading to the decision that was made.

It is clear that a group has more firepower than an individual, and an assembly of people has an expanded potential for new perspectives and integrative solutions. How then can five or ten capable persons meet together to solve a problem or make a decision, only to leave the meeting frustrated and having made little progress or having developed outcomes that are acceptable to only a few of the principals? In answer to this and other questions, the following is a discussion of the important obstacles to effective group functioning:

LIABILITIES OF GROUPS

Social pressures to conform. Sometimes majorities or powerful minorities—or even the boss—pressure people into going along with lower-quality decisions. In their desire to be good group members or to be accepted, people sometimes keep their disagreements to themselves or only voice them after the meeting to close associates.

Quick convergence. In a group there is frequently a tendency to seize quickly on a solution that seems to have support. The apparent acceptance of an idea can overshadow appropriate concerns for quality or accuracy. Agreement is often erroneously assumed to signal the correct or the best solution.

Furthermore, ideas of higher quality that are introduced late in a discussion may have little chance of real consideration. Research has shown that when groups are required to produce two solutions to every problem, the second solution is frequently the better of the two.

A dominant individual. Sometimes one person prevails because of status, activity level, verbal skills, or stubborn persistence—all of which may be unrelated to competence in the particular task facing the group. Since a leader is particularly likely to dominate a discussion, his or her skills at avoiding, and insights into, the consequences of excessive control are especially important.

Secondary goals or hidden agendas. Often individuals are working simultaneously on the assigned task and—covertly—on their own needs. Their hidden agendas may include personal pride, protection of one's position or department, desires for visibility or acceptance, or personality conflicts with others who are present. Some of these factors lead to attempts to "win the decision" rather than to find the best solution; other factors lead to moves for prominence, deference, and other responses.

Time constraints. Available time may restrict the group's potential. It simply takes more time for a group to make a decision than it does for a single individual. It also takes a good deal of time for a group to develop the skills and procedures required for effective work—that is, to capitalize on the assets mentioned earlier and to limit the liabilities inherent in any group effort.

Problems with disagreement. Issues are often sharpened, and therefore clarified, when there are differences or conflicts between members of a group in defining the problem, gaining preferred solutions, obtaining information, and establishing perspectives. However, because disagreement afflicts people differently, it may also block progress due to hard feelings between individuals. Some people experience disagreement as a cue to attack; others react to conflict and controversy by freezing and withdrawing.

When disagreement is well managed, new ideas and innovative solutions are often the outcomes. When differences between people are seen as sources of new information rather than as obstacles to be overcome, solutions tend to be more creative.

Premature discussion of solutions. Confusion and conflict occasionally arise over proposed solutions because there is not yet sufficient agreement or clarity concerning the problem to be addressed. Unwittingly, the different solutions are being offered to solve different problems. Both the quality and the acceptance of solutions increase when the seeking of solutions is delayed until both goals and potential obstacles are identified.

Identifying and mobilizing the resources of a group and overcoming the obstacles to effective group functioning are keys to a group's success. The quality of a group's decision obviously depends on whether the people with the best ideas or those with the worst ideas are more influential. The declaration, "Let's get all the facts on the table and then make a decision," is a naive wish, as the foregoing catalog of the liabilities of groups indicates. Getting all relevant information on the table and ensuring that it receives an appropriate hearing is a very difficult task. It is to this task of effective leadership that we now turn.

EFFECTIVE LEADERSHIP

Once the decision has been made to assign a job to a group of people, the behavior of the group's leadership becomes critical to its success. It is important to recognize that the more the responsibility for leadership is shared by all members of a problem-solving group, the more productive and creative that group is likely to be—provided that this kind of behavior, where responsibilities are shared and group members take initiatives, does not threaten the formal leader (that is, the boss).

In problem-solving groups, effective leadership promotes the utilization of all members as relevant resources and ensures open and accurate communication among them. It is important, therefore, to understand *the leadership dilemma:* The more power a leader has, the more positive the contributions he or she can make to a group's functioning and to its procedures. On the other hand, the more power a leader has, the more his or her own behavior can be a barrier to the free exchange of ideas.

For most groups, the best solutions come with a *strong* leader working with *strong* group members. In this situation, conflict and disagreement tend to be creative and all resources have opportunities to be fully utilized. Such a situation occurs when there is a two-way initiative between the leader and other group members—not simply two-way communication, but two-way initiatives—and responsibilities for leadership activities are shared. This situation also assumes that the strength of subordinates, coupled with their assuming responsibilities for leadership functions, does not threaten the boss. As was said earlier, the boss can do more than anyone else to facilitate or block effective group functioning.

There are several things required from members of a problem-solving group in which leadership is conceived as a set of *functions* to be performed by anyone seeing the need, rather than as a *role* to be filled by the boss. These functions include encouraging broad participation by bringing others into the discussion and by protecting minority points of view, assuming responsibility for accurate communications between other group members, summarizing progress by pointing out where things stand at the moment, and questioning the appropriateness or the order of agenda items.

The more each of these requirements of effective leadership are shared and performed by all members of a problem-solving group, the more productive and creative that group is likely to be—provided this kind of behavior does not threaten the boss. It is the boss who can do more than anyone else to create both an unintentional "camel" as the group's product and to provoke the attitude among the membership that we have all experienced: "If I can only get through this meeting, then I can get some work done!" On the other hand, the boss can do the most to provide the conditions for effective group efforts.

In summary, some of the world's most productive and progressive organizations are managed by executive committees. Likewise, some of any organization's problems can best be handled by a committee or similar group of employees. This article is our attempt to provide some guidelines for when groups are a good choice for suggesting solutions to day-to-day problems in the life of a manager and some insights into how to make those groups function more effectively.

27

"I'd Like to See You in My Office"

Elanor Reiter

"I'd like to see you in my office." At this moment, somewhere in the world of business, government, or education, a manager may be making this seemingly straightforward remark to a subordinate. It's a simple statement; in fact, its simplicity is the source of its mysterious power. It takes only a moment—but so does the shooting of a curare-tipped dart. Like the dart, this simple summons evokes agony in the target. And since, in management, this result is usually unintended, it can and should be avoided.

In the no-nonsense, results-oriented world of business, it is to be expected that if a manager wants to see a person in his or her office, he or she should be able to say precisely that. After all, a straight line is the shortest distance between two points. Pity the harried manager, trying to do a job quickly and efficiently, who is given a pair of kid gloves to use.

From *Supervisory Management*, May 1976.

But all managers need to be aware of the weight of their "hand" in handling people. In discussions of interpersonal relationships, tactile images abound. We talk about "strokes"; we refer to a light touch versus a heavy-handed approach to management. When a manager says, "I'd like to see you in my office," he or she is, perhaps unwittingly, adopting the pernicious, heavy-handed technique— "management by angst."

GUILT AND FEAR

Management by angst involves using the guilt and fear of the unknown that is part of every adult to mold subordinates' behavior. Angst is more than mere anxiety; it is primeval dread of a seemingly inevitable catastrophe. Unfocused and irrational, angst is all the more disturbing in the logical, familiar, defined world of work; the dark shadows of angst are more ominous in the fluorescent-lit glare of the office. In transactional analysis terms, "I'd like to see you in my office" can transform the OK Adult into the guilty, not-OK Child. Here's how it happens:

Between the time a manager says, "I'd like to see you in my office" and the time the actual face-to-face encounter takes place, the subordinate imagines innumerable scenarios, all accusatory and catastrophic. "I'd like to see you in my office" usually evokes an immediate reaction of "What did I do?" or, worse yet (if childhood peccadilloes are remembered), "He (she) *knows*." All is lost. Truth will out. The jig is up. The principal has sent a note to the teacher, and the text is the same: "I'd like to see John (Jane) in my office."

"But," the manager may say, "I only wanted to know whether he's going to the farewell party we've having for Chuck next week." Well, if that's what you want to know, say so. Human nature abhors a vacuum. If you don't finish your sentence, if you don't say "I'd like to see you in my office about . . . a new photocopier we're thinking of buying," or ". . . a new benefit in the employee health plan," the employee will provide his own fearful multiple-choice: "I'd like to see you in my office about . . . a call I received from the nurse at your son's school," " . . . your car, which is parked in the president's parking space," or " . . . cost-saving measures that require us to fire you."

POWER PLOY

Like dynamite, management by angst can have its positive uses. It's an excellent tool for breaking down a person's defenses and leaving him or her open to any changes the manager may suggest. Having lived all morning with the imagined prospect of being transferred to Outer Mongolia, the subordinate is relieved—even, perhaps, pleased—to find out that he or she is merely being moved to a windowless closet in the basement. Management by angst is also an effective power ploy to be used against a subordinate who is getting too uppity. When the subordinate thinks, "He (she) *knows*," the manager can indicate by a cryptic smile and an eloquent silence that he or she is indeed omniscient—and, if not propitiated, will tell all.

Management by angst is not confined to the one sentence used here, although "I'd like to see you in my office" is certainly one of the most effective weapons. You can evoke angst through nonverbal means as well: You don't invite Jane to have coffee with you because you think she has a rush project to complete. (She thinks she's being rejected.) You're installing a new phone system and you stand out of John's earshot, looking at him (he thinks), and pointing in his direction (he notices) while you talk to the telephone company representative (who, John thinks, is a consulting efficiency expert).

If you were unaware that you were using management by angst—if, on the contrary, you are horrified and protest that you didn't know the gun was loaded—don't despair. By listening to yourself as well as to others, you will soon become aware of angst-evoking situations. The simple act of finishing your summoning sentences will probably help to solve the immediate problem.

LACK OF EMPATHY

Nevertheless, ignorance of angst is no excuse. Management by angst may well be the symptom of a far more serious deficiency: a lack of empathy. Perhaps you need to cultivate empathy by trying to remember your own feelings. Unless you've always been the president of an organization in which you're accountable to no one, you yourself have felt the immediate gut reaction to "I'd like to see you in my office." Recalling your own visceral tension will enable you to engage empathetically with your subordinate. If you think that empathy is a special gift, give yourself a present.

In an era of "assertiveness training," empathy may be an old-fashioned virtue. It is, however, as American as shooting from the hip at high noon. Maturity and self-awareness enable us to manage our own angst; immaturity and a lack of awareness of the feelings of others causes us to manage by angst.

28

Discipline in the Workplace Today

Randi Sachs

Two small letters—me—spell one big problem for today's supervisor. The 1970s were often characterized as the decade of the "Me Generation," especially for younger people. For the supervisor of the 1980s this means supervising people whose loyalties lie with "number 1"—themselves—and not with the company.

Young employees entering today's workforce have often had permissive parents and teachers who didn't discipline. These new workers were brought up and educated to "know themselves" and to strive for individuality.

As a result, the first day on a job may be quite a shock to them. Imagine, a list of rules and regulations they *must* work by. While some of these rules may seem obvious—just common sense—others may seem to cover trivial details or to focus on personal matters. However

From *Supervisory Sense*, Prototype/July 1980.

the employees may view the rules, though, the fact remains that they must adhere to them. If they have problems following the rules, the supervisor may find him (her) self involved in the "disciplinary process."

TEACH, DON'T PUNISH

The word "discipline" comes from a Latin word meaning "teaching" or "learning." Too often, however, supervisors use Webster's fourth definition of discipline—"punishment."

A management consultant who frequently works on supervisory problems described a too common approach to discipline:

Drew, a sales manager, had discussed with the consultant a problem he was having with Andy, one of his salespeople. Andy had been continually coming in late. When he did arrive, he would talk for long hours on the phone—obviously about personal business. Drew had been getting increasingly upset about Andy's behavior and was determined to "get back at him." He finally solved the problem by transferring Andy to an undesirable sales territory, citing his behavior as reason.

When the management consultant next spoke to Drew, she asked, "How are you doing with that employee you were having trouble with?"

"Oh him," said Drew. "I don't think I'll have any more trouble with him. I really nailed him good."

The management consultant looked at Drew, noting his satisfaction with the way he had dealt with Andy. "Drew," she said quietly, "I bet that individual really feels like he was nailed, too."

What, if any, are the problems that can arise from an employee feeling "nailed" by his (her) supervisor?

The first thing that is apt to come out of this is called "malicious obedience." Richard Grote, president of Performance Systems Corporation, describes an employee's attitude in this situation to be one of "I'll do as you tell me because I want to keep my job." What this means is that the employee "turns off" from the job, doing only what he or she is required to do by the job description and following all instructions given by the boss, literally. Any initiative or motivation that the employee had quickly disappears. In some instances, the employee may even work in subtle ways to sabotage the department's operations.

The second thing that can happen is that the employee may quit. This occurs when the individual doesn't need the job.

Given the inevitable results, it should be clear that nailing an employee is a negative rather than a positive form of disciplinary action. "We cannot get persons to behave better by treating them progressively worse," says Grote.

PREVENTIVE DISCIPLINE

Because of the emphasis new employees place on the importance of self, supervisors will have to learn to adapt their management techniques to deal with these newcomers. For example, it is up to the supervisor to introduce an employee into the work situation—whether it is an office or a factory—in a manner that does not threaten the employee's ego. Try to understand that after going through "formal processing" by the personnel department these new recruits may feel more like an identification number than a person.

"That's the biggest problem young people have going into jobs today—they aren't treated as individuals," says Myrna L. Cohn, human resource development consultant with Creative Consulting Concepts. "People think that when you work for a large corporation you give up your freedom—and that should not be the case."

How can you, as a supervisor, convince your new employee that he or she is not losing individuality by putting on a tie or a hard hat? The answer is simple: Treat each employee as an individual. Rather than simply reading off a list of rules to an employee, take the time to sit down and discuss them with him (her). "When a new employee comes aboard," says Cohn, "the supervisor needs to develop a complete understanding in him (her) of what the company policies are and why it is important for the person to adhere to them. Show the employee that he (she) is a unique part of the system, but stress that because the system is large, it is important to follow certain set rules and policies. The educational process is very important so the employee knows his (her) place in the system from the beginning.

Once this is understood, the individual can be held responsible for his (her) actions and must accept the consequences when he (she) violates the rules."

Hopefully, with this participative approach to preventive discipline you will never have to worry about the disciplinary process as it pertains to unacceptable behavior in the workplace. However, since people are imperfect human beings, you are bound to have a disciplinary problem sooner or later, and you'd better be prepared to deal with it.

THE HOT STOVE

Over the years guidelines have developed for the supervisor to follow in dealing with disciplinary matters. To make them easy to remember, they have traditionally been described in terms of the "hot stove." When administering discipline, the supervisor is supposed to behave like an old-fashioned, cast-iron stove. A hot stove:

◊ *Gives warning.* A hot stove sizzles, warning the person who approaches it not to touch. Likewise, a worker should know in advance that he (she) will get burned if the rules are broken.

◊ *Reacts immediately.* When a person touches a hot stove, it burns. Similarly, when an offense is committed, the supervisor should take action right away.

◊ *Is consistent.* A hot stove *always* burns. The supervisor should also enforce the rules at all times.

◊ *Is impersonal.* A hot stove burns anyone who touches it. So, too, the supervisor should not play favorites.

◊ *Doesn't apologize.* After a hot stove burns, it is silent. In like manner, the supervisor shouldn't lessen the effectiveness of disciplinary action by soothing the worker later.

◊ *Doesn't get emotional.* A stove has no emotions. Neither should a supervisor. However the worker may react, the supervisor should always stay calm.

This set of guidelines is indeed valuable for the supervisor who must deal with a discipline problem, but it does have one major flaw: It calls for a supervisor to be impersonal, and a supervisor cannot be impersonal in dealing with *individuals*.

While it is true that a supervisor must not play favorites, it is equally true that each employee is an individual and must be treated as such. If you react identically to each individual, you are showing your employees that each one is the same, that any problems or skills they may have will not be taken into account in the disciplinary process. People who have been encouraged to assert their individuality will not accept this treatment.

Mary Sue Foster, president of Foster & Wood Associates, agrees that the supervisor must deal with each employee as an individual. "The system as it works now is like an unyielding machine," she says. "We need to replace it with a machine that is more like the human body. The body is a machine, but it interacts with outside stimuli and adjusts to them."

This lack of concern for the employee as an individual is also inherent in the progressive discipline process that is so widely used—especially in union shops. In its simplest terms, progressive discipline can be described as "Four strikes and you're out." The process works like this:

Step 1. Right after a first offense, the supervisor ushers the worker into his (her) office and tells the employee to shape up or risk getting a black mark.

Step 2. If there is a second offense, the supervisor gives the worker a *written* reprimand—usually a formal "warning notice"—and says that further misbehavior will result in suspension.

Step 3. If there is a third offense, the supervisor lays off the worker for several days without pay.

Step 4. A fourth offense means termination.

In this process the supervisor is directed, again, to treat the employee impersonally. At each step the employee is informed that an infraction of the rules has occurred and that the consequences will be more severe if it happens again.

To illustrate how dangerous this can be, consider the following incident:

Amos was a stock boy at a large paper company. He had been having trouble getting to work on time. The third time he was late, Sharon, his supervisor, warned him that he would receive a written notice if he were late again.

Despite the warning he had received, Amos continued to come in late. Sharon had no choice but to follow company policy and suspend him from work for three days without pay. At that time, Sharon warned him that if he were late once more he would be fired. The discussion was brief and heated. Amos could hardly believe that he was being suspended for that reason.

"I get my job done whether I come in late or not. Most of the time I'm late because my car breaks down. If they paid me a decent salary here, I might be able to afford to get my car fixed."

"Amos, I can't be concerned about your transportation problems," said Sharon. "If your car doesn't work, take the bus, and stop being such a problem"

"But the bus . . . ," Amos started to say.

"Look, this discussion has gone far enough," Sharon interrupted. "You're suspended for the rest of the week. Take this time to figure how you'll get to work from now on. I'm warning you that if you're late again, you'll be fired."

For the next several months, Amos did manage to come in on time, but, as was inevitable, one morning his car broke down again. Amos was half an hour late; Sharon fired him.

In this case, although the supervisor followed the disciplinary guidelines set for her, the process proved a failure. "Discharge is not part of the disciplinary process," says Grote, "it is the *failure* of discipline." The only thing that Amos could have learned from this incident was that he would have been better off calling in sick than arriving at work late.

LEVELING

The goal of the supervisor today has to be one of dealing with an employee on an individual, adult-to-adult level. Instead of accusing an employee of wrongdoing, as Sharon did, Linda Schwarten, founder and director of The Conference Table, advocates the use of an approach to discipline she calls "leveling."

"There are two ways that you can level," she says. "The first way is to level like a bulldozer—you just run an employee down. The problem is solved, but the employee is left flattened.

"The right way is to level *with* an employee. Instead of saying to a secretary, 'You're a bad employee—you're always late,' describe the situation and the problem that the tardiness creates: 'The phones weren't covered today at 9 o'clock. What can we do about this?' Obviously, the employee has no choice but to promise to come in on time, but he or she was given the option of making that decision rather than simply being bulldozed, or ordered, to do so.

"The key here is to describe the quality of work that is needed and point out the difference from what is actually occurring. Don't evaluate the employee, *describe* the behavior in question."

Rather than viewing the worker as a wayward child, this approach treats him (her) as an adult: "Here's our problem. What would you say is the answer?" In receiving a challenge instead of a chewing out, and by being given the status of problem solver rather than problem causer, the worker comes to realize that the rules do have a purpose— that they are not merely some supervisor's whim.

When workers understand that rules are essential to efficient operation, discipline is easier to administer. In fact, "good discipline" exists where workers so thoroughly understand and accept the rules that they follow them automatically. Workers are then moved by the spirit of *self*-discipline—the most watchful, most effective supervisor that exists.

POSITIVE DISCIPLINE

Recognizing the advantages and disadvantages of both progressive discipline and leveling, Grote has developed a procedure that he calls "positive discipline." Although the steps follow closely those outlined in the progressive discipline process, there is a big difference in the supervisor's attitude. He (she) discusses the problem with the employee in a calm, nonaccusatory fashion and in the end asks the employee to make a choice. It works like this:

Step 1. After a first offense, the supervisor meets with the worker in private to discuss the problem. Instead of threatening disciplinary action if the worker doesn't straighten out, the supervisor stresses *why* the company has to maintain standards of performance. Reviewing what needs to be done, the supervisor says, "I am sure this is the last time I will have to speak to you about this."

Step 2. If the problem continues, the supervisor talks to the worker again—once more, without threats. The supervisor tells the employee the specific change that is required and asks the employee to confirm that he or she understands this. After the meeting, the supervisor writes a memo summarizing the discussion and stating the worker's willingness to cooperate. A copy is given to the worker.

Step 3. If the problem persists, the supervisor tells the worker, "The time has come for you to decide whether you wish to continue working for this company, which means sticking to the rules. Take tomorrow off to think over what you want to do, then come in and let me know what you've decided. If your decision is to remain with us, remember that any future problems will cause us to let you go. As a token of our faith in you, and as a sign that we do want you to remain, you will receive full pay for tomorrow."

That's the basic framework of positive discipline. How it's actually used in practice should depend on the seriousness of the offense. In the vast majority of cases, the offense will be minor—excessive tardiness, poor housekeeping, lengthy breaks or lunch periods, and small inefficiencies—and the supervisor may begin with Step 1. This should be done promptly.

If the worker commits a serious offense, the supervisor should begin with Step 2, the written reminder, or if necessary go right to Step 3, the leave of absence for decision making. Offenses that fall under these headings include smoking in restricted areas, sloppy workmanship, and unexcused absence.

What step the supervisor begins with depends on several things: the severity of the offense, the worker's previous record, what action the supervisor has already taken for similar offenses, and what step the supervisor believes would be more effective in bringing about a change in conduct.

Grote has some specific ideas on what makes Steps 2 and 3 worthwhile.

When undertaking, for instance, Step 2, the supervisor always meets and talks with the worker *before* preparing the written reminder—not the other way round. "There may be mitigating circumstances that the supervisor is unaware of before the conversation," Grote says. "Writing the notice after the meeting allows the supervisor to include any important comments or the commitment to change that the employee has expressed during the meeting."

In preparing the written reminder, he adds that it is frequently more effective to use a standard memo or plain piece of paper than a warning notice form. Employees frequently disregard the actual words written on a warning notice because of the inherent negative connotation of the form itself. Using a neutral memo form encourages the employee to read what has been written.

As for the paid day of absence, Grote says that this approach is far more likely to have positive results than the usual method of laying a worker off for several days without pay. "When workers return from an unpaid disciplinary layoff," he says, "the anger and hostility produced by the suspension frequently lead to reduced output, subtle sabotage, and other costly anti-organizational behavior. Paying them reduces the employees' need to 'save face' by striking back at the organization."

Another benefit of this method is its cost effectiveness. Grote states: "While the cost of paying employees for the one-day decision-making leave is a visible one, it typically is the *only significant cost* involved in using the system. Traditional unpaid suspensions for several days produce very high indirect costs in production disruption and the need to replace the missing worker for several days."

The figures bear out Grote's claims. In a group of 22 companies using positive discipline, 9,800 workers were given paid decision-making days of absence. Of these, 95 percent decided to stay on the job and 66 percent had no further disciplinary problems over the next 12 months.

HOWEVER YOU DO IT, DO IT!

Whether you choose to try leveling, positive discipline, progressive discipline, or something in between, be aware of one thing: Knowing the best way to discipline your subordinates will do you no good if you look the other way when problems occur in your department.

Today's workforce is harder to manage—there is no getting around this. And it makes the job of a supervisor that much more challenging. If you are to be an effective supervisor, you must make a commitment to meet that challenge.

In her work as a management consultant, Schwarten has seen most of the ways that supervisors react when they are faced with a discipline problem.

"There are three ways to cope," she says. "The first way is to fight back. But anger will not help the situation; it can only make it worse. The second way is flight—trying to avoid the situation. The problem with both these reactions is that they are as equally available to animals as humans. Supervisors must take the exclusively *human* approach in dealing with a discipline problem—be assertive. As distasteful as it may seem, it is the supervisor's responsibility to assert him (her) self and stand up for the organizational goals."

Assertion, says Schwarten, should not be confused with aggression. "Aggressiveness is the overexertion of assertiveness."

There are several reasons why supervisors choose the second method of coping with a problem—ignoring it—but none of these are legitimate excuses. Supervisors shy away from discipline because they are afraid of conflict. They are also afraid that if they discipline an employee, that employee won't like them anymore. While these fears are understandable, it should also be understood that discipline no longer need be either a "conflict situation" or a circumstance that results in the employee suddenly disliking the supervisor. If you, as a supervisor, treat the employee with respect, discuss the problem with an open ear, and allow the employee to participate in the process of solving the problem, then the discipline problem can truly act as the learning experience that it should be.

29

You Can Deal with Stress

Richard J.Walsh

Like most Americans, today's manager is living and working at a very fast pace. Managers need to find effective methods for dealing with the associated stress that afflicts anyone in a supervisory position.

Stress affects all levels of management, but supervisors and middle managers have their own stress problems. Some of them lack the authority to carry out their responsibilities—a problem sometimes compounded by poor communication from top management. The manager may even wonder whether he or she is doing his job adequately. And all managers must deal with economic uncertainty and rapid change.

WHAT IS STRESS?

What does stress mean to you? You might answer: "being in a pressure situation"; "having an uptight feeling"; "being nervous"; "feeling

From *Supervisory Management*, October 1975.

frustrated"; "having a feeling of tenseness"; or "being in a conflict situation." Stress can be any or all of these things. Here's a more complete definition of stress: "nervous tension that results from internal conflicts evolving from a wide range of external situations."

Stress is as much a part of life as joy, love, pain, or any other feeling. Some managers thrive under normal business pressures. They are able to meet tough production deadlines, for example, or execute projects that involve moderate to high risks. Research shows that under mild stress, many people tend to increase their performance.

But reaction to stress is a highly personal matter. What produces mild stress for one manager might be a traumatic situation for another. Therefore, we might say that stress is a person's reaction to a particular situation—that is, what he or she makes it—and not the situation itself. The nature and degree of stress felt depends on a person's ability to handle the situation to which he is reacting.

COPING WITH CHANGE

Research in the last decade has shown that major events in a person's life produce internal conflict, which in turn can produce stress that could lead to psychological or physical illness. Dr. Thomas Holmes and Dr. Richard Rahe from the University of Washington Medical School found that even such changes in ordinary life as a new job, a change in work responsibilities, or a vacation can trigger physical illness. Because people must spend energy coping with such changes, their resistance to disease may be lowered. The implication of these research results is that everyone has a given amount of energy—energy that may be depleted if a person must cope with several highly stress-provoking situations at the same time. The resultant decrease in psychological resources available for dealing with other problems will ultimately lower the person's resistance to illness.

In their studies, Dr. Rahe and Dr. Holmes developed a scale designed to determine the impact of life events. Called the Social-Readjustment Rating Scale, it indicates how much energy a person would use in a year to cope with life's major changes. The death of a spouse, for example, means a considerably greater need for adjustment than does the departure of a son from home. Losing your job is much more stress-provoking than having trouble with the boss. In using the scale to "test" a number of people, the researchers discovered that people who faced several stress-provoking events during the year were more likely to become physically ill than were those with fewer stress-provoking events.

You can try your own test along these lines. Count the number of major changes that have affected your life during the past year. If you discover that you have had several stress-provoking events (loss of your job, a business readjustment, a change in financial state, transfer to a different line of work, and so forth), you should realize that you are in the danger zone and may not have a good deal of energy to cope with additional difficult situations or resist physical illness. Although you can't control many such events, you can do some things to alleviate your situation: Postpone major purchases or investments that might cause financial worries, wait a little longer before moving into a new house or apartment, and certainly have a thorough medical checkup and plan a restful vacation.

ANALYZE YOUR LIFE STYLE

Behavioral scientists and doctors are beginning to agree that a manager's life style and behavior have a lot to do with the way tension affects him or her. Cardiologists Dr. Meyer Friedman and Dr. Ray Rosenman of the Harold Brunn Institute for Cardiovascular Research in San Francisco have reported on a behavioral pattern that is likely to produce heart attack or heart problems. This behavior pattern is referred to as "Type A." The person exhibiting the Type A behavior pattern constantly tries to achieve more and more in less and less time. His or her work is never finished. It's always go, go, go. Similar to this is Dr. Harold Mosak's description of a "Driver." A Driver is a person in constant motion; since he is a "workaholic," he is often an over-achiever. His work is never done, and this really bothers him.

The exact opposite of the Type A behavior pattern is called "Type B." The Type B person doesn't have a chronic desire to "beat the clock." He may have as much ambition and drive as his Type A counterpart, but he feels confident and secure and is able to be more relaxed.

Those with Type A and Driver behavior patterns live under nearly constant stress—stress that is, of course, created largely by the person himself. However, the Type A person is not totally to blame for his predicament. The business world has encouraged him in his Type A behavior. Everyone wants him to work harder and harder to get more and more done. However, the Type A person has gone beyond having achievement as a goal to make the frenetic pursuit of achievement his life style.

Every manager should check periodically to see whether he or she is exhibiting characteristics of Type A behavior or the Driver personality. Are you always in a hurry in everything you do? Do you always try to hurry others? Do you feel uncomfortable doing nothing every once in a while? Do you often have ten things going at once? Are you always too busy to enjoy your own accomplishments? If you answer these questions with an emphatic yes, you fall into the Type A behavior pattern. While it's not easy to change your everyday behavior patterns, you can and should do so for your own good.

REDUCE YOUR STRESS LEVEL

You can eliminate many stressful situations through effective planning. Start by structuring one day at a time. Then stretch to a week. By allotting time for rest and relaxation, you can do much to reduce your overall stress level. As you learn to control and plan your time effectively, you will gain enough control over your life to be able to prevent many stressful situations.

It's easy to see that ineffective daily planning creates stress. Consider the production manager who wants his employees to finish the small, easy jobs in the morning so they can devote the afternoon to a big, important contract. When the big, important contract isn't completed by the day's end, everyone is under deadline pressure. This is not the best way to manage—but ask yourself how often you run your own life that way. How many times do you try to get a lot of little things out of the way before you tackle a big problem?

SET GOALS AND PRIORITIES

It is important to establish daily goals and to set priorities. Most effective managers accomplish their most important objectives early in the day. Doing this, of course, assures that the important objectives will be accomplished. Managers who fail to plan and set priorities often face a stress situation at the end of the day simply because they used up their time doing less important work.

The establishment of long-range goals is also an importnat factor in reducing stress. Managers with only a general or vague notion of what they expect to accomplish in life often find themselves in conflict situations. You must shape your career goals so that they won't conflict with your marriage or your social life. It is possible to integrate your goals, but it often isn't easy. There are too many high-salaried but miserable managers who sacrificed their marriages and families to get ahead.

RELIEVE TENSION

Many successful managers use a combination of techniques to cope with everyday tensions. One manager talks with his wife over the phone. Because she listens sympathetically, he feels relieved after talking out his problems with her. Another manager talks out his big problems by visiting the in-house psychologist. A third relies on a chat with one of his peers.

Breaking the routine is another effective way to cope with daily tensions. One executive takes a midday walk to clear his mind before making a big decision. Another manager visits the company library and reads the sports page. A third makes it a habit to go out for lunch just for a change in scenery. Managers who see such breaks in the action as a waste of time are often the ones who don't understand the effects of stress. Everyone needs a release from tension; plowing through eight to ten hours of solid work will almost invariably increase tension.

Exercise can provide an excellent way of releasing the tension caused by stress. Regular exercise programs yield both psychological and physical benefits for managers who choose this avenue. After participating in a fitness program conducted by the National Aeronautics and Space Administration, nearly all the participants reported that they felt better; many said they had a more positive work attitude and less tension. Other research has shown that regular exercise at least three times a week increases both the efficiency and the strength of the heart muscles.

Taking a vacation is a good way to "recharge the batteries" and dispel tension. Even a weekend camping trip can help you relax. Some managers claim that transcendental meditation helps them relieve tension. A clean bill of health from your physician can also relieve anxiety and help you relax.

If you find yourself operating on the pressure-cooker theory of success, you need to find ways to lower the heat and decrease the pressure. It's up to you to determine which combination of activities will give you an adequate outlet for tensions and frustrations, but the task is not impossible.

Part Five

SPECIAL CONSIDERATIONS

30

What Is Your Absenteeism I.Q.?

J. Michael McDonald

How knowledgeable do you think you are about employee absenteeism? To find out, take the following test. More than 1,000 managers have taken the test in the past two years and, like many of them, you may be surprised by the results.

THE "ABSENTEEISM INTELLIGENCE QUOTIENT" TEST

Answer the following ten questions. Answers, accompanied by a brief discussion, immediately follow.

1. The median average absentee rate for U.S. companies in 1979 was close to (a) 2 percent, (b) 3 percent, (c) 4 percent, (d) 5 percent, or (e) 6 percent.

From *Personnel*, May–June 1980.

2. Large companies (defined as having more than 2,500 employees) have higher absentee rates than small companies (fewer than 250 employees). True or false?

3. Absentee rates are traditionally highest in midsummer and lowest in midwinter. True or false?

4. Women are much more likely to be absent than men, even when a comparison is made within a particular occupational group. True or false?

5. Absenteeism reached its peak in the United States in the (a) mid-1930s, (b) mid-1940s, (c) mid-1950s, (d) mid-1960s, or (e) mid-1970s.

6. Absences are fairly evenly distributed throughout all segments of the workforce. True or false?

7. Attendance-award programs have a positive effect on reducing absentee rates. True or false?

8. Home visits to check up on absent employees are used by approximately 50 percent of all companies in the United States on a regular basis. True or false?

9. Orientation procedures are not very effective in reducing absenteeism. True or false?

10. Counseling interviews are viewed as the single most effective corrective measure in controlling absenteeism. True or false?

ANSWERS AND DISCUSSION

1. The correct answer is *(b)—3 percent*. Most managers immediately guess 4 to 5 percent, and some even 6 percent. According to the Bureau of National Affairs (BNA), monthly absence rate in 1979 for all employees varied from 2.8 to 3.1 percent. Absentee rates tend to be higher in manufacturing (3.2 percent) than in nonmanufacturing (2.0 percent).

2. *True*. This should come as no surprise to most managers. In fact, BNA reports that firms with more than 2,500 employees averaged a 3.7 percent absentee rate, while firms with 250 or fewer employees had a rate of 2.8 percent. In the medium-size firms (from 251 to 2,499 employees), absentee rates averaged 3.0 percent. The reason for this is

that larger firms usually have greater problems with employees' feelings of impersonality and anonymity, lack of opportunity to participate in decision-making activities affecting their jobs, and a lack of control over the job itself—factors that increase absenteeism.

3. *False*. This answer may come as a shock to many managers, considering the temptation to take advantage of warm, sunny summer days. Absentee rates are highest in January and February, and then usually decline monthly until July, when absence rates are usually lowest, after which they steadily increase until they reach a high point in midwinter. Not surprising is the fact that the months with the lowest absentee rates are December (Christmas) and July (vacation time)—when extra money is needed and employees cut down on unscheduled absences.

4. *False*. However, the reasons for this involve some rather complex factors. According to Bureau of Labor Statistics economist Janis Hedges, studies do indicate that on the average, women have more unscheduled absences than men, but when comparisons are made between men and women in the same occupational group the difference becomes almost negligible. Factors other than sex tend to obscure the picture. For example, women are more likely to be new hires, work at lower-skilled jobs, and accept employment in lower-paid occupations than are men. Better predictors of absenteeism, says Hedges, are the skill level of the job, the age of the workers, the length of service, and the workers' job stability.

5. *The mid-1940s*. Of 50 managers, perhaps two will get this question right. Most will choose the mid-1960s, contending that this period of protest, upheaval, and social change was the worst period for absenteeism. However, in the mid-1940s, most able-bodied men in the United States were serving in the armed services, leaving behind a workforce consisting mainly of newcomers and/or oldtimers who didn't have the stamina or discipline required for many jobs. Large numbers of women, young people, old people, and marginally qualified and trained individuals—coupled with long working hours—contributed to a national absentee rate of nearly 8 percent in 1945.

6. *False*. A careful review of absence records reveals that high absentee rates tend to occur in certain jobs (with low pay or unpleasant working conditions); on certain days of the week (Mondays, Fridays, or

the day after payday); in certain shifts (3:00 PM to 11:00 PM or 11:00 PM to 7:00 AM, especially 3:00 PM to 11:00 PM on Friday or Saturday); in certain age groups (particularly the teenage-to-30 group); and nearly always with certain people ("chronic" absentees).

Most absenteeism studies confirm Pareto's Law of Maldistribution; that is, a vital few account for a disproportionately large share of the problem. In a recent hospital study, for example, less than 13 percent of all employees accounted for over 48 percent of all absences.

This holds true for most workforces. A small group of employees is responsible for most of the accidents, lost time, grievances, problems, and so on. Therefore, any absenteeism control effort must focus on the chronic absentee.

7. *False*. Studies of attendance award programs are few and far between. Those that have been published claim that the programs do have a positive effect, but close examination reveals that most programs are either short-term in their effect or actually reward those employees who would have come to work even without an award as an incentive. There are some exceptions, however. Attendance-award programs set up on a "shortened-success cycle" (for example, a week or a month instead of a year) usually produce good results. Lottery award programs on shortened-success cycles seem to work especially well: Even chronic absentees have a chance of winning an award if they can manage perfect attendance for, say, a week. The problem, however, is that when the rewards are removed, absentee rates often gradually return to their former level.

8. *False*. Most companies rarely resort to this method of checking up nowadays (mostly because they fear a charge of "invasion of privacy"), although it used to be common practice. However, some companies—and especially individual managers—make it a practice to occasionally call an employee at home when he or she is absent simply to find out how that individual is doing. This method is used most often with persistent, chronic absentees who have shown a pattern of fabricated excuses to avoid coming to work.

9. *False*. In fact, research conducted at Texas Instruments shows that orientation, if it's properly conducted, can not only cut absences dramatically, but also reduce turnover, waste, and training costs as well as increase productivity. In a classic orientation experiment with

female assembly-line operators, Texas Instruments found that the most significant part of orientation was the "human" side—the socialization of the new employee. Teaching the employee the "rules of the game," the problems she would encounter, and even the boss's likes and dislikes regarding the employees—all before she actually started work—helped reduce the employee's initial anxieties about the job and heightened the employee's chances of success.

10. *True*. When it comes down to brass tacks, the most effective way to control absenteeism is still consistent supervisory follow-up and counseling. The irony in this conclusion, however, is that although according to the Bureau of National Affairs most companies rank counseling services as the single most effective corrective measure in controlling chronic absenteeism, less than half of all companies require follow-up interviews with returning absentees. Even more ironic is the fact that very few supervisors or managers receive sufficient training in counseling skills. To be effective in turning around a chronic absentee, a manager must possess the skills to confront the employee in a positive, constructive way and then help that employee find his or her own solution to the problem. It's not a hit-or-miss proposition.

RATING YOUR AIQ

To determine your Absenteeism Intelligence Quotient, add up your number of correct answers and look up your profile below.

Zero to 4—"Impaired intellect." You probably slept through company training courses. Otherwise, check your reading ability. Of 1,009 managers who took the test—representing all levels from president, vice-president, and plant manager down to assistant supervisor—only 2.8 percent, or 28, fell into this category.

5 to 6—"Borderline bright." You possibly have some misconceptions about people and can benefit from additional training. One hundred and three managers, or 10 percent of the total, were in this category.

7 to 8—"Sophisticated supervisor." You know a lot but not enough, and you probably resisted some test questions. Training would reinforce your existing knowledge of absenteeism. Nearly 50 percent, or 502 managers, scored this high.

9 to 10—"Gifted with greatness." You've probably been around quite a while, tried all the whiz-bang management techniques, and are now back to basics. You are likely to do well in helping conduct a training course for new supervisors because you know why people come to work. A sizable number—376, or 37 percent—had either near-perfect or perfect scores on this test.

31

Preventive Measures Against Marginal Performance

Charles D. Lein

Have you ever heard a supervisor say, "It's tough to get good people anymore. People just aren't as dedicated as they used to be. Why, when I was a kid. . ."?

Have you ever spoken this way yourself? Unfortunately, most supervisors would rather blame a subordinate than blame themselves for a worker's poor job performance. Supervisors often won't take responsibility for the actions of their subordinates or try to motivate and direct a marginal worker.

Why do supervisors give up so easily? Probably because they think that the effort they put in won't pay off in improved job performance. They don't realize that they could actually prevent more marginal performance before it begins. They don't realize that once

From *Supervisory Management*, May 1973.

they have identified a marginal performer, they can do a great deal to help him improve on the job.

Marginal performance is seldom the result of inability to do the job—though it often seems otherwise. The causes of marginal performance are numerous and run the gamut from personality problems and conflicts to inadequate supervision and training; from improper placement to misunderstandings about duties and reponsibilities. Social and cultural conflicts at the workplace may be another cause when the worker is required to do something that he considers unethical. Then there's the Peter Principle at work: A worker is promoted to his level of incompetency and must remain there for the duration of his career. The fact that someone is an outstanding salesman doesn't mean he will be an outstanding sales manager. In most cases where an employee quits or gets fired, the supervisor could have prevented such a final move—if he had understood the problem, its origin, and its possible solution.

AN OUNCE OF PREDICTION

Take the case of Hank Richmond, for example. Hank was a contract reviewer for a large insurance company. Popular with his co-workers and good at his job, Hank had consistently garnered "outstanding" ratings on his performance reviews. When a vacancy arose in the higher level contracting-approval section, Hank's supervisor recommended him for promotion because of his past performance. But the supervisor failed to analyze Hank's *potential* performance.

As a reviewer, Hank was involved in the complete preparation of insurance policies. The company issued a wide variety of policies; seldom were two identical documents prepared in any one day. Because of Hank's expertise in selecting the proper policy provisions according to the underwriters' decisions, his co-workers often consulted him on tough cases. Despite taking time to help others, Hank was always among the top producers in policies prepared, a fact reflected on the weekly measurement sheet.

Hank's new job was drastically different from his old one. Instead of preparing contracts, Hank now checked those prepared by others. He had to forgo the challenge—and pleasure—of interpreting the underwriters' decisions. The checking job consisted in looking for errors in the reviewers' work. Five others did the same work as Hank and they were highly experienced; Hank missed the old days when he was consulted by his peers. Finally, the new job gave Hank less control over his work. In the former job, the production report was a weekly total, so Hank could compensate for a slow start by picking up in the latter part of the week. On the new job, there was a daily count, so Hank had to maintain a high daily output.

The result of Hank's promotion was a sharp drop in his performance. Not wanting to appear ungrateful for the promotion and for the few dollars more a week it paid, Hank still seemed to be his congenial self. But his work gradually became the poorest in the approving section and, in the subsequent work review, his performance was rated as "fair." Hank was fast becoming a marginal employee. His new supervisor attributed the change to "personal problems," since Hank's wife had recently given birth to their first child, and there were no visible signs of any other changes or difficulties.

If Hank's new supervisor had been more aware of the requirements of the job in relation to Hank's background, he never would have gone along with the promotion. Even after Hank was promoted, the new supervisor could have done something to help Hank—but only if he were aware of his original mistake.

TAKE PREVENTIVE MEASURES

It's difficult enough to discover that you have a marginal employee whose status might be of your own making. It's ten times more painful if you aren't able to learn from the experience. What can you do to prevent the development of a marginal employee? Here are some guidelines:

Tell a new employee exactly what's expected of him. You should tell him what the organization expects, what his primary and secondary responsibilities are, and what you expect. Your explanation should go far beyond a mere job description.

In order to clarify individual responsibilities for a worker who is not new to the organization, it may be helpful for both you and your subordinate to write out in detail what each of you considers to be the responsibilities and duties of his job. Frequently, these lists may not coincide. The result: a subordinate who feels that he is doing his job to the best of his ability, and a boss who feels that the worker is doing only half his job.

Set objectives. Once you have identified job responsibilities, get together with your subordinate to set specific, measurable goals on a periodic basis: daily, weekly, monthly, and/or annual. Encourage your subordinate to develop his own goals and to transfer as many of his successful methods from his previous job as possible.

The establishment of such objectives will help your subordinate know what he is required to do in order to attain an acceptable performance level. It will also help him identify priorities. Setting specific objectives will be helpful when you have to evaluate your new subordinate.

Make realistic predictions. When you set objectives, don't assume that excellence in one job will mean excellence in another. Take your subordinate's personality and background into account. Try to evaluate the factors that made him successful in his previous job and determine which of them will be present in his new position. Try to find out what new demands will be made on him and what previous experience he has that will help him meet those demands. This is particularly important if the worker has been transferred or promoted into your unit.

Be supportive. Once specific objectives have been agreed upon, you should try to provide the necessary support to help him achieve the agreed-upon performance level. In the case of a worker who has been marginal in the past, you must try to help him gain more self-confidence as well as provide him with technical training. This can be accomplished best by building a series of small, but meaningful, successes into his work experience.

Compare performance with objectives. Evaluation and feedback are essential in working with the marginal as well as the achievement-oriented experience.

Conduct frequent evaluations. Many supervisors do not evaluate their subordinates often enough. Unfortunately, the evaluation process is usually a once- or twice-a-year affair. You should make an effort to evaluate your subordinates—particularly the new or the marginal ones—at least every other month.

An example of a frustrated employee who rarely received

feedback was Sally Smith. The only kind of communication she got from her supervisor Michael Harrad—who was currently preparing her performance appraisal—was a comment on her perfume or a request to bring him a computer printout. She began to feel neglected and eventually quit.

Learn to accept feedback. The feedback process should flow in both directions. Whenever you evaluate or deal with a subordinate, encourage him to open up and discuss any problems that he might be having in meeting established objectives. These open-ended conversations will strengthen your relationship with the subordinate and may help clear up any problems that are bothering him. You may be surprised at how quickly many problems disappear when they are aired. Inability to meet a deadline, lack of information in a specific area, personality conflicts often resolve themselves, given this kind of free-flowing conversation.

WHEN HE NEEDS HELP

Sometimes none of these preventive measures will work, and you'll find yourself with a marginal worker on your hands. You know that something's wrong and you want to try something to deal with the problem instead of ignoring it or firing him. Here's what you can do:

Don't waste time. If you spot a deficiency in a subordinate's work, plan for an immediate, informal interview—even though the time for formal appraisal is months away. By waiting for the formal review, you will only permit the problem to compound itself; the longer you let an employee operate in the belief that all is well, the harder it is to tell him that his work is below average. The time to stop a person's bad habits is immediately.

Develop a strategy. Once you've decided that a worker needs help, prepare for your talk with him. Review his personnel record to acquaint yourself with prior strengths and weaknesses. Is he a slow learner? Does he fail to keep accurate notes? Does overtime adversely affect his work?

When you confront him with the problem, create a relaxed atmosphere, one in which the worker will feel encouraged to share his views and listen to yours. Let him know exactly where he is weak and how he can improve. Finally, reach a mutual agreement on objectives and deadlines. A reasonable goal will provide an incentive for the worker and a method of showing that he wants to cooperate with you.

Try to find a remedy. Traditional efforts at finding a remedy that will help a problem employee—coaching, counseling, training, management by objectives—are often very productive.

Document your discussions. Much of your effort will be wasted if you don't record the steps you have taken. A written record gives you something tangible to review if the employee's problems prove to be chronic or if they recur. Also, it is indisputable proof that the worker was alerted to his weaknesses and that goals for improvement were established. Conversations provide only fleeting memories, and an employee who feels that he has been overlooked at increase time may conveniently forget them altogether. By documenting your interviews —and by including goals and deadlines—you'll be able both to help the worker improve and to help yourself realistically evaluate his improvement efforts.

Follow through. Any golfer will tell you that the ball will go neither straight nor far unless you follow through in your swing. Similarly, the degree and accuracy of the worker's improvement will depend on your willingness to invest time in his efforts. After your review and discussion of his work, make certain that he feels free to come to you if problems remain or develop. Sometimes an employee's problems are aggravated by the fact that he's afraid to ask his supervisor for help. If you ever reach the point where you might have to terminate an employee, you'll want to be certain that you offered every possible assistance, including your own accessibility.

Learn from experience. Few jobs are more difficult than confronting a worker with his deficiencies. Naturally, you will find some approaches more fruitful than others. When you hit upon one that produces results, use it again. You might have to adapt it to each worker's personality, but that's the secret of good personal relations. Furthermore, as you uncover causes of poor performance, apply what you learn from one case to the next. Knowledge gained from one experience may give you an edge in dealing with a future problem.

NO OTHER ALTERNATIVE?

If you have tried all of the above approaches to dealing with a marginal employee, and he still doesn't improve, you can try transferring him to another area in your department or in the company. If that doesn't work, you might consider demoting him to a job that you know he can do well.

If these alternatives are not possible or if the worker will not accept these alternatives, you will have to dismiss him. This requires considerable preparation. Work closely with your personnel department. You'll have to provide comparative production figures and evidence of your attempts to improve the worker's deficiencies by counseling him.

Although termination is an unpleasant procedure, it is necessary when all else has failed. Workers whose feelings you don't want to hurt have a habit of becoming thirty-year, unmovable, disgruntled people whose careers might have been different if they had been forced to confront their shortcomings.

It's tough to make the decision to fire someone. But a supervisor with maturity and a sense of responsibility will be able to recognize deficiencies and take positive actions to correct problems. In so doing, he is performing a service to his department, his company, and himself.

32

What to Do When Their Skills Aren't Up to Par

When I first got on this job, I used to run around doing everything myself. I'd go from one station to another—setting up for one guy, then going on to the next one, who'd be waiting for me to show him what to do.

Believe me, it was no way to run a department.

The trouble was that I didn't have one decent fitter in the whole bunch. Out of fifteen, only three were what I'd even call second-class, and that was being charitable. The rest of them were willing enough, but they just hadn't been in the business long enough to pick up what they needed to know.

Naturally, Jake Hagerty, the shop superintendent, had told me when he put me in charge that the front office knew I'd be running into problems, since we'd never had experience with this particular type of container before. It had been a matter of taking it on as part of the contract, or seeing the entire contract go to someone else.

From *Supervisory Management,* February 1970. Prepared by staff writers.

MAKING DO

That's why we set up the whole operation in a hurry. We cleaned out the old blacksmith shop in the back and ran some ads for qualified fitters. There aren't many qualified fitters floating around loose—which is why we took what we could get.

It was a tough situation. There we were, out in an unheated shed in the middle of winter, trying to produce some odd-ball fuel tanks, each one different from the next. There was hardly enough light to see by. In fact, I was getting to the point of throwing in the towel, even though it was the first chance I'd ever had to run my own show without anyone standing over me.

The main problem was the way I had to take most of the guys by the hand. Take Charley Ware, for instance. He'd worked in metal fabricating before, but every time it came to looking up the next step in the blueprint, he'd wait for me to figure it out for him. And while he was waiting, he and his helper would be huddled over the fire they had going in the oil drum next to the job.

"Charley," I told him one day, "why don't you take one of these prints home with you one day and figure it out for yourself? How are you ever going to make first-class if you can't work by yourself?"

A 9-TO-5 JOB?

"I wish I knew, Jimmy," said Charley. "Anyway, I like to do something different on my time off, don't you? I get enough of those blueprints right here in the shop."

"I spent a lot of my own time learning the job when I first got on," I told him.

"Yeah, I'll bet you did," said Charley, looking at Eddie Sanders, his helper on the job. They both laughed.

"Well, I did, damn it!" I said. "I used to go over to my Uncle Joe's just about every night and he'd show me how to read prints, how to lay out a job, just about everything he knew."

"Who's your uncle?" asked Charley. "Joe Fanelli, in the machine shop?"

"That's right," I said.

"But," said Sanders, "you have to be a relative for something like that."

"The hell you do," I said. I was starting to get a little sore. "If you two were to come to my house tonight, I'd go over a lot of these things with you. But you'd never come, would you?"

"I might," said Charley. "Where do you live?"

We figured out that it would take about forty-five minutes to drive from Charley's house to mine. "That's pretty far," he said.

"Well, if you come, you come," I told him. "And if you don't . . ."

"Yeah, he don't," said Sanders. "Just don't hold your breath."

That night, at eight o'clock, there was a knock on my front door. Charley was standing there, and so was Eddie Sanders. "Just happened to be in the neighborhood," said Charley.

I had to laugh. "Come on in and meet my family," I told them. "Then we can go down to the basement and do some work."

And work we did. I took a lot of the prints Uncle Joe and I had worked on and spread them out on the ping pong table; then we went over them point by point. The light was good, there was nothing to disturb us, and they listened to everything I had to say. I could tell from their questions that I was getting through to them. Before we even knew it, it was pretty close to eleven o'clock.

"You gonna do this again, Jimmy?" asked Charley, after we'd had some coffee.

"Just let me know when you're coming," I said, "and I'll make it my business to be here."

Jake Hagerty thought I was some kind of nut when he found out what I was doing. "You're expecting miracles," he told me. "It takes years to make a first-class fitter. If those guys were really serious about making it, they'd be going to night classes on their own time, and not bothering you."

ONE STEP AT A TIME

"Night classes are okay, Jake," I told him, "but this way they're getting exactly what they need to do a first-class job right here in the shop—

which is all I'm worried about. Furthermore, it's not that much of a bother."

Jake just shook his head and groaned. The funny thing was that right after he talked to me, Charley and Eddie told me that they'd signed up for some shop courses at the local high school. They also asked me if a couple of the other guys could come over to my house when they did. Naturally, I told them I'd take anyone who wanted to come.

All this was over a year ago, and a lot of things have changed since then. For one thing, we made out all right on the first contract for the fuel tanks, and now it looks as though we'll have as much work there as we can handle. The old blacksmith shop has been rebuilt, and the new lighting is adequate.

Charley and Eddie are first-class fitters, and so are a few of the other guys. Jake Hagerty wanted to keep on classifying them as second-class, but I told him there wasn't anything they couldn't do, as far as I was concerned. I didn't remind him of how long he told me it'd take to make a first-class fitter, but it might have been on his mind, because he did tell me one thing: "If anyone had said to me a year ago that you'd turn that bunch of shoemakers into a first-class crew, I'd have laughed and called for another joke." Considering that it was coming from Jake, I couldn't have asked for a finer compliment.

33

Performance Review: Confronting the Poor Performer

Robert C. McCoy

Although management has a reputation in the eyes of the public as being "tough-minded," this label is *not* applicable to nine out of ten supervisors confronted with a poor performer. While the all-too-typical manager (particularly at higher levels) is likely to deal fearlessly and decisively with facilities, materials, engineering, and economics, he or she all too often fails to deal realistically or positively with a stumbling subordinate.

This evasion of a crucial managerial responsibility is not a willful or deliberate evasion, but rather an unwillingness to "play God" or to engage in a potentially explosive or emotionally disturbing situation. Perhaps because of a widespread deficiency in managerial training, the fulfillment of this duty has become the *poorest part of management*

From *Supervisory Management,* July 1976.

performance and a weakness that is extremely costly to any organization.

In one company, three key production foremen positions had been occupied for two years by totally inadequate people (promoted from the ranks because they were "the best workers"). Despite daily demonstration of their inadequacy, they were never confronted. Finally, a new plant manager decided to face up to the situation. He reassigned the three foremen (who were actually relieved because they could handle the new assignments adequately without personal stress or the constant strain of knowing that they were doing a poor job) and replaced them with three effective supervisors.

In another case, "Good Old Bill" was promoted to a level well above his capabilities (because he was admired and had come so far in the organization). It wasn't until Bill had a mental breakdown that the mistake was recognized and admitted.

A SUCCESSION OF COVER-UPS

In many companies it has become a practice to employ bright young college graduates or MBAs, put them on a fast track to a high-level position, and base their future on their supervisory success during an eight- or nine-month trial period. Some succeed and some fail—but that's not the real problem. Rather, since their success is to be judged on their performance during a brief period of months, these bright young men and women certainly do not stir up trouble by dealing with inadequate performance around them. Instead, they "cover up" or "wire around" the problem—so the same unsatisfactory performers manage to stay in position, performing poorly, through a succession of short-term supervisors. In the long run the organization cannot avoid being adversely affected. Misuse of manpower is as destructive to an organization as misuse of physical and financial assets.

WHY PROCRASTINATE?

Why do so many managers avoid firing an obviously incompetent employee? It is not at all unusual to see otherwise dynamic leaders procrastinate when it comes to dealing with a subordinate who is failing on the job. Some rationalize: "He may not be the best there is, but he may be better than his unknown replacement." Or, "Maybe he'll quit pretty soon, anyway." One personnel vice-president claimed that unionization almost succeeded several times in one of his company's divisions because of inadequate foremen. The division periodically added wage increases and fringe benefits, but avoided the real problem—inadequate foremen. The division's managers seemed to be waiting for a "Mr. Wonderful" to come along and handle the problem.

Some managers dodge the firing issue completely by delegating the task to a subordinate. One manager called his immediate subordinate in at five o'clock one evening and told him to "ask Fred to stay a little late tonight"—and then to discharge Fred after everyone else had gone home, "to save a disturbance in the organization." Some executives are willing to pay high fees for external consultants to handle this admittedly distasteful part of the management job. But such "outsider action" is never in the best interests of anyone concerned. Action must be taken by the responsible executive or manager. A consultant may help *coach* a manager in planning the action and may work with the subordinate, if desirable. But allowing an outsider to assume a manager's responsibilities and do his "dirty work" can only damage the manager's relationships in the organization and water down his or her image, self-confidence, and productivity.

A BETTER METHOD

What is needed is a method for handling inadequate performers that is (1) less threatening and distressing to the boss; (2) more contributory to management effectiveness, profit, and performance; and (3) more humane and developmental for the unsatisfactory performer.

Here are some stages in this proposed approach:

1. *Adopt a realistic attitude toward poor performance*. Recognize that procrastination is fair neither to the individual nor to the organization—even though it may seem kind on the surface. Recognize that no poor performer can go on making an inadequate contribution forever. When economic conditions worsen (and when he may be several years older), he will be the first to be caught in the "crunch"—

and his chances of finding other employment will be much lower than they currently are. Realize, too, that a person who is working over his head is not meeting his own emotional needs and is very likely to develop physical or psychological problems that can be costly to his family, himself, his organization, and society in general. Though firing may be distasteful, it may also be the best medicine for his "work illness." Isn't it better to help someone start a new career while there is still time than to preserve his inadequacy until it is too late to do something about it? Remember that management also has a responsibility to others in the organization—that the maintenance of "bad apples" can lead to lowered standards and lower productivity, culminating in potential disaster for all.

2. *Deal promptly with inadequate performance.* If performance standards are nonexistent or very low, a worker may make poor performance his career pattern. Therefore, the work of each subordinate should be "inspected" as well as "expected" promptly after his assignment to a job. Begin immediately to help a new worker become productive and valuable to the organization. Many managers concern themselves more with a subordinate's approach than with his output. Whatever methods a worker uses, he should be *judged* by his work results. These results should be measured quickly and regularly to prevent poor performance and to help the poor performer improve.

3. *Plan your actions.* Set up a plan and a timetable for coaching and counseling the underperformer.

4. *Involve the employee in charting his own course.* Take a cue from MBO (management by objectives). Sit down with the underperformer and develop mutual objectives with him; let him know that his performance will be measured in terms of how well he achieves them. MBO enthusiasts say that this is the best way to develop people. Study after study in behavioral science indicates that the "people developing" supervisor achieves much greater productivity than do those who limit themselves to "task orientation." The manager who, with the assistance of the employee, develops a factual and results-oriented method of keeping score on job performance will not so readily dodge emotionally distasteful situations. Instead, if he develops reasonable standards and measures performance periodically, both he and the employee "know the score" and are in a position to move toward a fair resolution of performance problems.

5. *Establish a "D (Determination) Day."* When an employee's performance is not acceptable, the manager and employee should get together and agree that by a specified time, one of the following must have occurred: (1) The employee's performance will have improved to an acceptable level; (2) the employee's work will have improved enough to justify more developmental work; or (3) the employee's performance will still be unacceptable and he will be asked to resign or will be fired. The employee who isn't working out will have gotten the message and may well start looking for another job.

6. *Act effectively and decisively.* Most managers cope with technical problems by preparing a plan of action supported by documented facts and evidence; they follow through by meeting established deadlines for action. The effective people-problem solver follows the same route. If he needs extra help to build his confidence, he might role-play his approach with a confidante, the personnel manager, or a consultant. He will probably find that when he is well prepared and confident, the encounter is must less distressing and distasteful than he had expected.

7. *Recognize your social responsibility.* The executive or manager who has failed to take action on unsatisfactory performance and has procrastinated for a significant portion of an employee's working years probably has a social responsibility to maintain that employee for the rest of his working life. This can be costly, but it is only fair. If a manager has allowed a poor performer to slide along for 20 years (or roughly half of his working career), it is that manager's responsibility to locate another job in the organization where the person can work for his remaining work life without doing any damage. (If this 20-year figure doesn't seem fair to you, establish one that you can live with.) If, on the other hand, a manager does not feel that he has accumulated a lifetime liability for an employee, he should, on the basis of an established termination period related to length of service, aid the underperformer in making an effective job search or career switch. Many companies today provide professional vocational counseling and coaching as well as job-search assistance at company expense.

THE BENEFITS

The manager willing to follow these steps in dealing with a poor performer can expect to reap some of the following benefits:

◇ Since the manager knows he has taken the best course for the employee and the company, he will not be guilt-ridden.

◇ The company free of "bad apples" undoubtedly has a better future.

◇ The employee who has faced his own poor performance and either improved it or realized that he is in the wrong line of work is certainly better prepared to face the future.

◇ The fair-but-firm style of management demonstrated in this approach is likely to increase your credibility in the eyes of subordinates and to strengthen their adherence to productive performance standards.

Given the fact of varied jobs requiring different qualities and characteristics and varied people with unique abilities, interests, capabilities, and levels of motivation, there are bound to be some "misfit" situations. Personnel selection techniques are being improved, but perfection is still a long way off. Therefore, dealing with poor performers continues to be an important responsibility of any effective leader. No successful manager can afford to ignore the problem. He or she must deal with incompetence by establishing reasonable performance criteria, evaluating subordinates' work fairly and continually, confronting a failing employee promptly, providing constructive criticism and improvement tools or techniques—and, when all else fails, firing the employee who has shown he cannot meet minimum performance standards. This last step must be taken while he still has a good chance of changing careers or finding a more suitable job.

34

Softening the Blow of "You're Fired"

Angelo M. Troisi

When Jim Smith didn't get a raise on his employment anniversary date, he didn't worry. He knew his salary was higher than that of others at his job level, and he thought that the company had passed him over simply to bring the salaries of his co-workers in line with his. So, Smith was shocked when five months later the general manager of the organization told him he was fired.

The general manager, in turn, was surprised at Smith's reaction. He had assumed Jim would read his failure to receive a pay increase as an unmistakable signal that the company found his work performance unsatisfactory.

The differing interpretations of this particular superior and subordinate, compounded by their failure to communicate with each other, made a painful experience—termination—even worse.

Terminations, unpleasant as they may be, are a fact of life for any

From *Supervisory Management*, June 1980.

company. For the sake of the employee, they should be handled with humanity and, for the sake of the company, with care and efficiency.

AVOIDING THE DIRTY WORK

Because most supervisors tend to avoid firing anyone, they don't learn how to carry out this difficult but important task. But whether you are prepared or not, sometimes termination of an employee is unavoidable. If you feel you have done everything possible to motivate an employee and to train him or her properly, and you have come to the conclusion that the employee is not salvageable, then you have in effect reached a decision to terminate the person. It's important, though, that you do it right.

In any termination, three steps must be handled thoroughly and consistently. These steps are:

1. Justification for termination.
2. Termination settlement or severance package.
3. Conduct of termination interview.

Recent legislation designed to protect employees from discriminatory employment practices demands that company-initiated terminations be well documented. Before an employee is terminated, the supervisor should be able to prove that:

1. The employee's job description was regularly reviewed to determine if the employee was performing the duties described.
2. The correlation between the employee's salary and the description of the job was reviewed.
3. His or her performance reviews were carefully studied.

EVALUATION—A VALUABLE TOOL

It is important to both the employer and the employee that the company conduct annual or semiannual performance reviews. These should be submitted in writing and should be kept separate from salary reviews. There is a great deal of literature available for study on how to conduct a performance review, if your company does not already have a policy on this.

For a performance review to be an effective tool, supervisors must be totally honest with employees about their work. Otherwise, supervisors may find that their good workers are frustrated at being evaluated the same as poor workers. This frustration can, and often does, lead to their resignation. Even more serious, a performance evaluation system not administered honestly and uniformly can open the door to discrimination charges. In fact, many corporate attorneys believe that companies should not fire a person based on one manager's input. They are fearful that the terminated employee would charge that it was a case of discrimination or personal differences.

Once the employee's poor performance is determined, management should take corrective action. If the company continues to reward the marginal performer, he or she will assume that there is no problem. The employee's salary, which could climb to substantial levels, supports that assumption. Presupposing you have developed a valid job description from which to evaluate your employee, you should list the employee's failed objectives in job-related tasks. If an employee is given ample time and opportunity to improve performance and does not, then the company, armed with objective documentation, should terminate the employee.

FACING THE TRAUMA

Although the emotional impact of being fired varies with the individual, studies show that the trauma associated with termination is so great that it can be compared in intensity to divorce or the death of a loved one. Shock, depression, anger, self-pity, confusion, and loss of identity are some common feelings and reactions. The person is filled with anxiety and self-doubt about the prospects of finding a new job, the reactions of family and peers, and finances. The individual may be extremely bitter and negative about the future to the point of seeking revenge. He or she may go to work for a customer or competitor, file a lawsuit against the company, or spread malicious rumors. Since such negative actions can substantially damage a company's reputation and can have a serious effect on its recruiting efforts, community image, and employee morale and loyalty, it is in a company's best interests to handle terminations as positively and sensitively as possible.

The news travels fast when an employee is fired, and the effect it has on other employees depends in large measure on how the company handles the firing. If the employee is treated fairly and offered the kind of assistance needed during this critical period, it tells the rest of the employees that if they were to be fired, the company would provide help for them, too. Treating the employee with concern and consideration helps to bolster the company's image with all the employees.

SOMETIMES THERE'S AN ALTERNATIVE

Before firing an employee, the company should make an effort to see whether he or she might be able to function positively in another position in the company. We have seen a number of situations in which an employee was fired, began working with us in the outplacement process, and was then rehired when another department within the company became aware the individual was available.

SETTLEMENT ARRANGEMENTS

Companies handle settlement arrangements in many ways. Some have written policies with carefully derived formulas to arrive at an amount of severance pay and its method of distribution. Others merely express verbally a vaguely defined amount of time for job hunting.

Once a decision to terminate has been reached, though, the best approach is to put the settlement in writing. This way, the company gains better cost control, better records for future use in manpower planning, and legal documentation that confirms the settlement arrangements. For the fired employee, having the settlement terms spelled out establishes the finality of the situation. That is hard to accomplish with a verbal exchange, since the individual will not be thinking too clearly and will hear only what he or she wants to hear.

As outplacement counselors, we see value in a letter of termination because it helps us to advise the employee about financial pressures that will have an impact on his or her campaign for a new job.

The termination letter should cover the method of distributing severance, the disposition of benefits, and employment assistance to be offered by the company.

EMPLOYMENT ASSISTANCE

Employment assistance in the form of outplacement counseling is a strongly recommended option in settlement arrangements because severance pay alone is not enough to solve the employee's problem. A newly terminated employee is in emotional turmoil and may feel ill-prepared to embark on the search for a new job. The individual may feel unable to market himself or herself or feel too old to be able to get another job. The employee may have no idea how to begin looking, lack the experience to be easily marketable, be in a technical discipline that is not readily in demand, or have a salary level that is high in relation to skills or job level. To have at this crucial time assistance in getting back into the job market can be invaluable. And from the company's standpoint, the sooner the former employee finds a job, the lower the company's separation costs.

THE TERMINATION MEETING

You have documented the reasons for the employee's termination, put together a fair settlement package, and are now prepared for the termination meeting. If your package is indeed fair and includes outplacement counseling, it should be clear that the company will try to make the transition as easy as possible and will provide a large amount of support.

There is no good time to fire someone, but there are some times that are worse than others—for example, birthdays, anniversaries, just before a holiday, and on Friday, late in the day.

We find that in the morning people are generally stronger, fresher, and better able to deal with the situation. The emotion that is stirred translates itself very quickly into energy used for positive and negative action. And if the termination interview is handled right, the employee will move in a positive direction.

Never fire someone on a Friday. When you do, you maximize his or her potential for negative reaction. He or she has two days to feel abandoned and alone, to think of a way to protect his or her family and assets from this harm. Some actions can include bad-mouthing the company to friends, spreading malicious rumors about you or your company, and possibly suing for discrimination.

KEEP THE MEETING BRIEF

There is no absolute "right way" to conduct a termination interview. Even in the case of a layoff resulting from a downturn in business, and in which other employees are affected, you must remember that the employee will feel anxiety and pain. Whether this hurt is displayed outwardly depends on the person.

The discussion should be conducted privately and should be kept brief. Move quickly to the reason for the meeting.

"John, the reason I've asked you to meet with me concerns the company's current financial condition and its effect on you. We are laying off a number of employees, and you are one of them.

"This has not been an easy decision to reach; however, it's one that was made out of necessity. The company has taken many factors into consideration and is prepared to assist you in a number of ways that are spelled out in this letter."

At this point, pause and wait for a reaction before going on further. Sometimes, you will have to do a lot of agreeing with the employee about the injustice of it all. At other times, there will be a need only to listen.

If the employee's performance has been a factor, and the employee raises the issue, address it.

"John, we have had discussions in the past about your performance, and that was a consideration; however it was not the only one that went into this decision.

"Although we've had differing views of your performance, I'm certain that you'll do well in your next job since I'm confident that the performance issues we've discussed will be a consideration in your selecting your next job. I'll give you every support possible in a reference check and will stress the economic condition of the company as being the primary factor in your layoff."

Encourage the employee. It may be appropriate to identify the strengths that he or she will be able to take to another job. Remember, the employee is not apt to hear much of what is said after being told of a layoff. The task of going over severance, references, and other important details should be done again, by an outplacement counselor or a member of the personnel department. Suggest that the employee feel free to come to you with any questions or ask you for any advice you can give.

DON'TS

A most ineffective way of handling the termination interview is to try to depersonalize the meeting. An insensitive supervisor calls the employee into his or her office and says:

"John, your services are no longer needed. This decision was based on some performance problems. As for your severance package, I don't have any details, but I'm sure the personnel department can answer your questions."

John, feeling hurt and shocked, responds, "I don't understand; just six months ago you gave me a raise."

The approach taken by this supervisor shows a total disregard for the employee. It also indicates that the supervisor has not performed his or her job properly if he or she can recommend a raise for an employee and follow it up six months later with a termination due to poor performance. A termination due to unsatisfactory performance should not come as a surprise to an employee.

Equally bad is the supervisor who informs the employee while passing him in the hall that the "personnel department wants to discuss something with you." Both approaches signal a poor supervisor who is ready to pass on the dirty deed to someone else. The supervisor apparently assumes no responsibility in the matter, even though the employee worked for him or her day in and day out.

ADDING IT ALL UP

To make terminations as positive and as problem-proof as possible, you should (1) develop a formal evaluation system that is fair and complete and that can form the nucleus for decisions about promotions as well as terminations, (2) develop a severance package to meet individual needs, (3) deliver the news of the termination early in the day and early in the week when the employee is best able to deal with the news, and (4) assure the employee that the company will help maximize his or her potential for rapid reentry into the job market.

By following these steps, you can extract positive employee and public relations for your company from what could have been perceived as a negative action. At the same time, you can help an employee turn a job ending into a job beginning.

35

How to Nourish the Creative Employee

Donald W. Myers

The best supervisor is not necessarily the one who tries singlehandedly to come up with solutions to organizational problems. A more important quality is the ability to channel employee ideas into the mainstream of the organization. To do that requires an understanding of the care and feeding of the creative employee.

The following quiz is a test of your capacity as a supervisor for managing creativity. It is divided into four parts: the human elements of creativity, the impact of the organizational environment, the effect of management philosophy, and the cultural aspects of creativity. Be honest with yourself in answering the questions, and try not to look at the answers before giving your opinion. Answer each question as true or false. The correct answers are explained beneath each question.

From *Supervisory Management*, February 1981.

THE HUMAN ASPECTS OF CREATIVITY

1. *Creativity and personal growth are interrelated.*

TRUE. When employees are treated as adults who can creatively contribute to the success of the organization, they mature as human beings. An environment conducive to creativity is a prerequisite for self-fulfillment since creativity is in the main a personal expression of one's self. The individual releases creative energies that provide personal fulfillment and satisfaction, which according to Abraham Maslow is an indication of a "healthy personality."

2. *Employee creativity is the result of planned management action.*

FALSE. Creativity will exist independent of management's actions. Management's role is to direct the creative behavior. As an example, one researcher found that where work methods were strictly prescribed, employees engaged in a variety of creative activities, including different types of games, purposeless antics, and singing. In this case, the creative behavior that was used to counter job monotony was harmless. Creativity can, however, have more harmful manifestations, including clever methods to restrict output—even sabotage. It is the nature of the frustrated employee to either withdraw by engaging in day-dreaming and absenteeism, or to exhibit aggressive behavior in overt violations of organizational rules.

3. *There is no proven correlation between creativity and employee performance.*

FALSE. Many managers feel that creativity has a detrimental effect upon productivity. They believe that employees who are thinking about ideas are wasting time that should be spent producing. But research conducted by myself and others shows a statistically significant correlation between employee creativity and job performance. Creative employees seem to have a zealous regard for long hours and hard work.

4. *Creative problem solving is a function of the left hemisphere of the brain.*

FALSE. The right half of the brain controls the creative thought process used in solving problems. It is also the source of thought in initiating new programs and analyzing contingencies. The left half of the brain controls logic and decision making based on the routine and familiar. While right hemispheric thought leads to new hypotheses, it is the left side that verifies and rationally analyzes those hypotheses. Studies have shown that in the proper environment people can be induced to utilize the right half of their brains and thus develop their creative abilities.

5. *Supervisors could be aided considerably if only there were some means of measuring creativity.*

FALSE. There is already a considerable body of research regarding the measurement of creativity. The problem is putting those findings to work.

THE ORGANIZATION

6. *Opportunities for employee creativity are limited in most organizations.*

TRUE. The opportunities for creative expression are limited because organizations have not encouraged employees to tackle the myriad problems that every organization faces. Intel Vice-Chairman Robert N. Noyce, for one, believes that one of the reasons Japan is winning the competitive industrial battle with the United States is that U.S. manufacturers discourage innovation.

7. *Extrinsic rewards like cash and praise are needed to arouse the creative abilities in employees.*

TRUE. While intrinsic rewards are important, they cannot be the sole basis for encouraging creativity. Researchers have found that extrinsic reward systems have a significant impact on employees' creativity. The energies employees expend in creative efforts are a function of their desire for a particular reward and their expectation of receiving it. Employees value recognition in the form of money and praise (extrinsic rewards) as well as in the form of meaningful work assignments (intrinsic rewards) that allow them the freedom to choose methods and procedures in accomplishing tasks.

8. *One of the principal deficiencies of the scientific management of Frederick W. Taylor is that it ignores the contribution of employee creativity.*

FALSE. Taylor was perhaps the first person in management to

recognize the creative efforts of employees to cooperatively reduce productive energies. The confusion about Taylor stems from the fact that he advocated scientifically determined methods of work. Consequently, he is criticized for having been insensitive to the human aspects of work and in favor of a more task-oriented approach to management. While some of the criticism may be valid, it cannot be said that he was unmindful of the effects of employee creativity on efficiency.

9. *Creativity is an individual process that involves four stages of ideation—preparation, incubation, illumination, and verification.*

FALSE. Elton Mayo, writing on the Hawthorne studies, noted that positive group creativity could be obtained by asking for group solutions to problems and by consulting the group about proposed changes. He also found that group involvement assured commitment to the accomplishment of goals.

10. *Inflexible organizations prevent employees from exhibiting their creative talents.*

FALSE. Inflexible organizations require employees to be more creative in adapting. Gordon Allport has said that creativity is fundamental in personal adaptation to organizational life. The problem for management is the direction of creativity. Many arbitration cases testify to elaborate disciplinary procedures designed to coerce employee compliance to inflexible rules and procedures.

MANAGEMENT PHILOSOPHY

11. *The creative potential of employees is limited.*

FALSE. Your answer to this question reflects your philosophy of management. Douglas McGregor says that Theory X managers would answer true while Theory Y managers would say false, believing that creativity, like other human characteristics, is distributed in varying degrees among people. One of the paramount demands upon managers in the 1980s is to tap the creative potential in employees.

12. *Creativity can be developed in employees.*

FALSE. While the answer to this one may seem tricky, the concept is not. Employees develop their creative talents, not management. Organizations can aid employees in their development of latent creative abilities, however, by providing an encouraging work environment. The proper atmosphere consists of a management philosophy that recognizes the value of creativity and nourishes ideas with job descriptions that are not tightly constraining, a reward system that is fair, and supervisors who communicate with employees.

13. *Suggestion programs are necessary to ensure constructive creativity.*

FALSE. While suggestion programs can be excellent for channeling creative energies, they do not guarantee constructive commitment. Systems like suggestion programs can promote employee creativity only if management demonstrates its willingness to recognize the importance of creative ideas. While both the system and the philosophy are important, the latter is more significant because it establishes the rationale for a system's existence. Mary Parker Follett said that people are not going to think creatively unless there is a reason for them to do so.

14. *The objective of employee creativity is to obtain ideas that increase the efficiency of the organization.*

FALSE. As many or more benefits result from the by-products of employee creativity than from the direct application of ideas. In my research, I have found that safety, for instance, can be improved when employees and managers are asked to focus their creative energies on finding ways to reduce accidents. A by-product is a heightened safety-consciousness among employees in their daily work. When employees are challenged to think creatively about their work, they seek to know more about their jobs and in the process become more competent and efficient. This self-development aspect of creativity is continuous as employees attempt to gain increasing amounts of knowledge to improve existing skills. This cyclical development can also promote adult personality development. Certainly the organization benefits from the direct application of ideas, but it profits to an even greater degree from the maturative process in which employees seek greater responsibility, become self-regulated, and develop as people.

15. *The immediate supervisor determines the quality and quantity of employee creativity.*

FALSE. Top management, through its organizational objectives, determines the quality of employee creativity. Supervisors only reflect the concerns of top management.

THE CULTURAL ASPECTS

16. *Creativity and intelligence are related.*

FALSE. In a study I conducted, there was no evidence of a difference in creativity between 100 mentally retarded employees and 100 nonretarded employees engaged in the same work and employed in the same organization. Other studies have also failed to indicate a correlation between intelligence and creativity.

17. *Creative employees are usually long-haired types who are constantly dreaming up impractical schemes.*

FALSE. There may be creative employees who fit that description but for the most part there's no point in trying to identify creative people by their physical features, personal attire, and so forth. The best way to tell is to ask employees for solutions to problems. Familiarity with workers will make their abilities clear enough— provided the organization really wants ideas, treats employees fairly, and gives them adequate recognition for their initiative.

18. *Employees usually have little interest in using their creative abilities to help the organization.*

TRUE. Researchers have noted that employees usually have little inclination to be constructively creative in their jobs. One of the principal reasons for this is the cultural pressure for conformity. Regimentation begins early in life at school and continues through the work career. During that time expressions of creativity are too often subjected to criticism and even ridicule. Not enough effort is made to stimulate and recognize creativity through intrinsic (meaningful work, opportunity for personal growth, and the like) rewards and extrinsic (money and praise) rewards. The result is inertia and apathy.

19. *Research and development is the most appropriate function for creative employees.*

FALSE. All organizational functions are appropriate for employee creativity. While there is a tendency to view research and development as the principal—even the sole—domain for creativity, experience has shown that for businesses to remain competitive, employee creativity is needed at all levels and in all functions. The most appropriate place for its use is where the need is greatest.

20. *Managers do not appreciate the importance of employee creativity in organizational efficiency.*

FALSE. Most modern-day managers realize that creativity is important. The problem is that they don't know what to do about it. As one manager said in a seminar I recently conducted, "I know all about creativity—you should hear the excuses I get from employees who show up late for work on Monday mornings." That's the negative side to creativity. Unfortunately, the positive side is not nearly so evident because employees are often frustrated in their creative efforts.

36

Conducting an Internal Compliance Review of Affirmative Action

Kenneth E. Marino

Affirmative action regulations were conceived and implemented to equalize employment opportunities for certain groups of people—initially identified as ethnic minorities, with the subsequent inclusion of women—who were affected by past discriminatory actions. More recent legislation has broadened the definition of affirmative action target groups to include veterans and the handicapped.

Affirmative action regulations apply to all branches of the federal government, including government contractors and subcontractors whose contract meets or exceeds a specified minimum dollar value and whose workforce meets or exceeds a specified minimum number of employees. Firms competing for government contracts are required to

From *Personnel*, March–April 1980.

identify underutilized target groups by job category, design a plan with goals and timetables to eliminate the underutilization, and apply a good-faith effort toward meeting those goals.

As federal contract compliance officers—or Equal Opportunity Specialists, as they are formally called—will explain, the acid test of any affirmative action plan is the increased proportions of minorities and women in various job classifications. When designing an affirmative action plan, human resources management can choose either of two broad strategies to pursue—the "good faith effort" strategy or the "quota" strategy—each with its own risks to the organization.

THE GOOD-FAITH-EFFORT STRATEGY

The overall objectives pursued in the good-faith-effort strategy are the identification and modification of patterns of behavior that may have contributed to the exclusion or underutilization of minority groups or females in certain job classifications. Actions are sought that will open up the organizational system to these individuals and communicate the opportunities to both current and prospective employees.

Specific actions to implement this strategy might include establishing a training program to enable minority-group members to better compete for entry-level jobs, placing advertisements where they can reach target groups, and supporting day care services or flexible working hours for women with small children. The emphasis is on diagnostic and remedial action; implicit in this approach is the assumption that if existing impediments within the organization can be identified and eliminated, the desired results will follow.

This approach involves a risk to the organization, however—a risk that derives from the conciliatory powers of the compliance officer. If the desired results are not achieved, the organization must demonstrate that the actions undertaken constitute a "reasonable effort" to hire or promote specified numbers of individuals and that failure to do so results from factors outside its control. Should management fail to do this, it will find itself in an unenviable negotiatng position. The threat of economic sanctions through contract termination and legal action through EEOC gives the compliance officer leverage in conciliating any additional program actions or procedures to be undertaken in the future. In the absence of results, management would have little power to resist any recommendations that the compliance officer might make.

THE QUOTA STRATEGY

The quota strategy is a natural extension of the good-faith-effort strategy. In this case, human resources management seeks to minimize the risks of conciliation. Instead of emphasizing modifications in behavior patterns and operating procedures in anticipation of results, the quota strategy mandates results through hiring and promotion restrictions. That is, results are not left to chance, because hiring goals are operationally treated as employment quotas.

Just as with the good-faith-effort strategy, there is a risk involved in using quota system. The court case brought by Brian Weber against the Kaiser Aluminum and Chemical Corporation is a case in point. Weber, a white employee, claimed he was excluded from a crafts retraining program because of his race. To relieve underutilization in skilled crafts jobs, Kaiser had stipulated that at least one black or female employee be admitted to the program for every white male. As a result, minorities and females with less seniority than Weber were admitted to the program.

The Supreme Court recently ruled that Kaiser's plan was consistent with the intent of Congress when it passed Title VII of the Civil Rights Act of 1964, and therefore is legal. This decision is quite narrow in that the Court refused to delineate between permissible and impermissible affirmative action plans. It stated only that Kaiser's plan at that specific plant was permissible.

Through future court decisions or legislative action, the characteristics of permissible quota systems should become explicit. However, until such a time, employers pursuing a quota strategy may face charges of reverse discrimination.

FINDING THE MIDDLE GROUND

The legal question raised springs from two fundamentally contradictory public policy instruments—the Civil Rights Act of 1964, which prohibits discrimination on the basis of race and sex, and Executive

Orders 11246 and 11375, which demand preferential treatment for certain individuals based on race and sex. Throughout its relatively short public tenure, affirmative action has operated under this inconsistency. The issues remaining to be resolved are (1) when does preferential treatment become discrimination and (2) under what circumstances will discrimination be temporarily permitted?

These legal uncertainties indicate that, for the present, a strategy based on quotas should be rejected and the attention of the human resources manager directed instead toward improving the effectiveness of an affirmative action plan based on the good-faith-effort strategy. Such improvements might reduce the risk inherent in conciliation in two ways: First, the more effective the program, the greater the likelihood of achieving hiring goals and thus avoiding conciliation altogether, and second, in the event the goals are not met, the good-faith-effort defense can be strengthened.

These are several actions that contracting organizations can take to meet the minority/female hiring goals specified in the affirmative action plan. Naturally, some will have a more pronounced effect on workforce composition than others: For example, a contractor can require the firm's equal employment policy to be posted in all work areas, but incorporating affirmative action progress into the performance evaluation of supervisors with hiring responsibility would be more instrumental in achieving the hiring goals.

It is the responsibility of the contract compliance officer to evaluate the specific actions undertaken by the contractor and determine whether those actions constitute a good-faith effort. The actions that are judged effective will, of course, vary according to the organization, its industry group, and the compliance officer in charge.

In an effort to define what actions constitute a good-faith compliance effort, a sample of 50 federal compliance officers was interviewed. The results provide (1) an analytical framework that human resources managers can use to identify any areas needing management attention and (2) some remedies considered effective by the officers.

THE STUDY

The study proceeded under two assumptions: first, that there is a limit on the number of specific actions a contractor might choose in designing an affirmative action program, and second, that compliance officers have determined on the basis of their experience which actions generally indicate a good-faith effort.

A list of possible actions was developed by (1) examining the documents prepared to assist the contract compliance officer in the evaluation process, and (2) interviewing the directors of contract compliance in the New England regional offices of two federal agencies. To judge how important each action is in evaluating a contractor's compliance effort, a questionnaire was sent to compliance officers in the ten regional field offices of one federal agency that had compliance responsibility over a broad range of manufactured products. The questionnaires were distributed by agency personnel and, when completed, were returned by mail directly to the researcher, thus preserving the respondents' anonymity and the confidentiality of their responses. A total of 50 usable questionnaires were returned for a response rate of 45 percent. The list of actions originally formulated is thought to be fairly inclusive, because although the respondents were asked to add other actions they considered important, their responses yielded no new evaluative criteria.

The respondents were asked to rate each of the 33 activities listed in the questionnaire on its importance in evaluating the compliance effort of a hypothetical contractor organization, described as having performed an acceptable workforce utilization analysis that indicated underutilization in several blue-collar and white-collar job groups. It was also assumed that acceptable goals and timetables for correcting the underutilization had been established. The mean responses for each activity and the standard deviation of the means are presented in Figure 36-1. The rating scale was scored so that a high rating indicates an activity considered important in the evaluation of the contractor's compliance effort.

In response to the hypothetical situation presented in the questionnaire, the compliance officers agreed that all 33 activities had some relevance in the evaluation process. While this finding may be of interest to the practicing manager and can assist him or her in initiating or redirecting specific activities within the organization, the immediate goal of the survey was to develop an analytical framework for evaluating the firm's entire affirmative action program. To this end, the data were analyzed by means of multivariate statistical methods to determine if and how individual actions might be grouped into more

Figure 36-1. Results of the questionnaire completed by contract compliance officers (N = 50).

Questionnaire Items	Mean	Standard Deviation
1. Evidence that the CEO or plant manager is seriously committed to EEO policy.	6.7	0.8
2. Evidence that the contractor treats violations of EEO policy with the same severity as violations of other corporate policies.	6.7	0.8
3. Evidence that the contractor's EEO coordinator has the authority to review all hiring and promotion decisions.	6.5	1.0
4. General awareness of the EEO coordinator with current problems, effectiveness of programs, progress toward goals, and other matters related to the contractor's compliance obligations.	6.5	0.8
5. Participation by the top facility executive (CEO, plant manager) in the EEO training and orientation sessions of line supervisors.	6.5	0.9
6. Posting of promotion opportunities within work areas.	6.5	1.0
7. Inclusion of affirmative action progress in the performance evaluation of line supervisors.	6.4	0.9
8. Availability of career-development counseling to all employees.	6.3	0.9
9. Involvement of the contractor's line supervisors in the establishment of affirmative action hiring goals.	6.3	1.0
10. Conversion of the contractor's seniority system from a department to a plantwide seniority system.	6.1	1.3
11. Evidence that the contractor has encouraged minority employees to refer other minorities to the contractor for possible employment.	6.1	0.9
12. Personal contact, by the EEO coordinator, with employment referral agencies such as the Urban League or Job Corps.	6.1	1.3
13. Direct notification to all eligible employees of promotion opportunities as vacancies occur.	6.0	1.5
14. Inclusion of predominantly minority colleges and universities in the contractor's campus recruitment activities.	6.0	1.4
15. Evidence that a formal EEO complaint procedure has been established within the facility.	5.9	1.3
16. Explanation of contractor's EEO policy during the new-employee-orientation procedure.	5.9	1.1

Questionnaire Items	Mean	Standard Deviation
17. Institution of minority-oriented training programs.	5.9	1.5
18. Retention of applications from unhired minorities to be reviewed as vacancies occur in the future.	5.9	1.6
19. Frequency of preparation of written reports evaluating progress toward affirmative action goals.	5.8	1.2
20. Sponsoring of a formal on-the-job training program.	5.8	1.4
21. Existence of a formal, written job description for most jobs at the facility.	5.7	1.1
22. Restructuring of traditional jobs in an effort to broaden the incumbent's work skills.	5.7	1.4
23. Specification of position, pay, qualifications, and other relevant information when notifying referral agencies of job vacancies.	5.7	1.3
24. Institution of a job rotation program in an effort to broaden employee work skills.	5.6	1.2
25. Discussion of EEO matters, such as program success, in the contractor's publications (house organ, newsletter).	5.4	1.4
26. Explanation of tuition refund and training programs during new-employee-orientation procedure.	5.3	1.5
27. Institution or support of a transportation program or car pooling service if the contractor's facility is not adequately served by public transportation.	5.3	1.4
28. Placement of employment advertising in minority-oriented print and broadcast media.	5.2	1.6
29. Display of contractor's EEO policy statement in work areas.	5.0	1.8
30. Participation in job fair and career day programs at area high schools.	5.0	1.2
31. Appointment of key management personnel for service on a community relations board or similar organization.	4.8	1.6
32. Willingness of the contractor to conduct tours of the plant and facilities for school groups and referral agency representatives.	4.7	1.5
33. Availability of the contractor's affirmative action policy for employee review (with customary deletion of goals and timetables).	4.7	1.6

The contract compliance officers were asked to rate each of the above items on their importance in evaluating the contractor's compliance effort on a scale of 1 (relatively unimportant) to 7 (very important).

general categories of compliance behavior. The result: questionnaire items fell into the following six categories for action.

1. Increasing the minority/female applicant flow.
2. Demonstrating top-management support for the equal employment policy.
3. Demonstrating equal employment commitment to the community.
4. Keeping employees informed.
5. Broadening the work skills of incumbent employees.
6. Internalizing the equal employment policy.

These areas of action provide not only a clarified view of the compliance effort, but also the desired framework for an internal evaluation.

Figure 36-2 identifies the overall objective of actions within each area and some possible tactics for pursuing them. The list of tactics is by no means exhaustive and certainly not meant to preclude any kind of innovative and creative activity on the part of a particular organization.

These six areas can also be viewed as organizational bottlenecks, impeding affirmative action progress in organizations. The objectives in each area are distinct and each area is, to some extent, critical to the effectiveness of the overall program. It should be noted, however, that some tactics can serve multiple objectives. For example, frequent contacts with local employment services are likely to demonstrate the firm's EEO commitment to the community and increase applicant flow as well. Similarly, the discussion of EEO matters at various staff or departmental meetings can both inform employees and emphasize management's support.

As a general prescription, management would be well advised to vigorously pursue all six objectives. In fact, for some organizations, this may be the key to a successful affirmative action program. However, each firm is unique—with its own labor market, technical sophistication, entry-level skill requirements, current workforce makeup, labor history, and so on—and to apply the general prescription may be costly and even counterproductive. It would be more effective to use the general case developed here as an analytical framework for identifying the most critical factors affecting progress in the organization and then concentrate resources and efforts on those factors.

APPLYING THE FRAMEWORK

Management should note that applying this general framework to a specific organization does not relieve the organization of its technical compliance obligations, which require (1) including the "equal opportunity employer" statement in recruitment advertising; (2) including an EEO clause in purchase orders and in subcontracts; (3) obtaining certification of nonsegregated facilities for contractors and applicable subcontractors; (4) displaying EEO posters prominently throughout the facility; and (5) notifying unions or employee representatives of affirmative action commitment.

The organization should have completed several data-gathering tasks before embarking on a good-faith-effort compliance strategy: (1) the utilization analysis data that specify which job groups, based on the relevant labor market availability, are underutilizing protected group members; (2) a tabulation of all applicants by protected group status and the disposition in terms of hires, nonqualifieds, and so on; and (3) voluntary and involuntary termination information, again by protected groups. These data identify problem areas in terms of underutilization and the human inflow and outflow of the facility.

The remaining task is to identify bottlenecks within the organization and apply appropriate solutions and control mechanisms. The manager performs an identical function with materials control, cash flow, quality control, and the other systems within an organization. Therefore, diagnostic skills and responsibility logically rest with management. Equipped with an understanding of what are considered action areas, management should be able to identify and solve problems and to defend the rationality of its actions to the compliance officer.

For example, underutilization in entry-level job groups should direct attention to either the supply or hiring rates of protected group members. If sufficient numbers of these groups are not being attracted to the personnel office, resources should naturally be focused on increasing that applicant flow and/or demonstrating affirmative action support to the local community. If, however, seemingly adequate numbers of applicants do not yield a significant number of new hires, job requirements and personnel procedures should be scrutinized. Management actions must be directed at demonstrating support for internalizing the affirmative action policy.

Figure 36-2. Framework for an affirmative action compliance strategy.

Areas for Action	Overall Objectives of Affirmative Action	Possible Tactics and Program Specifics
Increasing minority/female applicant flow	To insure that minorities and females are not systemically excluded from the communication of employment opportunities available in the facility; and to encourage those individuals to apply.	1. Include minority colleges and universities in campus recruitment programs. 2. Personal and regular contacts with employment referral agencies, such as Job Corps or Urban League. 3. Participate in job fair or career day programs at area high schools and vocational schools. 4. Place employment advertising in minority-oriented print and broadcast media. 5. Encourage current minority/female employees to refer other minority/female individuals to the organization (for example, memo, "finder's fee"). 6. Retain applications of unhired minority/female applicants for review as vacancies occur.
Demonstrating top-management support for EEO policy	To indicate to all employees that top management considers affirmative action and equal employment opportunity to be legitimate and important activities for the organization.	1. Prepare written reports evaluating progress toward affirmative action goals as frequently as other management control reports are prepared. 2. Involve the line supervisors in the establishment of the affirmative action hiring goals. 3. Appoint an EEO coordinator who is both highly visible and from a department other than personnel. 4. Participation by the top executive in the EEO training and orientation of line supervisors. 5. Route progress reports and related material on affirmative action through senior executives' offices. 6. Include affirmative action issues and progress on the agenda of departmental meetings.

Areas for Action	Overall Objectives of Affirmative Action	Possible Tactics and Program Specifics
Demonstrating EEO commitment to the local community	To indicate to the public and local labor market management's concern for equal employment opportunity and its sensitivity to the unique employment problems of the community.	1. Conduct tours of plant and facilities for interested school groups or referral agency representatives. 2. Appoint key management personnel to serve on community relations board or similar organizations. 3. Establish a formal EEO complaint procedure within the facility. 4. Specify pay, position, qualifications, and other relevant information when communicating vacancies to referral agencies. 5. Establish an on-the-job training program at the facility. 6. Institute a transportation or car pooling service if the facility is inadequately served by public transportation. 7. Establish or support existing child care facilities. 8. Initiate efforts to retrain or seek alternative employment for involuntary terminees.

Underutilization in skilled and professional job groups might be resolved by more aggressive and specialized recruitment activities focusing on a broader labor market. Organizations that prefer promotion from within must define and examine the internal progression paths to those jobs. Remedial action might take the form of job restructuring or rotation, improvement in the communication of opportunities, or internalization via modified reward systems or altered hiring authority.

CONCLUSION

Human resources managers today are faced with the necessity of pursuing affirmative action goals in order to avoid compliance enforcement penalties, and at the same time avoid charges of reverse discrimination. Unfortunately, this middle ground has yet to be legally defined.

The design of an affirmative action program that increases the number of hires and promotions involving target-group members without resorting to mandatory hiring quotas is the only course of action left open to the government contractor. It is hoped that, by relying on the collective experience of federal contract compliance officers, human resources managers will focus on the same critical areas scrutinized by the officers, and form a sense of what might constitute an effective remedy.

Applying the framework developed here to a particular organization does not depend on any unique management skills or additional data-collection efforts. As an evaluation tool to be used internally to appraise the affirmative action program, it will hopefully facilitate the achievement of hiring goals or assist in preparing a good-faith-effort defense.

37

Smoothing the Way for the Handicapped Worker

A. B. Zimmer

There was a time when many employers met their moral obligation to hire the handicapped by subcontracting certain routine production, assembling, and packaging tasks to sheltered workshops. Other employers met this same obligation by employing the handicapped at the subminimum wages authorized by the special exemptions of the Fair Labor Standards Act of 1938. In the view of some observers, particularly advocates of handicapped rights, there was a cruel irony in these examples of "handicapped employment." The critics saw these arrangements not as accommodation but as exploitation.

The year 1973 was a major turning point for handicapped employment rights with the enactment of The Rehabilitation Act. Companion legislation was passed by Congress the following year protecting the rights of Vietnam-era and disabled veterans in substantially the same manner. Thus what had been, at best, nothing more than a moral obligation to hire the handicapped has become a statutory

From *Supervisory Management*, April 1981.

requirement for employers doing business with the federal government.

Under Section 503 of the rehabilitation law, companies with federal contracts (or subcontracts) of at least $2,500 must hire and advance qualified handicapped individuals. Section 402 of the veterans' legislation mandates the same action for companies with contracts (or subcontracts) of at least $10,000. Under Section 504 of The Rehabilitation Act, thirty government agencies enforce similar requirements for companies receiving federal financial assistance, such as grants and other subsidies, outside of the normal procurement process.

For those employers not involved in federal-government-financed activities of any kind, the above requirements do *not* apply. However, close to 40 states and some local governments have passed laws that closely mirror the federal statutes in their protection of the employment rights of *all* handicapped citizens. In short, the prudent employer will take carefully planned and well-documented steps to employ *and* advance in employment qualified handicapped individuals.

Since federal and state handicapped laws place similar equal-employment-opportunity and affirmative-action obligations upon employers, supervisors must be well versed in their basic responsibilities.

In requiring that companies not only employ but advance qualified handicapped individuals, there is more than an implicit warning by the government *not* to stick disabled persons in dead-end jobs. Affirmative action and nondiscrimination by companies, even if not outlined in a comprehensive written plan, must cover entry-level up to executive positions in the following employment practices:

Advertising.
Recruitment and selection.
Upgrading.
Transfers.
Training (including apprenticeship programs).
Demotions.
Layoffs.
Terminations.
Compensation and benefits.

In terms of recruitment, positive efforts must be made to locate handicapped applicants. Employers no longer can sit back passively and wait for handicapped individuals to show up at the personnel office. For disabled veterans in particular, there is a mandatory state-employment-service job-listing requirement under Section 402 of the veterans law that mandates strict recordkeeping and reporting. General recordkeeping requirements for all handicapped applicants and workers include the maintenance of a complaint log and actions taken to resolve complaints. These records must be available to federal government inspectors investigating complaints.

Additional employer obligations include the designation of a company official responsible for affirmative action, the accessibility of facilities whether they are leased or owned, the careful review of physical and mental job qualifications to insure their validity, and the creation of a mechanism that allows handicapped applicants and workers not only to identify themselves but also to make recommendations on how they can be accommodated in a reasonable manner.

WHO ARE THE HANDICAPPED?

A more perplexing problem for some supervisors than understanding basic statutory obligations is identifying the different categories of handicapped workers who warrant special consideration. The federal government has provided employers with some guidance by stating that a qualified handicapped individual is someone with a physical or mental impairment that "substantially" limits one or more major life activities. Additionally, the individual is covered if he or she has a record of such impairment or is regarded as having such an impairment.

But what constitutes a handicapped condition? The federal government, refusing to be pinned down, doesn't provide employers with a precise definition. However, supervisors should be able to identify the following qualifying conditions: alcoholism, drug addiction, cancer, cerebral palsy, heart disease, mental retardation, diabetes, kidney disease, multiple sclerosis, muscular dystrophy, deafness, blindness, and mental or emotional illness. Some of the above conditions are hidden handicaps and require more acute observation by the supervisor who may be used to working with only wheelchair-bound individuals or others with obvious handicaps.

Once it is understood who the handicapped are, the next step is getting management to hire them. Unless top management supports the principle of handicapped employment rights, balancing this commitment with competing obligations toward racial minorities and women, the supervisor's efforts are doomed to failure. More to the point, it is unlikely that the supervisor will begin to make a sincere effort unless he or she perceives employment of the handicapped as a corporate priority.

Out of the executive offices must emanate a continuous stream of support. Intracompany memoranda must state, in unequivocal terms, a dedication to handicapped employment. Company magazines, newsletters, bulletin-board announcements, affirmative-action posters, employee manuals, press releases, and other forms of communication must reinforce this commitment. Financial incentives for managers and supervisors must be determined, at least in part, by whether or not this company goal is achieved. In addition, supervisors must be assured by top management that they will have the necessary funds to make workplace modifications to accommodate the special needs of handicapped workers.

When top management puts out the word to its supervisors that handicapped employment is a corporate goal, the same message must be telegraphed to the personnel department where the recruitment, selection, and hiring is normally centralized.

INVOLVING PERSONNEL

The supervisor's already difficult task of assimilating the handicapped worker is compounded without cooperation from the personnel department. Not infrequently, the supervisor will have to guide the personnel staff in its effort to find qualified handicapped applicants for his or her department. It is imperative, for instance, that the supervisor communicate to personnel all mandatory and optional job requirements. An imprecise job description can lead to the selection of a handicapped worker who isn't equipped to handle the particular job in question. For example, a warehouse position that requires frequent operation of a motorized industrial truck could not be filled by a person subject to periodic and uncontrollable epileptic seizures.

Particularly with respect to handicapped applicants, the outreach efforts of the personnel department should be a significant concern to the supervisor. If dexterous production workers are needed, for instance, the supervisor must insist that the personnel department work with handicapped referral organizations in the community that are capable of providing qualified candidates. Further, the supervisor should meet with officials from these organizations to describe in detail specific job responsibilities plus the skills and aptitudes needed to fulfill them. Supervisors should even consider conducting company tours for representatives of handicapped referral organizations. By developing rapport with even a few handicapped groups, the supervisor can be instrumental in refining the selection process. Meanwhile, the likely success of the new handicapped worker is enhanced and production schedules are maintained at acceptable levels.

Clearly, then, the supervisor, through close coordination and continued consultation, can make sure that the personnel department refers handicapped applicants who can function adequately on the job. However, even after careful recruitment and selection procedures are followed, handicapped applicants must still be tested to insure they possess the necessary job skills. Here, too, supervisors can insist that the tests measure only those skills needed to perform adequately on the job. Testing for unrelated skills that do not affect job performance will not only complicate the selection process unnecessarily but will often lead to charges of discrimination.

Medical histories must be evaluated vis-à-vis the applicant's ability to handle the job in question. Again, the supervisor must consult with the company physician to make sure that realistic, not mythical, medical guidelines are applied. By carefully assessing actual job duties and the accident record of the department, the supervisor can assist the company physician in making a practical reappraisal of the medical standards applied to new workers. The American Medical Association's *Guide to the Evaluation of Permanent Impairments* will be useful in determining whether or not a physical or mental condition is disabling and therefore worthy of special attention.

MAKING ACCOMMODATIONS

Assuming that the personnel department refers and the medical department approves a qualified handicapped person who can perform adequately on the job, the burden then shifts almost entirely to the supervisor to make what may be a revolutionary job situation operate in a routine manner.

For even a seasoned supervisor, the sudden arrival of a handicapped worker can be nothing less than traumatic, since the necessary adaptations may disrupt a comfortable system that has been functioning for years. Hopefully, the new employee will have discussed reasonable job accommodations with the personnel department prior to job assignment, and the personnel department, in turn, will have consulted with the supervisor as to the feasibility of such accommodations. Sometimes, simple adjustments, such as raising a desk for a wheelchair-bound worker or modifying the work schedule of an employee with kidney dysfunction (who must leave work early to receive dialysis treatment), will suffice. Other times, more elaborate accommodations will be necessary, such as changing the emergency warning systems for a blind or deaf worker.

Supervisors, over the years, have shown that the old adage "where there's a will, there's a way" can be applied to successful accommodation of the handicapped worker. Imaginative supervisors have eliminated the rotating shift responsibilities of an epileptic worker who needed a regular work schedule; provided air-conditioned work space for a worker with a respiratory ailment; secured a parking spot near the entrance for a worker in leg braces; provided cassette recorders for blind workers; allocated additional desk and shelf space for a blind worker's braille dictionary; and requisitioned a special typewriter for a one-armed secretary who was then capable of typing the necessary 55 words per minute.

All of the above accommodations were made with the particular needs of the handicapped worker in mind. In consultation with other company officials, however, the supervisor can advise as well on a number of general accommodations that will benefit *all* handicapped workers. For example, specially marked parking spots, ramps leading to entrances, and accessible doors and food service areas will accommodate all handicapped workers and not just the individuals under the supervisor's immediate jurisdiction. All of these accommodations, both specific and general, will make the supervisor's task simpler while they confirm the company's commitment to equal employment opportunity and affirmative action for the handicapped.

If the accommodation is inordinately difficult or expensive, then "business necessity" or "undue hardship" can be invoked by federal contractors and subcontractors (note: a number of state laws allow the same exemption). It is incumbent upon the supervisor to advise top management and the personnel department on whether or not the handicapped person is capable of performing the job with reasonable accommodation as opposed to unreasonable modification of the worksite or the work schedule. The handicapped individual needs to be guided into the right job, but all too often this important function isn't carried out by the personnel department. Thus, the supervisor is often in the rather unenviable position of assessing the potential abilities versus the overly restrictive disabilities of a worker who has yet to perform or has just started on the job. The supervisor must also be ready to recommend, with justification, the transfer of a hand-icapped worker to a more suitable position or—as a last resort—termination. Whatever action the supervisor recommends, he or she must provide ample, written documentation for the decision.

INTEGRATING THE EMPLOYEE

Once a handicapped person is hired, the supervisor should know how to integrate the new employee into the department. By showing special consideration to the handicapped worker, the supervisor may inadvertently create tension within his or her department and resentment among other employees. At this point, a good supervisor will defuse a potentially explosive situation. First, he or she will explain the company's statutory obligations to union representatives and other employees while pointing out that handicapped workers will be held to the same performance standards as other workers. The supervisor will counsel his or her workers for patience and understand-ing during the critical adjustment period faced by the handicapped worker. The supervisor will arrange for awareness-training sessions through the personnel or training department to acquaint workers with the attitudes and problems of handicapped persons. These sessions will focus ultimately on the abilities of the handicapped and their contribution to the work team. A number of handicapped organizations in the community will be anxious to make presentations on this crucial subject or to make available a variety of audiovisual programs.

Above all else, the supervisor's ingenuity, compassion, and consistency can be the most important ingredients in fostering the success of a capable handicapped worker who simply needs time to adjust to a novel work environment. Any demonstration of understanding must be tempered with predictable and disciplined supervision. Befriending the handicapped worker or, far worse, patronizing him or her will breed resentment among co-workers and further exacerbate any adjustment problems that may arise.

38

Clearing the Way
for the Growth
of Women Subordinates

DeAnne Rosenberg

Edith Bunker isn't the only woman who has been stifled. For years, women in business who have aspired to any position higher than private secretary or administrative assistant (the difference between the two is usually negligible) have had to jump much higher hurdles than men, have been given little training to help them clear those hurdles, and have been expected to run the race while chained to a typewriter and copy machine.

But although stifling continues in the Bunker household and elsewhere, it is decidedly less fashionable than it once was. Some companies have seen the very real advantages of developing and using all human resources. And government pressure has forced other businesses to practice equal opportunity employment. When a com-

From *Supervisory Management*, January 1976.

pany finds that most of its women employees are clustered in the low-responsibility, low-paying jobs, it can no longer claim that no women are qualified to move up. It must begin to offer all employees—women as well as men—the kind of training and development that will enable them to advance. And it must be willing to hire qualified women to fill jobs traditionally reserved for men.

Many businesses are frustrated by quotas and the feeling that they must overhaul their entire personnel operation—regardless of inconvenience and added costs—in order to comply with government regulations. Many complain that the government is forcing them to hire unqualified people. But if the government is forcing some businesses to spend more money and change some procedures, the increased productivity that comes with improved human resources management will easily cover the costs. And the law does *not* require any business to hire or promote unqualified people. It merely requires that hiring be based on ability alone and that all training and development opportunities be offered to all employees.

If you supervise women, what can you do to make sure that they have an equal chance of advancing? There are five basic areas you can check to make sure that women are receiving the same considerations as men:

1. *Job descriptions.* Give all subordinates job descriptions that specify the results and accomplishments that are expected during the course of a year. Most women's job descriptions are purposefully vague, while men's job descriptions can usually be defined in terms of expected results or output. Since promotions are made on the basis of results achieved on the present job, women with vague job descriptions are never sure on what basis they are being evaluated or what they must achieve to be promoted. What's more, no one else knows either.

The problem is basically this: When a woman's job encompasses everything and anything, she is unable to say, "That's not my job" because everything *is* her job. She becomes an undefined catchall for every loose-end job in the office, and so is responsible for the results of nothing; no one can see the effects of her effort, presence, and input.

2. *Added responsibilities.* When a woman is given additional duties, make certain that those new responsibilities are published.

Usually, when a man is given additional responsibility or authority, a memo is sent to everyone in the organization making them aware of that fact. But when a woman is given an increase in responsibility, it is too seldom announced or even formally acknowledged. Often her boss will decide that she is now going to take over the supervision of the workflow (not the people) of the steno pool. However, the steno pool regards her as one of them. They think this way: "What right does *she* have to tell us what to do?" Instead of handling her new responsibilities well, she fails because the people she is supposed to supervise refuse to be supervised by her. Her boss becomes convinced that she would make a poor manager and should forever remain right where she is—behind the typewriter.

When a woman is promoted or is given added responsibility, legitimizing her new position by publishing it is critical. It shows that the organization is behind her; top management has an interest and a stake in her success.

3. *Career planning*. Develop a career plan for each position designated as a managerial training slot.

What happens in many organizations today is that women slated for promotional opportunities are put into meaningless jobs—jobs with fancy titles that were nonexistent five years ago. There is no precedent to indicate where the present jobholder will go after successfully performing in the position. Moreover, because there has been no previous history in the position to indicate what constitutes good performance, there is no way to judge—no yardstick for appraising peformance. Usually these are staff jobs (EEOC coordinator, administrative assistant, and so forth) with little, if any, decision-making authority.

Historically, women have been placed in jobs that reward for following directions, not for making decisions. People in these jobs are given praise and recognition for doing things the right way rather than for getting things done. This is perpetuated when women are put into such "token" jobs. It is far better to put women into jobs that have always existed, where the desired results are a matter of record and where there is a basis for performance comparison between the woman and her male predecessors. Creating special jobs with fancy titles for women reinforces the myths that some duties are "women's work" (special jobs for the ladies) and that women are less capable than men in business. Women need equality—a chance to succeed or fail in exactly the same jobs men hold.

4. *Performance*. Set high expectations; demand good performance. Easy enough? Something we do with all our employees? One of the worst blocks to the development and growth of women can be the supervisor assigned to assist the woman manager trainee. He regards this assignment as one entailing high risk: If she fails, he fails. What's more, the eyes of the entire organization are on him, evaluating him as he struggles with this assignment.

Out of his own fear that his training ability might be called into question, and also out of a sincere desire to help "that nice little girl," he takes upon himself all her decision-making activities. That way she has no opportunity to make any mistakes. Nor does she have any opportunity for growth. He is so delighted when she does something right—anything right—that he leaves her with the impression that all she has to do is come to work every day and breathe. With that kind of low expectation, she comes to work every day and breathes—period. At the end of her designated training period, she is unable to handle the responsibilities for which she supposedly had been trained. As a result, more men become converts to the belief that women can't handle managerial responsibilities.

When a woman is deprived of meaningful duties, her sense of purpose and her interest in the job wane. Without the expectation of excellence, any employee will regress to a level of mediocrity. In such a situation, women begin to feel that managing is not worthy of an effort. Managers must be taught how to sponsor a woman manager trainee in order to prevent these things from happening.

5. *Management's virile image*. Be aware that the role model for the effective manager is masculine: The best managers are thought to be aggressive, competitive, firm, and hard-nosed decision makers. Women are thought incapable of being tough or, at best, they are considered unnatural and unwomanly if they can pull it off.

Now, faced with having to accept women in the management role, many oldtimers are also faced with a dilemma: Shall they accept only women who exhibit an aggressive, hard-boiled personality—women who seem "masculine"—or should they also accept women who seem gentle, intuitive, and kind-hearted? Can a woman (or a man) succeed as a manager without the tough virility of a John Wayne or a Humphrey Bogart?

In the days when people lived in caves, a woman wanted the strongest man to live with her to protect her from the wild dangers of the world outside the cave. Physical strength and virility were the primary requirements for *that* job. But management skills are quite different from caveman skills. Diplomacy is more important than brute strength when it comes to supervising people. Management is for people with intelligence, stamina, the ability to inspire and direct others, and tact. Neither sex has a corner on these commodities.

It might be helpful to point out to women who have been selected for management training that the male image of manager still persists and may cause some special problems. Then they can be prepared to deal with the problems. Eventually, the successful woman manager will be accepted, but such acceptance will take time. If each woman understands what she is facing, it will be easier for her to wait out final acceptance into the management peer group.

There was a time when most women were supervised for nongrowth futures. Today, the demand for skilled and knowledgeable personnel coupled with governmental pressures for equal opportunity in employment have made the future a little brighter for women who desire greater responsibilities in business.

39

Sexual Harassment: An Old Issue—a New Problem

Oliver L. Niehouse
Joanne Ross Doades

One of the most explosive situations facing American companies today is that of sexual harassment of female workers. The issue is not new, but its consequences are, as many companies are learning to their sorrow. And although the legal ground rules are both vague and contradictory, it is becoming increasingly apparent that managers and supervisors in most companies are ill-prepared to deal with the situation in a positive, meaningful way.

In the past, the sexual behavior between men and women on the job was considered a personal concern. Performance as measured by results on the job was all that seemed to matter to many in upper management. Any interpersonal problems between employees had to be resolved by the parties involved.

From *Supervisory Management*, April 1980.

The past few years, however, have seen an increasing number of complaints filed with the courts and with various equal opportunity agencies—complaints from women who claimed verbal or physical abuse or economic retaliation as a result of sexual noncompliance with a male supervisor or colleague. Although female complainants tended to lose these cases initially, the trend seems to be changing as courts and government agencies are increasingly rendering decisions on behalf of women employees. In addition, even in cases where companies successfully defended themselves, they usually won on technicalities regarding the complaint process rather than on the merits of the case itself. (For example, companies have won cases by demonstrating that the complainant did not use established channels for filing her complaint.)

Considerable legal costs can be incurred by organizations defending against such charges; the back pay and damage awards can be substantial. Yet, perhaps most important is the negative impact that such a suit can have on an organization's reputation. Thus it is important that supervisors understand some of the implications of the sexual harassment issue for themselves and their companies, and what can be done to minimize such problems.

THE SITUATION

First, it is necessary to understand what constitutes sexual harassment. This is no easy task—even the court system has shied away from a definition for years—but emerging from the confusion surrounding the sexual harassment issue are three factors that may suggest the direction future legal action will take.

1. *Although anyone can theoretically be a harasser and anyone a victim, it is usually a male who is accused of sexually harassing a female.* When early suits charged that sexual harassment of women was a violation of the Civil Rights Act of 1964, Title VII, companies successfully defended themselves on the grounds that no discrimination against one sex or the other was being practiced—in effect, "anyone, male *or* female, can engage in harassment." While this logic had initial success in the courts, the trend is changing. More recent thinking indicates that while women might theoretically harass men,

that does not make the harassment of a woman any less a violation of her civil rights.

2. *"Harassment" is not confined to economic retaliation.* Although there still exist enormous confusion and controversy regarding what constitutes sexual harassment, it seems that actions other than direct economic retaliation (transfer, lost promotion, dismissal) for sexual noncompliance are and will increasingly be considered harassment. Such other actions could include verbal abuse or any conduct directed against a female employee, based on her sexual difference, that creates an unpleasant working environment. This is analogous to the racial epithet situation where precedents have established that employers are required to act in cases where racial remarks directed at an employee have created an emotionally repressive working environment.

3. *The method of lodging the complaint is not as important as the complaint itself.* The issue of whether the alleged harassment actually occurred seems to be achieving greater importance than the manner of registering the complaint. At the same time, since an employee may feel that reporting a sexual harassment complaint may leave her open to intimidation and subtle forms of reprisal, the courts and EEOC rulings indicate that the complaint process must protect the complainant's privacy. In the future, the failure to do so may result in penalties for the employer.

While the legal fine points will probably be clarified over the next several years, one thing seems certain: The increase in on-the-job sexual harassment suits is going to result in significantly higher costs for employers in terms of dollars, lost productivity, and public opinion. It is therefore the responsibility of every supervisor to understand the far-reaching implications of the sexual harassment issue and to understand how he or she can deal with such potentially explosive situations.

MORALE AND PRODUCTIVITY

In terms of achieving unit objectives, a supervisor's most pressing concern is that a sexual harassment situation can seriously disrupt the work group's ability to perform at optimal levels. Testimony given during court cases, before equal opportunity boards, and in private interviews with working women who have been the victims of sexual harassment, indicates that conditions of extreme stress, tension, and distraction are created by such situations. The women themselves identified significant drops in their own productivity, a condition that often lasted months or in some extreme cases a year or more.

However, the disruption in performance from a sexual harassment situation is not limited to one person. While the harasser's performance on the job may *seem* to be satisfactory, it is likely that his aggressive and immature behavior is negatively affecting others as well. The evidence shows that a harasser rarely confines himself to one victim but instead uses his workplace as an arena in which to act out his obsessions on a succession of other workers.

Employees other than those directly involved in a harassment situation generally tend to become involved in one way or another as well. Friends and sympathetic co-workers may spend time counseling the harassed female employee, and the tension generated by the situation may subconsciously affect even those who remain on the sidelines. Under such conditions, the group's quality and quantity of work suffer.

Clearly, as the supervisor responsible for such a group, you would have a real interest in resolving the problem as quickly and as unobtrusively as possible, enabling employees to reestablish a more productive environment.

WHAT YOU CAN DO

Much of your success in dealing with a sexual harassment situation depends on your attitude toward the issue itself. You need to sort out and acknowledge your personal feelings on the subject. This is necessary so that you can treat all parties objectively and fairly. The more you understand your own attitudes, the better your chances for dealing with them in a constructive way and for ensuring that *your* actions won't negatively contribute to an already difficult situation.

If your company has an established policy for dealing with sexual harassment complaints, your job is then relatively easy—follow the guidelines that have been set. However, if your company is like most today, there are no procedures for you to follow. In that case, you should document the complaint as carefully as possible. Include a dated write-up of your conversation with the complainant and separately add any observations you care to make. You may or may not want to confront the alleged harasser at this point; but if you do decide to interview him, be sure to record the exchange you have faithfully.

You should then proceed to do either of the following:

1. *Report the allegation, or ask the employee to report the allegation, to any employee grievance committee that may exist in the organization.* Although many female employees are reluctant to file so formal a complaint, it is imperative that this be done. It is the most appropriate route for informing top management that a problem exists, and it will later protect you and your management from charges of mishandling the situation.

2. *Report the allegation to your superior if no employee grievance committee or other formal complaint agency exists within the organization.* You should keep a record of this and any other conversations you have with your boss on this subject. In addition, you should tactfully ask your superior what action he or she plans to take and request that you be informed of any future developments. The more you know about matters so seriously affecting your group, the better position you will be in to handle any problems that arise in connection with these complaints.

MANAGING FOR TOMORROW

There was a time when managers and supervisors were selected and promoted on the basis of their functional ability: The outstanding salesman became the sales manager, the best clerk became the office manager, the most productive lathe operator became the shift supervisor. The last decade has seen a trend away from this practice, and the 1980s promise to continue and intensify the emphasis on human relations rather than functional skills in managers and supervisors. One of the primary reasons for this change is the formal acknowledgment of the fact that an effective manager must be an effective leader, and an effective leader is one whose primary value lies in his or her ability to motivate others.

As a professional manager, you must be prepared to deal with sensitive and difficult employee-related matters in a way that will not only resolve the problem on an immediate basis but will strengthen the organization in the future as well. The issue of on-the-job sexual harassment is admittedly an emotionally charged, difficult one. Proper handling of it requires the same qualities you would bring to any employee-centered problems within your group: sensitivity, objectivity, and a balanced perspective. Your management will be relying on these attributes more and more in years to come, and the extent to which you possess them will determine your success in managing the increasingly difficult human relations aspects of your job.

Good supervisors are those who anticipate change and prepare for it before it is upon them. Although the sexual harassment problem itself is not new, the present and future implications of it, and the effects it will have on your organization, are. Now is the time to prepare yourself for the possibility that you will be faced with the problem, for the prepared manager is in control and is well on his or her way to resolving this problem.

40

The Problems of Perfect Employees

Jeff Davidson

Cathy Clark really knows her job. Not only that, but she sincerely seems to enjoy her work, and she shows it by working late when necessary and completing all her assignments on time. When her boss is bogged down, she also acts to relieve some of his work pressure. She likes the company, too, and is always quick to defend management's decisions.

You would say that Cathy's future is secure, and her chance for promotion is in the bag, wouldn't you? Well, not necessarily; even ideal employees can run into trouble on the job, and sometimes it is their competency and dedication that bring on the trouble.

The types of problems that can beset an ideal employee are often a result of others' attitudes toward him or her. Attitudes such as jealousy, suspicion, or even indifference toward an ideal employee by

From *Supervisory Management*, May 1980.

co-workers and superiors can work to turn an ideal employee into a frustrated one.

Jealousy

Often, an employee who diligently puts in a full day's work that leaves no time for extended coffee breaks and casual chats arouses the jealousy and/or suspicion of co-workers. Regardless of the "ideal" employee's intentions, the co-workers are ready to believe that this employee is an apple polisher, a traitor, or a "sell-out." When employees who give less than a full day's work and neglect their responsibilities encounter someone who does an outstanding job, defense mechanisms don't allow them to believe that this employee is just doing an excellent job, and that he or she enjoys the work.

Because of jealousy or suspicion, the ideal employee's co-workers may, unbeknownst to the boss, ostracize him or her in subtle ways. What happens? The ideal employee ends up doing many tasks alone, concluding that it would be easier to go his or her own route. If this does not suit the boss, the ideal employee could be destined for trouble.

Suspicious Employers

Believe it or not, co-workers are not the only ones to worry about a diligent performer. Many employers are suspicious of an ideal employee and will, in fact, actively seek "clues" as to why the individual is doing such a good job! The employer may have known or had an employee in the past who also exhibited a high achievement level and sound business skills only to learn too late this person (1) was preparing to start a business on his or her own; (2) was using the experience to attain a better paying job in another firm; or (3) was camouflaging his or her real interests, and these were contrary to the objectives of the firm. Thus as the "ideal" employee continues to work harder to impress his or her boss, a greater degree of suspicion may develop.

If, as a manager, you find yourself suspecting one of your employees of such motives, it may help to sit down with him or her and discuss the employee's career goals.

Undercompensation

Ideal employees naturally assume that they can look forward to an uninterrupted stream of increasing earnings. They have been, after all, highly efficient and effective in contributing to the total profitability of the firm. A problem, however, can result when it's time for a raise, and the employee, knowing full well how hard he or she has worked, gets less than was expected. The employer may feel that the increase in the employee's compensation has been fairly determined, or the employer may wish to give more but cannot because of company policy or financial standing. Whatever the reason, the employee still feels gypped. And a decline in his or her performance is likely.

Thus an ideal employee may be "ideal" only until the time he or she is disappointed with the next salary rise.

Exploitation

A trap that is easy for an ideal employee to fall into is exploitation by a superior. It is natural for the best employee to be given the toughest assignments, sometimes even when he or she already has a full workload. And the additional assignments will, more often than not, be unaccompanied by a promotion or raise as a means of recognition for the employee's efforts. These may be promised to the hard-working employee but not delivered until many months have passed.

Ideal employees can easily be taken for granted by their superiors. Managers must remember that even if an employee takes on a disproportionately large amount of work *consistently*, he or she still deserves recognition or a word of appreciation. To neglect this is a costly mistake that too often is recognized after the ideal employee has left the organization.

Bypassed for Promotions

Sometimes an employee is so good at his or her job that the chances for increased responsibility are lessened because the employer is reluctant to make the change. Thus many ideal employees find themselves underutilized. Rather than being given the chance to grow, they are relied upon to accomplish routine, current tasks.

Discounted Efforts

We all tend to discount psychologically the work done by others, even in our own companies. This is, in essence, a defense mechanism that keeps us from having to face up to the reality that someone else is doing a better job than we are. We are too ready to say that an individual who does good work is "bailed out by the typist," is merely "regurgitating former reports," has an "extremely limited range" and once away from his or her strength will falter, or is "putting out" now in anticipation of a raise or some other reward. This is a dangerous trap, not only for the employee whose work is psychologically discounted, but for those who are doing the discounting.

Office Politics

The outstanding employee is a high achiever and makes optimal use of his or her time. Therefore, he or she is quite often the last to participate in, or enjoy, the benefits derived from office politicking. Engaging in office politics takes time away from actual work, and a busy employee is often unaware of the entire phenomenon. A good employer, one might observe, should see past the politics and offer a reward based on achievements. In reality, however, we "reward" those whom we like, and emotional and human factors have a heavy influence in business decisions.

The Truth at All Cost

Finally, let's examine how an ideal employee can run into trouble on the job because he or she is unskilled in "CY" (covering yourself techniques).

The "Persian Messenger Syndrome" is one situation that confronts many employees. The syndrome got its name because in ancient times the King of Persia was known to reward those messengers who brought him good news and to cut off the heads of those messengers who brought bad news. Of course, the messengers who should have been rewarded were those that brought bad news because it's more difficult to bring bad news. But the King didn't separate the messenger from the news that he or she was bringing.

Unfortunately, the Persian Messenger Syndrome exists today throughout business and government. The ideal employee, upon presentation of a financial report or a numerical analysis, may determine that the dissemination of the bad news is in order. Unskilled in CY, he or she may candidly present the information, not reducing the degree of the bad news through careful use of descriptive adjectives. If the boss is like the King of Persia, this act can be tantamount to stepping on a land mine—even for the ideal employee.

What can be learned by an awareness of these problems that befall ideal employees? The first conclusion one might draw is that there may be more to being an "ideal" employee than productivity. If an employee's work habits serve to alienate him or her from co-workers and superiors, then perhaps that employee should channel a little energy into developing better relationships with these people.

The second lesson is one for supervisors of ideal employees: Be sure not to take advantage of such individuals, and try to hold onto them by all means available to you, including compensation.

Ideal employees are not easy to come by. By knowing what problems they can run into, you, as their supervisor, can help keep them *happy* and *productive*.

41

Alcoholic Employees Beget Troubled Supervisors

Donald A. Phillips
Harry J. Older

When talking with public service managers about employees with serious alcohol problems, we have been deeply impressed with the concern and obvious anguish they feel. We have also found them to be frequently under stress and showing symptoms of anxiety and frustration. Following our discussions, these managers often seem greatly relieved and say something like, "Is providing therapy to supervisors part of your job description?"

In many cases that was exactly what was provided. The therapeutic exchange, which often consists primarily of allowing the manager to express his or her feelings and accept them as legitimate under the circumstances, can free the person to take positive action—

From *Supervisory Management*, September 1981.

to initiate the confrontation that begins the process of referral and rehabilitation.

In our opinion, there are ways in which the attitudes and behaviors of supervisors parallel the attitudes and behaviors of their alcoholic employees.

It is clear that each alcoholic employee begets at least one troubled supervisor. It has not always been recognized that part of the responsibility of those of us in occupational alcoholism is to provide "therapy" to the troubled supervisor. But upon reflection, it is obvious that a supervisor who is to play a role in the rehabilitation process effectively, must be counseled in how to maintain an objective, consistent approach to the problems of the alcoholic employee and must be helped to understand how the employee's behavior is impacting the manager's own behavior. This is true even though it is recognized that the supervisor's "troubles" are transitory and are situationally determined.

ALCOHOLIC BEHAVIOR PATTERNS

The troubles of alcoholic employees are well documented. Discussion of the powerful negative feelings, the destructive behaviors, and the denial syndrome make up a considerable portion of the literature on alcoholism. In part, the illness is defined by a sense of inadequacy, guilt, suppressed anger, confusion, fear, loneliness, preoccupation, and low self-esteem. With this burden it is no wonder that alcoholics suffer an emotional paralysis that inhibits their entry into treatment and their subsequent recovery. In large part one measure of recover is the extent to which alcoholics can get in touch with, and become aware of, these feelings.

A similar list of symptoms and similar sets of behavior problems generally can be ascribed to the concerned supervisor. Supervisors of alcoholic employees become deeply troubled themselves. Many of the same strong feelings paralyzing alcoholics also immobilize them. H. M. Trice and Paul Roman, two researchers, identified four recognition stages that "significant others" (including supervisors) experience in dealing with alcoholic employees. These are:

1. Disrupted-but-normal—a period during which intermittent disruption of job performance occurs. Although patterns of

behavior deviate from expectations, they are neither frequent nor disruptive enough to indicate any abnormality.

2. Blocked awareness—while deviance in behavior may increase in amount and degree, the employee is still seen as "normal" because of blocks in recognition.

3. Seesaw—as the impairment of job behavior increases, significant others become indecisive about whether to define the behavior as a deviant-drinking problem or to regard it as "normal."

4. Decision to recognize—the accumulation of abnormal behavior finally tips indecision toward recognizing the behaviors as abnormal. The appropriateness of referral to some treatment facility is recognized.

In the "blocked awareness" stage reported by these researchers in their book *Spirits and Demons at Work*, the supervisor represses strong feelings of anger and confusion. This stage is similar to the denial syndrome that the alcoholic undergoes, and it is essentially identical to the denial process experienced by spouses early in the development of the alcoholic problem. In the third stage, seesaw, these strong feelings can no longer be denied but are countered by other equally strong feelings of guilt, inadequacy, and fear. While preoccupied with the situation (and devoting an inordinate amount of time to fretting about it), the supervisor is at some point immobilized by an ambivalence fostered by these conflicting feelings. At others he or she is spurred to angry outbursts and irrational behavior, in the sense that the supervisor threatens the alcoholic, having no intention of carrying out the threat.

A supervisor at this stage needs counseling to provide reassurance that these ambivalent feelings and irrational actions are normal and even legitimate adjustive responses to the difficult situation which the employee has placed the supervisor. Then the supervisor is ready to hear specific suggestions for dealing with the employee and with the chaotic work situation that may have developed.

GAME PLAYING

Alcoholic employees have an uncanny knack for manipulating the feelings of supervisors. In many cases they sense the onset of angry outbursts and know how to play for the counterfeelings that will block supervisory urges to act decisively. A favorite ploy is the whipped-child syndrome characterized by the hangdog look and the "I can't do anything right" verbalizations. Almost invariably these behaviors tug at parental heartstrings, and suddenly a supervisor finds himself or herself comforting and supporting rather than confronting the alcoholic employee. At other times outbursts of righteous indignation by an employee will frighten the supervisor into backing off.

Alcoholics have a great deal of experience at playing these games. Unless they know what is going on supervisors do not have a chance. They need an understanding of the dynamics of these manipulations and specific techniques for dealing with them in ways that lead to timely and appropriate action. In the absence of objective, consistent behavior by the supervisor, situations develop in the manner portrayed in the supervisory training film "The Dryden File" produced by Newsfilm, U.S.A. In it, Matt Cirker, the boss, angrily threatens Tom Dryden over his latest performance problem. In a matter of minutes Dryden de fuses the anger and has Matt engaged in gentle "parental" stroking—perhaps a bit more rational than his angry outburst but equally nonproductive. To make matters worse, Tom isn't the only victim of Matt's anger. Matt's secretary suffers through two angry outbursts that are due to Matt's feelings of frustration in dealing with them. Matt's secretary, like many employees, is defenseless and must endure silently. It becomes clear that this type of behavior affects other employees, fellow supervisors, and the overall productivity and morale of the organization. It also, of course, can reach beyond the workplace to affect the families of supervisors.

To Matt, his performance is exemplary. He has Tom's pledge to do better. And isn't it much more pleasant filling the role of a nurturing parent than the ulcer-ridden, anxiety-provoking role of critical parent? Never mind that both are unproductive. Matt's bad feelings maybe miraculously soothed, but Tom is free to drink and fail again. The real confrontation has been put off.

Matt knows that he is procrastinating. He recognizes that he is not living up to his responsibilities as a manager. He suspects that other employees in his unit recognize the situation and look down on him for his inability to handle it effectively. And, perhaps worst of all, he may know just barely enough about alcoholism to have a vague underlying fear that he is contributing to the illness of the alcoholic employee.

Supervisors need to sort out these feelings. One important step in dealing with them is to begin to understand how they came about.

TROUBLED SUPERVISORS

The most important feelings that the supervisor will have (and, again, see how closely they parallel those of the alcoholic employee) are:

Anger. The angry feelings of supervisors toward alcoholic employees are triggered by broken promises, poor work performance, and absenteeism that requires continual adjustments of schedule. The supervisor may also feel self-directed anger at his or her inability to change the employee. We all become angry at our impotence in the face of situations that we don't understand—such as unpredictable and irrational behavior—and that's what the alcoholic employee is all about. And nothing seems to work, at least for long. The supervisor must be helped to understand that these feelings are normal and that positive actions designed to be helpful to the employee will relieve them.

Guilt. Supervisors also may feel guilty. They may ask themselves "What have I done wrong?" or "Why can't I handle the situation?" These are feelings of inadequacy: "I'm a poor supervisor. If a were a better one I'd be able to handle the situation." Since we tend to avoid situations with which we feel inadequate to deal, the supervisor tries to avoid a confrontation with the alcoholic employee.

Fear. Supervisors are often fearful of getting into discussions about employee problems that they view as highly personal. Many are fearful of the loss of control coming from anger. Some may fear criticism in return for some real or imagined failing. Perhaps some supervisors fear criticism of their own drinking behavior. And behind it all is a fear of, or at least a strong tendency to avoid, unpleasantness.

Ego involvement. Another strong psychological factor in some cases is ego involvement between supervisors and employees. This is usually the case where they have been together for a long time. The supervisor often feels that he or she has molded the employee, and therefore identifies with the employee's successes and failures. The supervisor feels responsible in some unexplained way for the employee's problem. In "The Dryden File," Matt, in a conversation with his own boss, assumes great responsibility for the person Tom Dryden has become.

Denial. One of the most striking similarities between what supervisors experience as they attempt to cope with alcoholic employees and the course of progressive alcoholism is the manifestation of denial. The "blocked awareness" stage described by Trice and Roman is clearly a form of denial and is analogous to the type of denial found in the families of alcoholics. We have all heard supervisors describe employees they know to be alcoholic. They stoutly maintain that job performance is still acceptable. Only on close questioning do they admit to examples of deteriorating job performance.

Even after supervisors can, at an objective and intellectual level, no longer block out the deviant behavior of their employees, they often continue to engage in denial. They may refuse to "see" blatant types of deviant behavior. This will frequently occur after a supervisor has made an unenforceable threat. To see it would require the supervisor to act in an unacceptable manner. Feelings of ambivalence are very intense and serve to block constructive action by giving the supervisor a rationale for procrastination.

Supervisors have great difficulty seeing themselves as part of the problem—another form of denial. But if they are tolerating an employee with deteriorating job performance and are engaged in the unproductive see-saw phase, they themselves have a managerial problem. At the very least they have become part of the problem rather than remaining detached and objective about it.

BARRIERS TO ACTION

There are other obstacles to effective supervisory action—long-felt prejudices or fears generated by the management system itself. Supervisors sometimes do not act for fear of a discrimination complaint, justified or not. In cases where these fears are groundless, adequate documentation generally insures that a complaint will not be pursued. Even if pursued, there is little likelihood it will be upheld. Still, such a possibility may generate very real fears in supervisor and these fears must be recognized and dealt with.

Union action in the form of a grievance that may eventually lead to arbitration is often cited as a barrier to supervisory action. Trice's research on the implementation of one government program, however, indicates that union awareness and involvement in the alcoholism program increases the likelihood of supervisory action. Where union and management have a clear understanding, supervisors have little to fear. The indication is that they are beginning to understand this.

The system is sometimes identified as a barrier—that tangled web of regulations and rules that govern our work lives. How many times have we heard public service supervisors say, or imply, "What difference does it make? You can't fire a federal employee anyway?" Granted, the process of termination in any organization has a system of checks to ensure that the rights of employees to due process are not violated. But it is not impossible, in any organization—including a government agency—to remove an employee.

Of course, removal is very unlikely if timely referral by the supervisor is made. Most employees will accept counseling as an alternative to discipline. Of those who do, 65 to 80 percent will get well. That's the experience of one federal program over the past four years.

In those cases where employees refuse counseling or are not successful in their rehabilitative efforts, if performance continues to be a problem, it is a supervisory obligation to take appropriate disciplinary action, even up to removal. This is not the outcome that supervisors should seek, but it *does* resolve a management problem. If supervisors do not live up to their administrative responsibilities then they themselves are contributing to the creation of other problems. Employees who see a poor performer go undisciplined, for whatever reason, will themselves fall into sloppy work habits. If they are forced to take over the work of the undisciplined alcoholic, they may even complain to management.

Supervisors attempting to take appropriate disciplinary action need support and encouragement. Frequently they are punished (in their eyes) by nit-picking as they wend their way through the disciplinary process. Eventually, they may see only two alternatives, a choice between being viewed (and viewing themselves) as ineffective because they take no action, or continuing to "fight the system" and taking positive assertive action. Placed in this difficult box many supervisors view the former alternative as less painful.

These are some of the feelings that plague even the best of

supervisors who have to deal with alcoholic employees. In work setting where occupational alcoholism programs are functioning, therapists work with supervisors to help them recognize these feelings.

REENTRY

Besides helping the supervisor to do something about an employee whose drinking problem is affecting performance, therapists also counsel supervisors on helping an employee who is coming back to work after coping with the problem. There is a period of reentry shock in which supervisory behavior can markedly affect the probability of a successful readjustment by the employee. The employee will probably not be completely back to optimum performance capability and will be filled with self-doubts concerning both work effectiveness and the ability to remain sober. The individual may have strong guilt feelings and be embarrassed about meeting with former peers, a situation that may provoke aggression and overt anger.

The supervisor should be prepared to expect these things and to deal with them. Of particular importance here is the delivery of substantial amounts of positive reinforcement for those new behaviors of the employee that the supervisor wants to maintain—for example, promptness, sobriety, attendance at AA sessions, improved work performance, and the like. Also, a positive work relationship should be maintained between employee and supervisor after the employee's reentry so that any problems can be dealt with before a relapse on the part of the employee occurs.

Most supervisors want to be good at their jobs. They also want to help their employees resolve their problems. However, supervisors develop strong feelings similar in nature to those of alcoholics when they try to deal with these troubled employees. But recognition of this and help through specialized counseling to accept the legitimacy of their own concerns can assist supervisors in coping with the problem in objective, constructive ways.

Part Six

LABOR-MANAGEMENT RELATIONS

42

New Directions for Labor-Management Cooperation

Donald N. Scobel

The status of quality-of-worklife (QWL) efforts in the United States can be characterized by two seemingly opposing statements:

◇ Nothing significantly new is happening in the workplace.
◇ So much new is happening that it is virtually impossible for one person to keep track of it all.

Amid this apparent dichotomy, QWL is a glowing enigma. It is at the same time a theorist's smorgasbord and a pragmatist's hunger. It is thunder to the behavioral scientist and an eerie silence to the drill press operator.

Statistically speaking, few American workers are touched by innovative approaches to what goes on at the workplace. Autonomous work groups, industrial democracy, supervisory boards, participative decision making, and most of the other terms in the evolving QWL

From *Management Review*, February 1977.

vocabulary are just that in the mind of the American worker—
vocabulary. The concepts that roll so easily off the tongues of
behavioral scientists, consultants, theorists, and even some politicians
have simply not been heard of, let alone experienced, by more than a
token sample of U.S. workers.

Even within some of the larger organizations exploring QWL and
participatory activities, only a small percentage of the workforce has
been touched by what is going on. For example, in the Eaton
Corporation, where some of us have been involved with worklife
change efforts for over seven years, worker involvement has yet to flow
beyond about 15 percent of our U.S. employees. Although we are by
no means satisfied or complacent, we are nonetheless pleased with
even this scope of osmosis within a complex organization in so short a
time.

A number of companies—General Motors, AT&T, Dana, Midland
Ross, Weyerhaeuser, and others in the Fortune 100—are supporting
various shades of QWL efforts toward worklife change. So are major
unions such as the United Auto Workers, the United Steelworkers,
and the Machinists. Even some communities such as Columbus, Ohio,
Salem, Oregon, and Jamestown, New York, have embarked on QWL
experiences. But if you ask almost anybody in these organizations and
communities what is going on, they will probably answer "Quality of
what?"

Thus it is true that "nothing significantly new is happening at the
American workplace" provided "significantly" refers only to the
percentage of American workers involved in or affected by that change.
The adequacy of the statement ends abruptly at that limitation,
however; it is a valid statistical statement that blankets a world of
relevant and vital activity. For hiding among the statistical bullrushes
is a veritable Moses of emerging and adventuresome new worklife
experiences.

WHAT QWL IS ALL ABOUT

1. *The major effort in the United States is not transpiring at the
legislative level as in Europe and elsewhere abroad.* Although there is
indeed substantial long-standing legislation affecting the workplace
and people within it, the movement under way in this country to

improve the climate of worklife is essentially grass root. Efforts to harmonize worklife are originating at the source—the workplace itself. The trend is for doers of disharmony in worklife to find their own reparations.

To be sure, proposed legislation ranges from mandating participative councils to providing seed money for sincere home-grown change efforts. Enactment, however, is not imminent, and on the American scene so far there has been no effective legislative thrust. The up-from-the-bottom history of labor-management relations in this country has nurtured some degree of worker involvement in his own destiny (the post-World War II development of major labor unions is one example) for the past four to five decades. It is reasonable to expect then that shopfloor solutions will continue to be sought and found. "Harmony by law" lacks an American ring.

2. *Much of what is happening in the American workplace is considered proprietary by the institutions doing it.* Hence, much more is occurring in the United States than is publicized. Perhaps even more important than proprietary reasons, many change efforts seek anonymity to protect the credibility of their own endeavors. Companies and unions alike don't want their own people thinking their efforts are motivated by public relations or even supplier or customer relations purposes. Like most newborn things, fresh QWL efforts are tender and delicate and need some initial protection from the cruelties of the environment.

3. *The American QWL experience to date has taken place in the factory, in the office, wherever the workplace may be—but not in the boardroom.* No major thrust has come from management, unions, government, or anyone else for employee representation on boards of directors as the way to effect constructive change in the worklife experience. This seems consistent with the grass-root characteristic of American worklife development. Decision involvement is sought at the level the employee himself implements, or at the level that tangibly alters, an aspect of the employee's worklife.

WHERE SPECIFIC DOORS OPEN FOR QWL

Quality of worklife in this country can be compared with an area, say a room, that can be entered through a number of doors. Each entryway represents a different approach to the same objective—to change the climate of the workplace, make it more effective, get more people involved in its dynamics, and unregiment some of its unnecessary restrictions so as to make it a more fulfilling life experience.

Improvement Sharing Plans

We are seeing a significant resurgence of improvement sharing plans, often called Scanlon or Rucker plans, which seek to give all employees in an organization a share in the improvement of the sales-volume-per-labor-input ratio. The important aspect of these programs, however, is not so much the economic sharing as the involvement processes that accompany this approach. These plans normally call for participative evaluation committees composed of both nonsupervisory people and supervisors, office staff together with factory hands, union members with nonunion employees; crosscuts of the workplace that normally interface only in conflict situations are thus interfaced in a constructive, cooperative process. An economic committee of all strata reviews, even computes, freely disclosed relevant economic data.

These sharing plans surfaced some years ago as a model of labor-management peace, but unfortunately the time was wrong. The fires of labor-management conflict were still too hot to envision peace. But now that many traditional relationships have matured, these processes of sharing are beginning to spring up like crocuses.

The Collective Bargaining Table

This door to QWL is not yet really open, but is slightly ajar. Even so, two major examples of QWL flowing from the bargaining room have slipped through—the auto industry and the steel industry.

In 1973 the UAW and General Motors Corporation agreed to jointly explore a humanization of the workplace. But neither party heralded this expression of intent as the major outflow of negotiations. In fact, the major result of the talks was not "humanization of the workplace" but somewhat the opposite—how to "get the hell out of the workplace," at least after 30 years of service. (It was the year of the 30-and-out pension.) This exploratory expression didn't just blow away, however, and now, in a way even quieter than the interior of one of their automobiles, GM and UAW are jointly experimenting at a number of the company's facilities.

The other significant bargaining outflow into the world of QWL originated in the steel industry where the Big 10 steel makers and the United Steelworkers have formed employment security and productivity committees to explore QWL efforts that do not interfere with usual collective bargaining subject matters. This approach grew out of the impact of foreign competition on domestic steel operations and a general recognition that some of the so-called productivity schemes so prevalent in steel had rusted to the point of counter-productivity. This committee structure, however, is formal recognition that the labor agreement is not the only solution to people problems. There are some better ways to cooperatively improve both business competitiveness and the meaningfulness of worklife.

Nonetheless, not too many QWL efforts will originate at collective bargaining time. The GM-UAW joint study provision, for example, did not spread to Ford or Chrysler in their recent talks. But it is becoming evident that however QWL begins in a unionized facility, it must in time brashly interface with the content of the labor agreement. There are some mistrusts in the labor agreement that cannot remain forever buried in a time capsule to be opened at a future date. QWL efforts and the labor agreement are a twain that must meet relatively early-on.

Joint Labor-Management Committees

Several joint labor-management committees arose not out of collective bargaining but in a variety of other ways. For example, Theodore Mills, executive director of the National Center for Productivity and Quality of Working Life, through his leadership of the Center and through related organizations, has seeded several current joint labor-management QWL efforts. An Ohio QWL project provided thrust for a similar approach within my own company, Eaton, as well as two efforts between a city management and various units of its organized municipal employees.

Characteristic of the joint labor-management committee approach are expressed commitments to a joint effort by high-level company and union executives. A joint committee is then formed at the plant or facility level to direct specific QWL efforts that come into play. Most joint committee approaches are under the initial guidance of external change experts who serve as catalysts to the processes of change. When the motor runs under its own power, the catalyst is supposed to silently steal away. Most joint committee approaches extensively survey the workforce or design other feedback mechanisms to periodically seek employee inputs and to measure the effectiveness of change.

The Job Enrichment Approach

This approach to changing worklife is perhaps the best known route in America. Certainly it is the most theorized and written about and may, in fact, touch the most people. If early Taylorism is likened to cracking an eggshell into its smallest pieces, then job enrichment—the process of redesigning jobs to provide a greater degree of employee responsibility—would be putting Humpty-Dumpty together again. In its earlier stages, most job enrichment effort was designed by management or a legion of consultant-disciples and then unilaterally put in place in the factory or office. More recent efforts, although still managerially initiated, involve the job holders themselves in the redesign of work structures.

Autonomous Work Groups

In this model, jobs are enriched and juxtapositioned in a way that lends to the formation of work teams that are given autonomy or quasi autonomy for determining task distribution and sometimes self-supervision of other aspects of worklife. Most of these efforts also are management-initiated, but do involve employee input all along the way.

The autonomous workgroup concept recognizes also that job enrichment is not the whole ballgame. Other aspects of worklife need enrichment if people are to come to work enthusiastically. Job enrichment pales if everything else in the worklife scenario remains unchanged. Autonomous workgroup experience has touched Procter & Gamble, General Foods, and TRW, to name a few. But these efforts are like a handshake within these large corporations and are by no means lovingly embraced throughout.

The Small Shop

Perhaps the most unheralded door to American QWL experiences opens to "small-shop" America. Usually with fewer than 150 employees, usually singly owned, and usually simple and homogeneously structured, these innovative companies are often led by someone who feels it important to provide a meaningful worklife opportunity for his or her employees. These bosses then stumble upon the revelation that their social consciousness seems to link to the fact that their businesses are immensely profitable.

In past eras this phenomenon was labeled paternalistic, but the creative small businessman today knows that the societal river flows onward, and a Big Daddy who imposes his benevolent life style upon his industrial family would today create a tin roof hotter than hell.

The contemporary small business innovator is far from paternalistic. He knows a creative workplace is essentially designed and implemented by the work society itself. Most of us know some happy, just plain factory or office people whose satisfaction with their worklife is enviously magnificent. Most often they work at one of those tucked-away, small factories where an alert and industrious workforce is really involved and its members really care about each other.

The New Plant.

A QWL approach that relates somewhat to the small-shop model is the newly constructed factory. Many companies of all sizes have vowed that their new plants would not reproduce the same old humdrum worklife culture. The new facility in a fresh, new environment looms as a human resource development laboratory—an excellent place to test the water, to try new approaches, and to involve people who have not been acculturated by the classic industrial conflict syndrome.

Some of these new workplaces have been criticized either as plastic societies where people are carefully manipulated into a nonunion mold or as little ideologies that bear small resemblance to the nitty gritty world. The criticisms are sometimes true. Often, however, these new workplaces offer quality worklife experience.

The essential thrust usually seeks to erase the traditionally disparate value system between factory and office worklife. The policies of factory life are stripped of unnecessary regimentations and constrictions. Meaningful communications in all directions are designed to flow freely. Factory and office interface is provided at almost every turn. Policies are designed as flexible building blocks instead of unyielding cell blocks. Many activities are orchestrated by committees of voluntary participants. These places are usually horizontal in organizational structure with very few supervisory tiers. They are often logical beginning points for larger companies that want to learn how to initiate QWL at their traditional workplaces, and innovative exposure at new plants provides basic training in the art of change.

Creeping Humanization

This is a significant movement in American industry that behaviorists would more likely classify under that amorphous umbrella called organizational development. In this mode an organization, usually under its own tutelage, realizes that its results orientation and human resource development operate off the same camshaft whereas in the past these were felt to be opposing systems.

This change in organizational style takes many forms. Often the structure of the organization is changed to bring interdisciplinary involvement in problems that cross traditional functional lines. Great strides are made in identifying leadership potential, and there is a management development surge to sharpen interpersonal skills, to develop enlightened managerial style, to implement win-win situations, and to study ways of affecting organizational behavior.

FORERUNNERS OF CHANGE

Although these activities may not in themselves change the worklife experience at office and factory levels, they often are the forerunners of such change. Participation in them helps managers to begin to think more elastically about cultural influences. And in many companies a change in worklife culture begins to flow. There usually is little fanfare, no formally structured joint committees, no behavioral catalyst, no exhaustive survey of long-known and -identified dissatisfactions, and no official projects, programs, or experiments. Instead, change is introduced on a gradual, participative basis.

One human process after another is examined and revised to

provide greater involvement, concern, trust, and effectiveness. Maybe the hiring process is changed to constructively involve the union, supervisors, and employees so that applicants learn all about that workplace. Some communications processes are changed, and people who don't ordinarily attend are invited to production control meetings and engineering process meetings. The plant news-sheet is turned over for editing and writing by a voluntary editorial board of factory, office, union, and supervisory people. A food service committee composed of employees is given full authority within fiscal guidelines to direct that activity.

Certain decisions are made from time to time by a vote of those affected. Meetings are held where factory people, union members, office employees, and engineers discuss viable process improvements. And scores of involvement processes slowly begin to take hold one at a time and gain credibility. The workplace begins to learn how to reshape itself, to discard change processes that fail, and to institutionalize the ones that fulfill. Little by little, constructive, winning processes displace the losing, conflict situations. The employees, their union, and their company begin to interrelate in ways that sustain each other in dignity, enrichment, and constructive purpose.

NEED FOR COOPERATION AND PERSISTENCE

These then are some of the doors that in this country open to enriched worklife experience. I have attempted no comparative evaluation of these entryways and am in no position to do so; there are probably very few persons who have walked through all. There is a tendency, however, for the proponents of each approach to believe theirs is truly the front door. In a pluralistic-business society each door no doubt works smoothly at some places and is hopelessly jammed at others. Also, many doors are not even discussed here. But it is important that QWL enthusiasts work together and revel in the multiplicity of their approaches.

A corollary concern is the imperative to admit failure. I have seen even in myself such enthusiasm for a particular approach to succeed that when failure knocked with the subtlety of an air hammer, there was still a tendency to sweep it under the rug rather than evaluate and deal with it. Not every approach fits, and failure must be laid bare if the free American QWL movement is to grow.

43

Walking the Supervisory Tightrope Between Management and Labor

Michael S. Golding

In the ever changing business scene, one fact remains the same: You, the first-line supervisor, are still the single most important person in your company's relationship with the workforce.

To your subordinates, in many respects, you are the company. Most of the decisions, schedules, promotions, raises, and other information affecting them come through you and are largely controlled by you. It's your responsibility to oversee your department's operations and manpower needs; meet production schedules; know the technical aspects of your operations; keep multiple records; and train, discipline, evaluate, and promote your subordinates.

However, for the supervisor in a unionized organization, the job

From *Supervisory Management*, December 1979.

entails more than just direct supervision of employees. He or she must be familiar with the union contract, enforce and interpret its rules and provisions, and, in general, administer the contract terms on a daily basis. It is both a difficult and vital task.

Actually, the basics of a good labor relations policy should not differ appreciably whether your firm is unionized or not. A good rule of thumb in labor relations is to make and administer your policies and rules as if a strong and militant union was staring down your throat every step of the way. If your shop is not unionized, this may help prevent a union from trying to come in and organize. Union or no union, it should help reduce the number of grievances in your organization as well as to uphold your decisions in cases that do arise.

UNIONS—A FACT OF CORPORATE LIFE

Whatever one's personal feelings about unions, they are here to stay. Unions have been a part of the American industrial scene as early as the Revolutionary War period. The history of organized labor in the United States has been a turbulent one, with constant struggles for growth and survival over the years against less-than-enthusiastic business and government leaders. In 1935, Congress enacted the National Labor Relations Act. This landmark piece of legislation protected the right of the American worker to organize and bargain collectively, thus guaranteeing labor unions continued existence and growth, if not unqualified support.

Today's powerful labor unions combine local, state, and national groups into a large, loose confederation. A single local may be part of a state and an international union within its federation. Each member local is highly autonomous and handles its own affairs (negotiating contracts with employers, admitting and disciplining members, collecting dues, and handling grievances), calling on its parent groups only for assistance and advice. Each local has its own executive board, consisting of a president, vice-president, secretary, treasurer, plus various committees and a number of shop stewards. Smaller firms usually have only one steward; larger companies have a steward in each department or division.

THE DUTIES OF THE SHOP STEWARD

As a supervisor, you are in frequent contact with your shop steward. Therefore, we should take a closer look at his or her function in the organization.

The shop steward is an unpaid union official elected by co-workers. The steward continues to hold his or her regular job and handles union affairs during working hours on a part-time basis, with the company agreeing to compensate the steward at his or her regular wage or salary.

The most important duty of the shop steward is to handle employee grievances. Other duties include recruiting new members, keeping members informed about union decisions, and getting support for union activities and programs.

You should realize that at times the steward in your department must take a position with which he or she may not necessarily agree, just as you must adhere to decisions made by higher management with which you disagree. Although you and the shop steward are going to be on opposite sides of many disputes by the very nature of your jobs, a constant state of guerrilla warfare need not exist. By achieving a good working relationship with the steward, this potential "thorn in your side" can become a valuable source for feedback concerning your employees' attitudes. He or she may warn you about any discontent or difficulties that may exist before they flare up into major problems or grievances.

You should keep your steward informed about what's happening in management. As a supervisor, you are not obliged to, nor should you, share decision making with the union (except when the terms require union approval). However, try to let him or her know about management decisions, particularly your own, before they are publicly announced.

Recognize that the steward's function is to investigate grievances. Allow him or her reasonable time to do the job thoroughly and properly. In turn, the steward should understand that your function is to get your department to achieve the highest production level possible, and to get a "fair day's work" from everyone.

BASIC PRINCIPLES

Good rapport and cooperation between management and labor are vital if an organization is to function efficiently. Following are some requirements of a good labor relations policy that you, as supervisor, should follow. The first and most important relates to communications. While good communications are important in any organization, in the unionized plant or company they are essential.

Good Communication Channels

Communication channels should be direct and official. Direct channels are desirable because they are simpler, vaster, and more reliable. Grapevines are inevitable in most organizations, but their negative effects can be neutralized if information is regularly conveyed first through official channels.

Here are some other rules on communication.

1. *Use several appropriate channels.* Select a number of communication methods that can be used to convey your message to your employees. You might consider posting information on bulletin boards, publishing a company newsletter, preparing handouts, or making announcements at meetings. It's a good idea to use multiple channels of communication and repeat your message as often as needed.

2. *Give your instructions in reasonable proportions.* Don't expect employees, even long-term ones, to absorb and understand lengthy or detailed instructions. Be patient—give each worker as many directives as he or she is capable of grasping at one time, and be prepared to repeat them again until they are understood.

3. *Keep employees informed about organizational matters.* Nothing upsets an organization or a department more quickly than a sudden and unexplained change in the ground rules, particularly those affecting job security or wages. You should notify your people in advance about any changes in policy and tell them whether or not the decision was your own, explain why and how it was reached, the reasons for it, and its probable effect on the workforce. You might

discuss the situation with the shop steward so you can identify what might be a potentially sensitive area. Also, pay attention to your subordinates' reactions to such an announcement; it may be quite different from what you anticipated.

4. *Be truthful*. Mutual trust is a key element in the supervisor-subordinate relationship. If you want honesty from your subordinates, you must first establish your own reputation for honesty. Don't make promises, hoping that your superiors will agree with you. If the situation is touch and go, say so frankly,. But once you have stated what you or the company will do, be sure it's done.

5. *Keep lines of communication open at all times*. Your people should feel that they can speak to you about things that are troubling them. An open-door policy is essential for successful supervision.

6. *Solicit feedback*. Do you know how your people view their job, the company, the rules, and so on? Encourage your subordinates to speak out during meetings. Another good idea is to adjust your schedule so that once a week you spend time on the floor. Observe your subordinates as they go about their jobs, and listen to what they have to say.

Let's now look at some other ways that you as a supervisor can support your organization's labor effort.

Be Fair and Impartial

Most firms allow their foremen or supervisors considerable latitude in assigning tasks and making schedules. In making assignments, don't play favorites. Try to distribute the "lush" jobs and the routine jobs as evenly as possible; rotating them is usually a fair practice.

Weed Out the Poor Workers Early

It's important to identify early in the game those employees who don't fit into the organizational structure. You should not put off making a decision, hoping that the worker will improve or waiting for the next economic downturn or seasonal slack so that you can lay him or her off. Most union contracts stipulate a probationary period, after which time an employee can be legally terminated. Delay can invite a grievance complaint or a lawsuit.

Accentuate the Positive

How can you do this?

When correcting an employee as to how a job should be done, emphasize the way you want it done rather than criticizing him or her without making clear what the correct method is.

Give positive reinforcement. Employees, no matter what their position, need to feel that they are accomplishing something. A simple "nice job" or "You did that very well, Joe," once in a while can do wonders for your employees' morale and productivity.

Encourage Employee Creativity.

Subordinates can be a great source of new ideas, suggestions for improvement, and so on. Listen to their ideas, and if they're good, try to implement them. If they're not feasible, explain to your subordinates why, and thank them for making the suggestion. Remember, also, to give individual subordinates credit for their ideas. Nothing will poison morale quicker than for the supervisor to get the credit for someone else's inventiveness.

Praise in Public, Criticize in Private

For some individuals, criticism can be an ego-crushing experience. Hence the first rule in disciplining a subordinate is to do it kindly, constructively, and privately. Negative criticism will only leave an individual frustrated, confused, and resentful long after the cause of or reason for the criticism is forgotten.

Establish and Follow Sound Written Disciplinary Policy

The longer you are in management, the more you realize the importance of and the necessity for a well-thought-out, written disciplinary policy. Such a policy provides you with a step-by-step procedure—approved by upper management and sanctioned by the union—for dealing with and punishing undesirable behavior. Another reason why a written disciplinary policy is important is that your subordinates will know what the rules are and what the penalties are if the rules are broken. But remember to apply disciplinary procedures consistently and immediately after the offense. Otherwise, you will be inviting a union grievance suit.

If you don't have a disciplinary policy the following steps will help you in establishing one for your department or for your entire organization.

1. *Decide what types of problems and situations you will probably encounter.* The most common kinds of undesirable behavior are absenteeism, tardiness, and insubordination. But there might be other problems peculiar to your type of organization or industry. Find out from your peers and superiors what they might be. Jot them all down in outline form, for clarity's sake.

2. *Research existing contracts and policies.* Study your firm's union contract and, if possible, the disciplinary policies of other companies. See where your ideas and theirs might conflict or agree. Next, find out how the provisions have been applied in the past and what precedents have been set, and modify your own policy accordingly.

3. *Write your policy in clear, easy-to-understand language.* Eschew legalistic jargon and long, drawn-out sentences.

4. *Clear your policy with the authorities.* Before you publish your policy, clear it with your immediate superior and also with the personnel department. Then discuss it with your shop steward. Consider making minor changes if they will make certain parts more palatable to labor. Then, reclear these with your superior.

5. *Distribute your policy to your subordinates.* Give copies to your subordinates and post copies conspicuously on appropriate bulletin boards. Hold a brief meeting to explain key points and answer any questions about the policy that may be raised. Also send a copy to the personnel department, the shop steward, and other involved parties. It is essential that everyone be aware of what the terms of the policy are before you begin to enforce them.

There will be times, of course, when total agreement between management and labor is not easily attained or not attainable at all. However, most of the time, an understanding can be achieved that will be beneficial to both sides. Being a supervisor, particularly in a unionized company, is somewhat like walking a tightrope, but finding the proper balance between both sides is the key to your success—to achieving the well-being of your subordinates and company.

The Contributors

JOE D. BATTEN is President of Batten, Batten, Hudson & Swab, Inc., a consulting firm in Des Moines, Iowa.

O. A. BATTISTA is Chairman and President of Research Services Corporation in Fort Worth, Texas.

ROBERT R. BELL is Chairman of the Department of Business Management at Tennessee Technological University in Cookeville, Tennessee.

DONALD T. DALENA is a member of the public relations staff of United Steelworkers of America in Pittsburgh, Pennsylvania.

JEFF DAVIDSON is Senior Associate of IMR Corporation in Falls Church, Virginia.

KEITH DAVIS is Professor of Management at Arizona State University in Tempe, Arizona.

JOANNE ROSS DOADES is a consultant with Ronald Doades and Company in New York City.

CURTIS E. DOBBS is Manager Services Supervisor of Ernst & Whinney in Dallas, Texas.

PETER F. DRUCKER is a widely published author of books and articles on management and a consultant who specializes in business and economic policy and in top management organization. He is Clarke Professor of Social Science and Management at Claremont Graduate School in Claremont, California.

MARION FARRANT is a freelance writer in South Pasadena, California.

FRED E. FIEDLER is Professor of Psychology and of Management and Organization and also Director of the Organizational Research Group at the University of Washington in Seattle, Washington.

MICHAEL S. GOLDING is Principal of Michael Associates in Elmhurst, Illinois.

MARION E. HAYNES is Employee Relations Associate with the Head Office–Employee Relations of Shell Oil Company, Houston, Texas.

RICHARD I. HENDERSON is Assistant Professor of Management at
Georgia State University in Atlanta, Georgia.

MARGARET V. HIGGINSON is a consultant to the Department of
Management Research of American Management Associations in
New York City.

FLORENCE M. HOYLMAN is a consultant with Organizational
Consultants in West Lafayette, Indiana.

BEVERLY HYMAN is Principal of Beverly Hyman and Associates,
Communications & Training Consultants in New York City.

LOUIS V. IMUNDO is President of Management Perspectives,
Organizational Development Consultants in Dayton, Ohio.

LAUREN HITE JACKSON is Senior Organization Research Analyst
with the BF Goodrich Company in Akron, Ohio.

GRANVILLE B. JACOBS, at the time his article was written, was a
writer who specialized in management subjects.

RAY A. KILLIAN is Vice President, Belk Store Services, Inc. in
Charlotte, North Carolina.

CHARLES D. LEIN is Chairman of the Department of Business
Administration at Weber State College in Ogden, Utah.

EDWARD L. LEVINE is Associate Professor of Industrial/Organiza-
tional Psychology at the University of South Florida in Tampa,
Florida.

RENSIS LIKERT is retired Director of the Institute for Social
Research at the Unversity of Michigan and heads his own
consulting organization in Ann Arbor, Michigan. He is a widely
published specialist in organizational theory and management
practice.

KENNETH E. MARINO is Assistant Professor of Business Administration at the University of Kentucky in Lexington, Kentucky.

ROBERT C. McCOY is Associate Professor of Management of the
College of Business, Eastern Michigan University of Ypsilanti,
Michigan.

J. MICHAEL McDONALD is Assistant Professor of Industrial Management at Clemson University in Clemson, South Carolina.

J. THOMAS MILLER III is President of Leadership Seminars
Associates in Duncan, South Carolina.

MARK G. MINDELL is Manager of Organization Research and
Development with the BF Goodrich Company in Akron, Ohio.

DONALD W. MYERS is Associate Professor of Management at the
School of Business Administration, Winthrop College, in Rock
Hill, South Carolina.

OLIVER L. NIEHOUSE is President of Oliver L. Niehouse & Associates, a consulting firm in Forest Hills, New York.

DAN H. NIX is Director of the Center for Management Development at J. Sargeant Reynolds Community College in Richmond, Virginia.

HARRY J. OLDER is a clinical psychologist and consultant on the Employee Assistance Program with NASA in Washington, D.C.

DONALD A. PHILLIPS is Manager, Alcoholism and Drug Abuse Program, U.S. Civil Service Commission in Washington, D.C.

BEVERLY A. POTTER is a training consultant in Stanford, California.

THOMAS L. QUICK is a Directing Editor with the Research Institute of America in New York City.

ELANOR REITER, at the time her article was written, was a Training Program Developer with the Allstate Insurance Company in Northbrook, Illinois.

DeANNE ROSENBERG is President of DeAnne Rosenberg, Inc.

RANDI SACHS, at the time her article was written, was an editor with AMACOM, a division of American Management Associations in New York City.

LEONARD SAYLES is a professor at the Graduate School of Business of Columbia University in New York City.

DONALD N. SCOBEL is Manager–Employee Relations, Research and Development at the Eaton Corporation.

JOHN J. SHERWOOD is Professor of Organization Psychology and Administrative Services at Purdue University in West Lafayette, Indiana.

ARTHUR SONDAK is President of Personnel Management Services in Matawan, New Jersey.

ANGELO M. TROISI is President of Troy Associates, Inc. in Boston, Massachusetts.

SANDRA A. VAVRA is Staff Sales and Motivation Manager of the Home Federal Savings and Loan Association in San Diego, California.

RICHARD J. WALSH is Director of Staff Development for American Appraisal Associates, Inc. in Milwaukee, Wisconsin.

HEINZ WEIHRICH is Associate Professor of Management and Organizational Behavior at Arizona State University in Tempe, Arizona, and writes frequently on management and behavioral topics.

A. B. ZIMMER is President of Eliot-Yeats, Inc., a consulting firm in Washington, D.C.

Index

abrasive manager, treatment by, 41
absenteeism, as people cost, 129–130
"absenteeism intelligence quotient" test, 233–237
accountability, and "boss" communication, 170
achievement drive, as leadership trait, 4
action instrumentation, as leadership behavior factor, 11
Adult ego state, 27, 32
affirmative action
    good-faith-effort strategy and, 272
    and handicapped persons, 284
    purpose of, 271
    questionnaire, 276–279
    quota strategy and, 273
Albrecht, Karl, on employee social system, 121
alcoholic employees
    behavior patterns of, 308–309
    game playing and, 309–311
    reentry by, 314
Allport, Gordon, and creativity, 267
American Medical Association, on disabling conditions, 287
anger
    as employee reaction, 44
    as supervisor reaction, 311
arrogant manager, treatment by, 41
ask, as DAD component, 179
assembling resources, communication and, 66
attitude
    listening and, 84
    and poor performance review, 252
authority, and managing, 37
autocratic leadership, and TA, 28, 31
autonomous work groups, as labor-management cooperation, 322

background, as communication barrier, 74

Baird, Johm, Styles of Management and Communication: A Comprehensive Study of Men and Women, 37–38
balanced existence, as quality of manager, 20
Barnard, Chester I., on leadership, 11
barriers
    and alcoholic employees, 312–314
    to communication, 73–77
Batten, Joe D., on managers, 17–23
Battista, O. A., on managers' mistakes, 182–186
behavior, communication as affecting, 71–72
behavior patterns, of alcoholic employees, 308–309
beliefs, as communication barrier, 74–75
Bell, Robert R., on evaluating subordinates, 133–142
belonging and affection, as employee need, 113–114
benefits, as people cost, 129
benevolent/autocratic leadership, and TA, 28, 31
Berne, Eric, Games People Play, 26
Blake, Robert, on team style management, 39
blocked awareness, as behavior pattern, 309
boss's time, use of, 167–168
Bradley, Patricia, Styles of Management and Communication: A Comprehensive Study of Men and Women, 37–38
Burrows, Martha, on women as managers, 38–39

career planning, and women workers, 293–294
catalyst, communication as, 81
change